Relocating
the Leisure Society:
Media, Consumption
and Spaces

Editors:
Jayne Caudwell, Steve Redhead,
Alan Tomlinson

LSA

LSA Publication No. 101

Relocating the Leisure Society:
Media, Consumption and Spaces

First published in 2008 by
Leisure Studies Association
The Chelsea School
University of Brighton
Eastbourne BN20 7SP (UK)

A catalogue record for this book
is available from the British Library.

ISBN: 978 1 905369 12 6

Cover design and page layout Myrene L. McFee

Cover Photo © Dreamstime.com

Printed and bound by CPI Antony Rowe, Eastbourne

Contents

RELOCATING THE LEISURE SOCIETY: EDITORS' INTRODUCTION

There was a time when professionals and academics in leisure studies and related areas such as physical education believed that their subject was the key to a better future. Hal A. Lawson, of the University of Washington (USA), writing in the journal *Quest* in 1974 talked of the need for a "creative endeavour in the search for alternatives" in the future of physical education and sport. Adopting an avowedly optimistic approach to the future, he wrote: "The society characterized by mass leisure and affluence is within man's grasp, awaiting only the necessary effort" (1976: p. 236). This was a (pre-feminist) physical education professional's well-intentioned interpretation of debates concerning automation, the emerging affluent society, and political claims of the time that Western liberal democracies were beyond ideology, based on a consensus of happy and contented capitalist consumers. The scenario here was a harmonious state of affairs in which all leisure seekers would find their appropriate outlets, as long as there were enough trained and well-meaning professionals available to guide them in the right direction (should they need such guidance). Earlier concerns, less shaped by a belief in the arrival of affluence for all, had long recognised that leisure also had its problem side. British author W.E. Simnett observed, in the year following the end of World War II, that productive machinery, shorter working hours, and holidays with pay could create a challenge of "too abundant freedom", making the majority "dangerously emancipated from our labours" (1946: p. 9). Simnett was a liberal interventionist for whom the promise of leisure meant educational intervention: people would need to learn how to use leisure, and the subtitle of his book emphasised the imperative of 'how to enjoy' leisure, with instructional chapters on reading, poetry, maps and social service, as well as sport, cycling, walking and media/popular cultural forms. But he also recognised that there would be no solution to the 'problem of enforced leisure or unemployment' until a way was found to abolish the 'paradox of poverty in the midst of plenty'. Nevertheless, it was the optimistic side of Simnett's vision that prevailed in a spirit of post-war rebuilding in Britain. Forty years on, way beyond the 1950s and the Conservative Harold Macmillan's pronouncement to the British people that they'd never had it so good, the faith of Labour's Harold Wilson in the white heat of technology, and the economic and political vicissitudes of the years culminating in the emergence in power of Margaret Thatcher's reforming conservative administration — and four decades after Simnett's optimistic projections — a different tone prevailed in writing about leisure and the so-called leisure society. Jeremy Seabrook's study *The leisure society* (1988) challenged the core assumptions of 'the promise of leisure', premised as that was on a "growth-and-expansion dynamic of capitalist society ... an appealing prospect to people whose lives have for so long been shaped by labour" (p. 182). Seabrook, sceptical of the liberating possibilities of such a model of the leisure society still based in the economics of capitalism, called for a vision of liberation in which a more "modest and equitable plenty" could be explored: "in which leisure would not be something cramped and threatened, dependent on money, and would cease to be a commodity" (p. 185). Another twenty years on, Seabrook's eloquent critique reads like a vision of hopelessly utopian idealism.

What happened to the leisure society then? Our conference-framing question for the 2007 Leisure Studies Association Annual Conference was designed to stimulate reflections on previous visions and analyses, and on contemporary trends in leisure practice and consumption. And it is interesting to look back at what has driven scholarship and critique in our field, as a means of framing our understanding of how trends in the field have changed. Very different in tenor and context, the three writers cited above share one characteristic at least: a commitment to the moral potential of leisure, its capacity to contribute to self-improvement, or to the more general social good. This sort of stance was depicted in Robert A. Heinlein's 1961 science fiction novel *Stranger in a strange land*, in which a "Dr Horace Quackenbush, Professor of Leisure Arts at Yale Divinity School, called for a return to faith and cultivation of spiritual values" (Heinlein, 1968: p. 71). The Leisure Studies Association is a broad church, though a moral stance on leisure is not, we understand — certainly not yet — fundamental to its constitution: but debates about the nature of leisure, and sometimes its moral dimensions, remain the Association's core business. And it is still more important to undertake such inquiry at a time when it is not the 'leisure society' that is seen as the dream of the future. Rather, when the dream of a knowledge economy provided for by the cultural and creative industries dominates the rhetoric of providers and politicians, accessible categories such as work and leisure, and their changing interdependency, are central to any understanding of contemporary society and culture.

In Britain, early in 2008, the Department for Culture, Media and Sport combined with the Department for Business, Enterprise & Regulatory Reform and the Department for Innovation, Universities and Skills to publish its manifesto cum policy report entitled *Creative Britain: new talents for the new economy*. The stated aim of this report was "to improve the quality of life for all through cultural and sporting activities, supporting the use of excellence. And champion the tourism, creative and leisure industries". Music, film, fashion, architecture, television, computer games — Prime Minister Gordon Brown listed these, in his Foreword to the report, as evidence of the renowned, undeniable 'force of British creativity' recognised by people 'across the globe'. Unlock the creative talents of all, Brown urged, for all the world sounding like a harbinger of a new leisure utopia in which the boundaries of producer and consumer become blurred in a flurry of overlapping creative activity. The spirit of the government document is admirable, the intent to blend cultural, business and educational/training policy bold. But read on in the report and the specifics — the sport, the leisure, the tourism highlighted in the stated aim — are notably vague, for the most part absent. No such policy can be effective without a sense of the trends in those sectors, and a more analytical perspective on the significance and potential of particular sorts of leisure activity and provision — where these might actually overlap with training, where business spills over into cultural production. Here, we have at least one answer to our conference-framing question: the leisure society is now the society of the creative industries, populated by droves of potentially unlocked talents in a new knowledge economy. It is an invigorating vision, but one which must be met with caution because it is premised on assumptions about what people do or are seen to want to do, rather than what they actually do and realistically aspire to do. Leisure Studies can continue to contribute to our knowledge of these utterly essential questions, and in doing so demonstrate that, while the dream of the leisure society may have faded, the need for leisure studies has never been greater. This collection of studies [one of two volumes: see also Gilchrist and Wheaton, 2008][1] illustrates the value of rigorous and focused analyses of specific leisure practices and spaces that can inform the wider debates about the nature of the cultural industries, the creative industries and the knowledge economy. In the volume we divide the contributions into three themed sections: media cultures and their relationship to leisure practices of women and young people; leisure and the complexities of consumption, including debates surrounding work, consumption and leisure lives, and lifestyle discourses; and tourist spaces, embracing traditional and emerging tourist visitor and travel attractions.

In section one **Sue Thornham** draws on two recent projects concerned with media and cultural industries to highlight emerging issues for feminists. The projects reflect her ongoing engagement with feminism and media studies and her recent qualitative research with young women living in China. She makes effective use of the 'makeover' trope and applies the idea to three areas of concern. Firstly, she outlines the shifts in 'Western' feminist media theory over the last three decades, involving the claims of post feminism. Secondly, she considers the 'spectacularized self' through a focus on television shows such as Channel 4's *Ten Years Younger,* and, finally she offers an analysis of Chinese femininities. Thornham illustrates how media, in the 'West', produce ideas about women's bodies and how young women in China use media, namely magazines, to reproduce particular versions of embodied femininity. The analysis shows how feminists (and this includes a critique of post-feminism) can analyse cultural differences when issues surrounding the media remain similar in both countries.

Lesley Fishwick, Elizabeth Sillence, Pamela Briggs and Peter Harris continue the focus on women's engagement with media through an analysis of how women use Internet sites to acquire knowledge about their bodies, more specifically their menopausal bodies and hormone replacement therapy (HRT). In their introduction they contextualise the use of the Internet in relation to notions of health, the body and healthy bodies, and discourses of surveillance. The research findings presented are taken from a larger project that involved 15 women, aged between 41–60 years, and at various stages of the menopause: these findings suggest that the women engage in processes of negotiation, and navigation, of Internet medical/health information. Interestingly, the research demonstrates that "the menopausal women in this study do not just inscribe their bodies with Internet medical discourse. Rather, embodied experiences as well as Internet information/knowledge inform the women's health choices" as they make sense of their changing bodies.

Donna Wong also focuses on the Internet in her discussion and analysis of sport and new media. She considers the Internet to be 'new media' leisure technology and demonstrates the ways those interested in the media and sport can take account of people's use of the Internet. The analysis draws on a larger research project with three groups of people defined by age, 11–15yrs, 16–24yrs and 25–35yrs. She argues that we are currently in a liminal phase of mediated sport and research is required in order to assess the impact of digital leisure technology on young people's involvement in sport. Wong explores three main research themes: access; the relationship between new media and sport; and displacement and engagement (with media). 'New media' is defined in relation to existing media and also in relation to existing research on sport and the media. Importantly, Wong addresses the moral panics surrounding new media usage and sedentary lifestyles. Her preliminary findings suggest that a link "exists between the use of sport-related new media and taking part in physical activities". More specifically, "it appears that interest in the digital version of sport can encourage participation in sport itself".

In section two, **Tim Robinson**'s contribution applies a specific economic analysis to aspects of what he calls 'market failure' in the area of work, leisure and the environment. He tackles the issue of 'work-life' balance and discovers that in many countries where thirty years ago there had been a decrease in work time, since then work effort has in fact increased (or at least stabilised). Robinson concludes that that there is a vicious circle of overwork and over-consumption in place. He argues that the economic analysis which he provides should be employed to support policies in 'market economies' that would both protect the environment and eventually bring about the reality of the 'leisure society' which has been prophesied for so long.

In the second contribution, **Robert A. Stebbins** contends that leisure and consumption are separate processes and cannot be equated. For Stebbins the study of consumption is mostly concerned with mass consumption and relates to leisure primarily through purchases manifested as 'mass leisure'. However, he argues, not all leisure can be classified as mass consumption, or even as consumption of any kind: a critical distinction is whether the leisure component of the activity is directly and solely dependent on the acquisition of something or whether the acquisition of something is a prerequisite to a set of conditions which make the activity 'leisure'. In Stebbins's view, whereas economists regard the act of acquisition of a good or service as at the heart of consumption, a 'leisure studies' approach places the accent elsewhere and in doing so sheds new light on modern-day consumption.

Lee Davidson continues this concern with the core meaning of leisure activity in showing that committed mountaineers today centre their lives around a demanding leisure activity in an era when commitment and continuity in leisure and in life generally are regarded as in decline. She draws on biographical narrative interviews with mountaineers from New Zealand to show the difficulties in maintaining a leisure lifestyle in what Zygmunt Bauman has termed a condition of 'liquid modernity' within a context of globalisation. The temptations of consumer culture are constantly in conflict with the 'lofty ideals' of mountaineering. In particular, Davidson traces the 'divided commitments' that the participants face in the transition from solid to liquid modernity, as the mountaineers in her interviews find, literally and metaphorically, that the ground tends to shift from beneath their feet.

The concern with leisure cultures and lifestyles is given an historical focus in **Carolyn Downs**'s consideration of the 'changing face of gambling' in her analysis of working-class gambling cultures. In particular, she explores the issues surrounding the Gambling Act (2005), and provides an historical account of working-class gambling culture during the twentieth century. Downs questions the impact of the recent Act on "groups that may be culturally vul-nerable to gambling harms". Discussion details the particular behaviours of working-class gamblers, as well as various forms of legislation that ultimately seek to regulate, and tax, gambling. Gambling is shown to be increasingly available: for example in addition to pools, lottery draws, bingo and betting shops, there exist high-stakes, high-jackpot fixed-odds betting terminals and Internet gambling. Downs highlights, implicitly, the relationships between gambling, economics (individual finances) and consumption, so offering a thorough account that raises important points for future analysis of gambling as a leisure activity.

The third section comprises four contributions which take stock of particular cultural spaces, tourism sites and spaces in North America, England, and Australia. **Nicky Ryan**'s analysis and exploration of advent of art hotels as signifiers of luxury in contemporary society, based on a case study of the recently opened Gramercy Park Hotel in New York, shows how the grand urban hotel has been re-imagined: in the case of the Gramercy Park, as a 'Bohemian Hotel'. She notes for example that the building has been refashioned, with the creation of a lobby space which resembles an artist's studio. She further argues that the bohemian lifestyle which the hotel signifies is emblematic of a new kind of luxury, at once idiosyncratic and individualistic, targeted at a "footloose, affluent and increasingly art-savvy leisure class". Through the case study Ryan demonstrates in an innovative way how culture has become central to the knowledge economy in general and the process of the creation of global corporate identity in particular.

Steve Hayler reviews the place of live entertainment in the package of the traditional English seaside resort, drawing upon unique data-bases generated in his own ongoing studies, and policy documentation issued by the UK government's Department for Culture, Media and Sport. He also considers the role of the local authority, the providers of the local state, in the provision of entertainment, so collapsing any crude notion of private and public provision for the seaside holidaymaker. Hayler concludes that a "new morphology is emerging as seaside live entertainment changes to sit somewhere between the exclusive entertainments provided at the early spa resorts and the traditional live entertainments provided during the period of mass tourism". He adds that this could be "part of a broader shift which is seeing seaside resorts being transformed into 'towns by the sea'". In this trend, the 'cultural offer' of live entertainment both away from the sea and by the sea is increasingly alike, as seaside live entertainment moves away from traditional seasonal provision towards a provision of a mix of 'low' and some 'high' provision.

Glyn Bissix, Nick Baker and Leisel Carlsson focus upon the Roosevelt Campobello International Park and assess the effects upon visitor patterns of stricter immigration controls between Canada and the USA. They show, in this rigorously conducted case study, how intensified homeland security measures implemented since September 11, 2001 have had the unanticipated consequences of inhibiting free-flowing tourism across the USA-Canada border.

Impulse or casual visitor numbers have fallen, and the authors recommend that a more aggressive marketing strategy be adopted by the facility managers. The study draws upon an on-line survey and Bissix *et al.* provide a valuable discussion of and rationale for the use of such a data-gathering method. The Park is the site of the former summer home of Franklin D. Roosevelt, the 32nd President of the United States, and the study shows how the intensified security measures have contributed to general visitor decline, and notes the impact on ageing visitors to whom the site has appealed on the basis of its historical resonances. More optimistically, the authors conclude that the site's historical value may "increase in the years to come as its antiquity grows".

Clare Lade's analysis of the value of cluster theory concludes the section and the volume. Her focus is on Australia's Murray River, and the advantages that the river provides for development of related, or at least contiguous, leisure activities. Adopting a case study method, Lade took four regions as a basis for her investigation into attitudes towards competition and the receptiveness to cluster development in order to increase competitive advantage along the river. A survey of business providers was complemented by in-depth interviews with selected main representatives of tourism and development organisations. Lade concludes that however much potential for competitive advantage cluster development has, much also depends upon the "presence of strong leadership and the ability for related and supporting industries in the region to work together...". Nevertheless, and despite some differences between the regions, all expressed a "regard for high innovation within development".

The LSA continues to promote an open-minded approach to the study of and research into leisure. The array of topics and cases covered in this volume is testimony to that commitment. In probing behind the policy rhetoric underpinning the 'leisure society' postulated in the middle of the twentieth century, and parallel political visions and models now sweeping leisure into the creative industries, it is vital that the range of leisure voices be listened to, the variety of leisure lives narrated and reported, and the multitude of leisure spaces studied and understood. Many of the contributions to this volume use a case study method; most are based upon a qualitative methodology and openness to interdisciplinary approaches. They capture the specificity of place, the meanings of lives, the niched provision by leisure providers. As such, they disavow over-arching generalizations and are valuable contributions on which to draw in answering the question '*What ever happened to the leisure society?*'.

Jayne Caudwell, Steve Redhead, Alan Tomlinson
May 2008

Note

1   See p. 190 of this volume for details of the companion volume.

References

DCMS (Department for Culture, Media and Sport) (2008) *Creative Britain: New talents for the new economy.* London: DCMS, 22 February. See at www.culture.gov.uk.

Gilchrist, P. and Wheaton, B. (2008) *Whatever happened to the Leisure Society? Theory, debate and policy* (LSA Publication No. 102). Eastbourne: Leisure Studies Association.

Heinlein, R. A. (1968) *Stranger in a strange land.* New York: Berkley Books.

Lawson, H. A. (1976) 'Physical education and sport: Alternatives for the future', in Yiannakis, A., McIntyre, T. D., Melnick, M. J. and Hart, D. P. (eds) *Sport sociology: Contemporary themes.* Dubuque/Iowa: Kendall/Hunt Publishing Company, pp. 230–237.

Seabrook, J. (1988) *The leisure society.* Oxford: Basil Blackwell.

Simnett, W.E. (1946) *Leisure: How to enjoy it.* London: George Allen & Unwin Ltd..

ABOUT THE CONTRIBUTORS

Nicholas Baker is a recent graduate of the Bachelor of Recreation Management Program at Acadia University, Nova Scotia, Canada. Currently Nicholas is continuing his education at Algonquin College in their post graduate Geographic Information Systems program. During his time at Acadia University, Nicholas conducted research for the Irving Botanical Gardens on Campobello Island based around the visitor experience to the Roosevelt Campobello International Park.

Dr. Glyn Bissix is a Professor in Recreation Management and Kinesiology at Acadia University, Nova Scotia, Canada. His recent research and consulting has focused on climate change and local response; and the relationship between alternative transportation and recreation infrastructure. He is co-author of the text *Integrated Resource and Environmental Management: The Human Dimension* (CABI, 2004) and his recent scientific publications are in the areas of rural women and depression; community resiliency and sustainability; and community design and active living.

Prof. Pamela Briggs is the Dean of the School of Psychology and Sport at Northumbria University. She has been involved with the field of human-computer interaction for the past fifteen years. Since gaining her PhD in psychology from Nottingham University she has worked in the UK, Japan and has just returned from a research sabbatical in Canada. Pam has been a principal investigator on a number of UK Research Council projects, and is currently directing projects funded by the ESRC and AHRB. She is particularly interested in social technologies and her two main areas of research are trust in computer-mediated communication and psychological issues in visual communication.

Dr. Jayne Caudwell is a Senior Lecturer in the sociology of sport and leisure cultures at the University of Brighton (UK). Her work tends to focus on gender and sexuality, more specifically on-going debate surrounding social theories of gender and sexuality, and, women's lived experiences of sport. In addition, she is concerned with feminist epistemology and methodology. Her most recent publications are: Caudwell, J. (2008) 'Girlfight:Boxing Women', *Sport and Society*. 11: pp. 227–239; and Caudwell, J. (2007) 'Critically Queer: Possibilities for a Sport Studies of the Body', in A. Tomlinson and J. Woodham (eds) *Image, Power and Space: Studies in Consumption and Identity*, Oxford: Meyer and Meyer, pp. 83–96.

Liesel Carlsson is a graduate student at Mount Saint Vincent University, Halifax (Nova Scotia), in the Department of Applied Human Nutrition. Her current research focus is on food security and community food systems, which originates from past involvement with research around issues of genuine progress, nutrition, quality of life, health related inequalities, and rural community sustainability. Related publications include: Bissix, G., Kruisselbrink, D., Carlsson, L., MacIntyre, P. and Hatcher, T. (2005) 'Active Lifestyle, Physical Recreation and Health Outcomes of Youth in Two Contrasting Nova Scotian Communities' in K. Hylton *et al.* (eds) *Evaluating Sport and Active Leisure for Young People* (LSA Publication No. 88).

Lee Davidson is a Senior Lecturer with the Museum & Heritage Studies programme at Victoria University, Wellington (New Zealand). Her main research interests include leisure and identity, and the narrative construction of meaning, with her most recent research examining meaning and identity construction in the life narratives of New Zealand mountaineers. Recent publications include: Davidson, L. (2008) 'Tragedy in the adventure playground: Media representations of mountaineering accidents in New Zealand', *Leisure Studies* Vol. 27, No. 1: pp. 3–19; and Davidson, L. (2007) 'The meaning of mountaineering: A study of New Zealand climbers', *New Zealand Alpine Journal* 59: pp. 103–107.

Dr. Carolyn Downs is a Research Fellow at Manchester Metropolitan University (UK), based in the Research Institute for Health and Social Change. Her interest in gambling and society developed from her PhD which was a social history of bingo in Britain. Her main areas of research are gambling-related, but she also has active research interests in alcohol and young people, the sociology of religion and late-eighteenth-century radicalism. Forthcoming publications include 'Pirates, death and disaster: Maintaining a business network in the 1780s' in Margrit Schulte Beerbühl and Andreas Gestrich (eds) *Cosmopolitan Networks*, The German Historical Institute, London.

Lesley Fishwick is a Senior Lecturer and CETL associate in the Division of Sport Sciences at Northumbria University (UK). Her main research interests focus on sociology of sport, women and sport, sporting identities and the social construction of healthy bodies. Recent work includes an ESRC funded project examining the role of the Internet in health, and an ethnography of health clubs examining the commoditication of fitness. Currently engaged in a series of projects with SPLaTR (Sport, Learning and Teaching Research group) focusing on developing research innovation and enhancement in the area of learning and teaching in sport-related fields.

Dr. Peter Harris is a social and health psychologist working at Sheffield University (UK). His main research interests are in risk perception, the Internet and health risk perception and predicting health behaviour. He gained his PhD in psychology from the University of London and has worked with colleagues at the Universities of Pittsburgh, USA and British Columbia, Canada. Peter has well-established research interests in "unrealistic optimism" and is also interested in the broad question of the role of perceived risk in precaution taking.

Steve Hayler is Director of Research in the Faculty of Management at Canterbury Christ Church University (UK). His main research interests are the social, cultural and economic effects of the cultural offer at English seaside resorts. Steve's particular specialism within the cultural offer is statisitics relating to live entertainment performances at English seaside theatres. His forthcoming publications include: Bull, C.J. and Hayler, S.M. (2008) 'The changing role of live entertainment at English seaside resorts at the beginning of the 21st Century', in *Tourism Geographies.*

Dr. Clare Lade works as a researcher and lecturer in the School of Sport, Tourism and Hospitality Management at La Trobe University, Bendigo (Australia). Her main research interests lie in regional economic development, of which tourism may be considered a significant driver, and marketing of festivals and events. Her doctoral research involved examination of the competitiveness of regional centres located along Australia's Murray River. She currently teaches in rural tourism, marketing and leisure related units.

Steve Redhead is Professor of Sport and Media Cultures in the Chelsea School, University of Brighton (UK) where he directs research into accelerated culture. He is author, or editor, of *Repetitive Beat Generation* (Canongate, Edinburgh, 2000), *Paul Virilio: Theorist for an Accelerated Culture* (Edinburgh University Press, Edinburgh/University of Toronto Press, Toronto and Buffalo, 2004), *The Paul Virilio Reader* (Edinburgh University Press, Edinburgh/Columbia University Press, NY, European Perspectives, 2004) and *The Jean Baudrillard Reader* (Edinburgh University Press, Edinburgh/Columbia University Press, NY, European Perspectives, 2008) alongside many other books. He is co-editor of Berg's *Subcultural Style* book series.

Tim Robinson is Professor and Head of School of Economics and Finance at Queensland University of Technology (Australia) where he is also a researcher with the Institute for Sustainable Resources. He has authored numerous journal articles and conference papers, as well three introductory economics texts and two research books: *Economic Theories of Exhaustible Resources* (Routledge, 1989) and *Work, Leisure and the Environment* (Edward Elgar, 2006). In "another life", Tim was a Queensland champion sailor and oarsman.

Dr. Nicky Ryan is Principal Lecturer in Cultural and Critical Studies in the School of Creative Enterprise at the University of the Arts London. She has recently submitted her PhD thesis in the History of Art which is an examination into cultural-commercial collaborations and the interrelationship between corporations, artists, non-profit cultural institutions and governments. Research interests include the intersection between art and business, the contemporary museum, the concept of luxury, fashion spaces and exhibitions, corporate art collections and the art scene in Las Vegas. Nicky has been published in *Fashion Theory*, *The Art Book*, *ArtReview*, *Retail Week* and is a regular reviewer for the *Museums Journal.*

Dr. Liz Sillence works as a lecturer in the Division of Psychology at Northumbria University (UK). She graduated from Aberdeen University in 1998 with B.Sc.(Hons) in Psychology and then moved to Birmingham University to complete an M.Sc. in Ergonomics and Work Design. During this time she completed a placement with NCR investigating the requirements for an online financial adviser and subsequently gained funding by NCR to carry out Ph.D. research into digital communities. She gained a Ph.D. from Birmingham University in 2003 and is currently working on the "Bodies Online" project examining the use of the Internet for health advice.

Dr. Robert A. Stebbins, FRSC, is Faculty Professor in the Department of Sociology at the University of Calgary (Canada) and Visiting Professor at the University of Bedfordshire (UK). He received his Ph.D. in 1964 from the University of Minnesota. He has written over 200 articles and chapters and written or edited 34 books, including *Between Work and Leisure* (2004), *Serious Leisure* (2007), and *Personal Decisions in the Public Square* (2008). Stebbins was elected Fellow of the Academy of Leisure Sciences in 1996 and Fellow of the Royal Society of Canada (1999). He has been studying work and leisure for nearly 45 years.

Sue Thornham is Professor of Media and Film Studies, Head of Department of Media and Film, University of Sussex, Brighton (UK). She has contributed several edited, co-authored and single authored books related to feminist film theory, feminist theory and cultural studies and more recently television drama: theories and identities. She teaches subjects such as British cinema and viewing women, and supervises doctoral students interested in the application of feminist theory to film, media and culture.

Alan Tomlinson is Professor of Leisure Studies and Head of the Chelsea School Research Centre, University of Brighton (UK). He has published more than 100 articles, book chapters and books on sport and leisure, combining historical enquiries with sociological and cultural studies. He has researched and lectured in the Americas and Australasias as well as Europe. His work has been featured in print and broadcast media and has informed policy debates on the nature and value of international sporting events. He edited *The Sports Studies Reader* (Routledge, 2007) and is currently working on the *Dictionary of Sports Studies* (Oxford University Press).

Donna Wong is a PhD student at the University of Edinburgh (UK) (Physical Education, Sport and Leisure Studies). Her main research areas are in sport and mass media. She is currently working on her PhD thesis on 'Young People, Sport and New Media Leisure Technology'. She received a BA (Merit) from the National University of Singapore, earned a Masters Degree in Mass Communication at the Nanyang Technological University (Singapore) and completed a Masters in Sport and Recreation Business Management with the University of Edinburgh. She has previously worked with the Singapore Sports Council for 9 years.

I

MEDIA CULTURES:
LEISURE PRACTICES OF WOMEN
AND YOUNG PEOPLE

'FEMINIST THOUGHTS MAY CAUSE RESENTMENT. WE MUST BE VERY CAREFUL WITH THEM.' THREE MAKEOVER STORIES

Sue Thornham

Department of Media and Film, University of Sussex, UK[1]

This chapter brings together two recent projects. One is my return to the history of the relationship between feminism and media studies in the writing of *Women, Feminism and Media* (2007). The other is a very recent visit to China, where I was conducting research with colleagues from Zhongshan University, Guangzhou, for a project tentatively called 'New femininities and popular culture in contemporary China'. Both projects have involved a re-thinking of the relationship between media and cultural industries and feminism. Both have also involved consideration of another relationship: that between feminism and its unhappy but — so she assures us — entirely legitimate daughter, postfeminism. In this chapter I want to ask: first, how can we best think the postfeminist images of today's popular culture? And second, how can a look at a contemporary cultural context which is both very different and yet in some ways strikingly familiar help us to do this? To answer these questions I'm going to tell a story of three makeovers.

Makeover 1: feminism to postfeminism

Tracing the history of a feminist media studies, one very clear trajectory that emerges is the consolidation of feminism as a subject position. In 1983 Ann Kaplan's *Women and Film* began by stating that, despite ten years of feminist film theory and criticism, "undergraduate film students rarely learn much about it" and the work is "virtually unknown" to students and academics in other, related disciplines (1983: p. ix, p. 1). She concludes by hoping that "teachers unfamiliar with feminist approaches ... will be inspired to ... *build the perspective into* their current courses".

It's a modest request. Fast forward twenty years, to 2001, and we find the journal *Feminist Media Studies* opening its launch issue in very different style. "Over the past few decades," it states, "feminist media scholarship has flourished, emerging from a barely perceptible public presence to become a profound influence on the field of communications and across a range of disciplines, and gaining particular authority in cultural and critical studies" (McLaughlin and Carter, 2001: p. 5). It's a huge shift.

The title of Kaplan's *Women and Film* was very much of its moment. In Britain the 1970s saw conferences on "Women and Socialism" and "Women and the Media" (Women's Studies Group 1978: pp. 12–13) and the establishment of a Women and Film Group in London. The first book called *Women and Media*, edited by Helen Baehr, appeared in 1980. This "political project of Women and...", as Charlotte Brunsdon calls it (2000: p. 103), was determined to force the consideration of women *in* to already existing fields of study. Not all of its protagonists were working in academic contexts, and those that were were mostly postgraduate students. It was the politics of second-wave feminism (the 'Women's Liberation Movement') not the university which brought them together. Hence what now seems an uneasy mix of huge ambition and a distinctly tentative quality. Thus the first issue of the journal *Women and Film* in 1972 could proclaim that "The struggle ... begins on all fronts", and in it women will unite with "other oppressed peoples" (1972: p. 5), whilst not being at all sure of how to achieve this. As Charlotte Brunsdon observed, finding a position from which to analyse what she calls a sense of being "somehow, outside history, and both central to, and absent in, culture" (Brunsdon 1978: p. 20), "seemed almost impossible". Since to *really* answer the question "What about women?" it would be necessary to "think... differently about the whole field or object of study" (1978: p. 11), and thus to change it both theoretically and institutionally, it is not surprising that goals were often less ambitious. Women scholars sought to 'carve out' spaces within existing fields, to 'extend' current methodologies, to 'intervene in' academic discourses, and, even more tentatively, to 'envision the kind of transformations we need and want'.

But the difference between Women and Film and *Feminist Media Studies* isn't just one of tone; it's also one of terminology. The key term, the identity from which the editors *speak,* in 2001, is that of 'feminist' not 'woman'. 'Women' as a category appears only four times in the Introduction. The identity 'feminist', however, appears over 30 times, though it might be crossed by differences in "nation, race, ethnicity, class, age, physical abilities and sexual identities" (2001: p. 6). As Denise Riley has pointed out (1988), the category 'woman' or 'women', has increasingly been recognised to be an unstable one. Not only is it fractured within by structuring inequalities (of nation, race, class for example), so that to claim to speak *for or on behalf of women* can seem to be an act of cultural imperialism. But it's also the case that to speak as and for women is to remain bounded by a category whose characteristics — however subject to historical change — are still defined by and in relation to men. Feminism is anchored in that category. But to speak as a feminist is to claim an agency beyond such characterization.

This position, the position of feminist, is, then, a *critical* one, standing in a critical relation to patriarchal structures and institutions, but also to social constructions of femininity, the dominant identity position offered to women but experienced by them, in the words of Beverley Skeggs, as "almost impossible", "uninhabitable as a complete and coherent category" (1997: p. 102). It has increasingly become also a *theoretical* one, seeking to develop the theoretical frameworks which would move analysis past the paralyzing position described by Brunsdon in 1978. And finally it is, as I said, a *subject* position. When in 1970 writers like Cellestine Ware declared themselves to be "the new feminists", making claims for a "new feminism" which was also a "renaissance of feminism"(1970: p. 7) they were claiming both a history and an identity. In that sense, their claim was *performative*. That is, they were not only making claims to a shared and politicized identity, and hence to a position from which to speak; they were also *producing* that identity.

Post-feminism

The reason I return to this here is that in some ways — and despite the insistence of *Feminist Media Studies*, perhaps itself performative — this is a history which now seems in question. Angela McRobbie (2004) points to a 1990 article by Andrea Stuart as signalling a key shift. In this piece, "Feminism: Dead or Alive?", Stuart distinguishes between what she calls "professional Feminism" and a new "popular feminism", its "errant" but more attractive daughter. Whilst the former has retreated to the academy, she writes, the new popular feminism "comes at most of us through the media": in soap operas, TV drama, ads, women's magazines and popular fiction (1990: p. 30). This new made-over feminism, one grounded in consumption as play, belongs, she writes, to "ordinary women". It is "knowing and ironic", and it celebrates individuality not collective action, pleasure not politics. Since 1990, of course, Stuart's "popular feminism" has become first "power feminism" and then "post-feminism". But the article marks two important and interrelated shifts: a shift within popular media representations, and a shift in theoretical positionings.

The shifts in popular media representations have been well charted. 'Women's genres' have — at least superficially — been re-valued. Returning after 20 years to the subject matter of her 1982 book on soap opera, Dorothy Hobson found in 2003 that its (still male) producers now see it (or claim to see it) as "television that speaks your language", "a showcase", even the contemporary "replacement … for *Play for Today*" (from interviews in Hobson, 2003: pp. 41, 50, 51). But this has also been accompanied by an increasing space given to men within the genre. In fact most popular TV dramas are now hybrid forms — both generically and in their elision of boundaries between public and private spheres (an elision first critically remarked within *Cagney and Lacey*, where it was hailed as a triumph for feminism).

These elisions are even more striking in the huge range of 'reality TV' formats, where intimate relations are played out in public arenas previously reserved for impersonal debate and social action. What this blurring of boundaries *means* is, as we know, a contested issue. On the one hand, the collapse of boundaries between a feminised private and a masculinised public sphere has been seen as liberatory for women, even as a new, feminised incarnation of the public sphere (Grindstaff 1997, Shattuc 1997). On the other, whilst in these shows notions of 'the real' and 'authenticity' are as central as they are for news or documentary, this is very much a 'real' which operates in the domain of the *body*, and the 'real' of the bodies which are displayed is one of emotion and excess. Like other 'low' or 'body genres' (Williams 1991), then, 'the real' is manifested here not in words but through emotional and bodily display. It is the staged display of bodily and emotional excess which produces the show as media entertainment, and it is the transformation and containment of this excess which provides its narrative structure. In this reading, what we are seeing here is less the formation of a feminised public sphere than the reassertion of an old idea — that mass culture operates as the realm of the degraded feminine (Huyssen, 1986; Modleski, 1986).

Finally, there is the emergence of the 'post-feminist heroine' (or as McRobbie calls it, the new 'female individualism') in advertising and in popular film and TV drama. From the knowing and self-conscious sexism of the 1990s Wonderbra ads onwards advertising images, argues McRobbie, evoke, only to dismiss, an 'old' feminism. We can see a similar phenomenon within film and popular television drama, in texts hugely popular not only with audiences but also with academics (students and teachers alike) — there are at least seven academic books on *Buffy the Vampire Slayer* (WB and UPN, 1997–2003) and, as far as I could see from Amazon, three on *Sex and the City* (HBO, 1998–2004). These popular TV texts, all aimed primarily at a female audience, and all featuring young(ish), independent, usually single women in an urban environment, engage repeatedly with feminist issues, but in an ironic, playful, style-conscious and ambivalent way. Feminism itself belongs to the past; what characterises the post-feminist woman of popular culture is individualism, sophistication and choice.

As I said, to Stuart this new position belongs to 'us', the women she calls 'ordinary women'. The phrase recalls Charlotte Brunsdon's account of 1980s feminist television criticism. It was, she says, founded on a "differentiation of the feminist from her other, the ordinary woman" (1997: p. 194). But in Brunsdon's account the 'ordinary woman' is the (feminine) woman the feminist 'might have become', to be both rejected and defended, and above all understood. Stuart's 'ordinary woman' is very different. Indeed, we can argue that the relationship between the two (the feminist and the ordinary woman) has in some ways been reversed. It is no longer the case that the 'ordinary woman' — the woman who un-self-consciously *enjoys* popular cultural forms aimed at women (soap opera, or Mills and Boon or women's magazines) — stands as a rather uncomfortable shadow figure to the feminist subject, a figure she both incorporates and rejects. Rather, it is now feminism which is simultaneously acknowledged and rejected, a shadow figure for the post-traditionalist, post-feminist 'ordinary woman' whom Stuart both invokes (1990: p. 29) and claims to be. The feminist, Stuart writes, is now within the academy; she is white, middle-class, and probably — despite her own continuing sense of marginalisation — by now a professor. The post-feminist heroine of the new women's genres, on the other hand, offers a new point of identification: post-conventional, and characterised by freedom and choice.

This figure is not only a heroine within popular culture; she also offers a powerful identificatory position for the 'post-feminist' critic and theorist. As the category 'woman' has seemed to dissolve, and that of feminist is left behind, so the position of 'post-feminist'– with its paradoxical promise of closing the gap between 'feminist subject' and 'ordinary (feminine) woman' — has become increasingly attractive. Here is the cover blurb from *Introducing Postfeminism* (1999):

> In the shift from feminism to postfeminism, women have begun to celebrate difference rather than equality. The postmodern culture of the 1990s has already seen the emergence of a new female icon. Tough, sexy and irreverent, she does not see herself as a victim, and she wants power. But *having deconstructed women's oppression and reclaimed women's culture*, what does the future hold for post-feminism? [my italics]

In this book and elsewhere, postfeminism, in its theoretical guise, becomes a conflation of 'postmodernism' and/or 'postcolonialism' (or 'poststructural-ism') and feminism, thus appropriating a whole range of theorists who would see themselves as feminist. But whereas the postcolonial or poststructuralist feminist remains a *feminist*, in 'post-feminism' such an identity is no longer on offer. Feminism disappears: in *Introducing Postfeminism* it disappears — with breathtaking speed — as early as 1968. "Postfeminism", write the authors, "begins in 1968" (1999: p. 3).

Makeover 2: the specularized self

So what identities *are* on offer here, in this postfeminist media culture, and how are we invited to adopt them? I want to begin with an example from UK television, before turning rather further afield. My example involves the intersection of a transformation narrative very familiar from women's magazines with both the 'reality' genre and the promises of new techno-logies. In Channel 4's *Ten Years Younger* the transformative promise is to reverse the passage of time for its participants (or at least to turn back their 'poll age') through a series of expert interventions: dental and plastic surgery; hair, makeup and fashion training. As a result they will improve both their 'personal life' and their public visibility.

As women age, they become invisible in the public sphere. The *solution* is to change their clothes, their faces and their bodies, the *problem* not one of social structures but of inadequate self-management leading to poor self-esteem. Shirley, then, who is 41 but, when displayed to an audience of passers by, "looks 52", has "sagging skin, Deputy Dawg eyebags and tombstone teeth". Unlike her exact contemporaries Sandra Bullock, Elle Macpherson and Courtney Cox, she has failed to "work hard to look good". She will be restored to an *imaginary* earlier self, the shameful traces of her present (and past) inadequacy erased, and so avoid the horrific future predicted in a series of computer-generated images of her aging face. But first she must have her grotesque body exposed; her teeth are shown filed to stumps, her skin is peeled back and the fatty lumps on her face are removed one by one and displayed to camera. Finally she is reconstructed, ready for public display: passers by now judge her to be 38; she is "a new woman" and, asked to comment, says she is "speechless". Her job serving gourmet food is safe.

Like other reality TV programmes, *Ten Years Younger* is constructed as a competition, a race against time to complete a successful transformation. But its material is "the female body in disarray" (Mellencamp 1992: p. 274); the time to be beaten that of the aging process as visible deterioration; the process of transformation a survival guide which is also a training exercise in normalization. A re-made Shirley is restored to public visibility, but the gendered structures that insist that her visibility (and her employment) depend on the appearance of youth have not been challenged. Nor, despite the process of 'mediated visibility' in which the private body has been subjected to a public gaze, have the boundaries between public and private been eroded. As private body, Shirley is fragmented into body parts, each subjected to the disciplinary gaze of the camera; once re-made as youthful public self, the camera retreats, observing her at work with colleagues and clients, transformed, regulated, surviving.

"I defy you not to watch that moment when the curtain goes back, and the person sees what's happened to them", says the producer of one makeover show, quoted in the *Guardian* of September 14th, 2005. "It's almost the pornographic shot." It's an interesting analogy, and one we might follow a little further. Writing about the pornographic "money shot", Linda Williams, drawing on Irigaray, talks about the overcathexis of vision, the "rule of visibility" and "specularization" (1990: p. 116) that characterises a capitalist and patriarchal economy. The fetishised and specularized excess of the money shot, she writes, substitutes for actual loss — that of relation to the female other (and of the woman's desire and pleasure which the shot purports to, but never can represent). In the money shot of the makeover show, the climactic moment is no less an overcathexis of vision. Here, however, the intensity is invested in the female subject's successful production of herself as an object of display. If as Anne Cronin (2000) argues, we too are produced performatively as subjects in the moment of our intense identificatory engagement with these images, the subject position we are offered here is one characterised by what we might call an 'active femininity'. This subject position is the paradoxical promise of postfeminism: an active femininity manifest in the production of the self as an aesthetic object within a consumerist regime.

Makeover 3: Chinese femininities

I want to shift focus a little now. At first sight, the fashion/women's magazines found in today's urban China are not very different from their Western counterparts. Indeed, the Chinese versions are often franchises of Western magazines. Hearst Magazines International has published a Chinese version of *Cosmopolitan* since 1998, via a Beijing-based, part government–owned partner, Trends Magazine, and over the last almost ten years this has been joined by both Chinese franchises of Japanese brands (*Oggi* — since 2001, *ViVi*) and by home-grown titles (*iLook* and *Rayli*).

If we look at the magazines themselves, however, there *are* differences. In the Western versions we find both the slide to postfeminist irony that I was talking about earlier and, more disturbingly, what Angela McRobbie (2007) has called 'semihallucinatory images', in which the models seem inaccessible, unreal, post- or perhaps simply non-human. These most recent images seem to belong to a more uneasy postfeminism, presenting us with a femininity that knows itself to be, in Skeggs' words, impossible, uninhabitable. But they are images that seem, as McRobbie argues, not so much playful as haunted, their seductive quality that of Baudrillard's "attraction of the void" (1990: pp. 76–7), not an invitation to reflexive play.

In the Chinese versions the promises are much less equivocal. But they are no more promises of a coherent subject position than their Western counterparts, and the femininity they offer is, I would argue, just as impossible. To understand what is going on here, I want to move, in part, away from the magazines themselves and to the young women I interviewed in China about their magazine reading. The 20 or so young women I interviewed, in pairs or groups of 3 or 4, are all students at Zhongshan University, Guangzhou, aged between 20 and 24. This positions them in a number of ways. They were all born in the post-Mao era, so that for them there is an absolute historical divide between the *now* which they inhabit and the 'then' of their mothers; with the break between the two being the Cultural Revolution (1966–76).

They were also born in the era of the single child policy (inaugurated in 1979), and although not all were in fact single children, most were. They

Fashion pages, Oggi March 2007

are also the product of a fiercely competitive education system, in which
gender difference is not recognised — a legacy of the Mao years, when
gender equality (or sameness) became official state policy — and to get into
a top ten university like Zhongshan you have to be at the very top. Now,
however, they are nearing the end of their time as students and looking
outwards, towards employment, and here too things are distinctively different

Beauté de Kosé ad, *Oggi* **March 2007**

from the past. They are part of the first generation to have to compete for jobs (rather than being assigned them, as happened up to the mid 1990s), in a world in which gender difference, officially denied in their school years, is suddenly very pronounced. All thought it much harder for young women than for young men to compete in the labour market, and all thought they were a world away from their mothers. As one said, "They [were] in

a communist society ... but we're the first generation in the new China"
(A, interview 5).

So in what way is this femininity, that they must now learn to inhabit,
an impossible position? And what has this to do with the postfeminism I
discussed in relation to Western popular culture? To answer the first question,
I want to identify two major — but highly contradictory — interpretive
structures (or repertoires, to use Joke Hermes' term) through which these
students discussed the images they found in the magazines. The first is
that of usefulness: the students persistently stressed the *use value* of the
magazines:

> I enjoy reading magazines because, first, they are useful for what,
> er for me. For example I want to buy some new dress in this summer
> and what can I buy? What is the fashion? I will read the magazine
> and find the answer. (A, interview 3)[2]

> I will read some useful parts and some important parts, for example
> they will tell you how to make you like er elegant er a career woman
> er in modern times. They can tell you how to make your skin
> beautiful, how to dress very gracefully. I think they're very useful.
> (P, interview 1)

But this is always accompanied by an insistence on the second key interpretive structure: that of daydream or fantasy — an *escape* from the real
which is at the same time a half-believed vision of a *future* real. Here's "B":

> For me, I always look with the colourful pictures just to relax. It's
> always so beautiful. Never to read this very closely, never to read
> this *** [*translator*: carefully] carefully, never read this carefully,
> because I er for me, you know the economics for me is not very good,
> so I have no money to buy this clothing, to buy these decorations,
> so I always look at these pictures, all so beautiful. Maybe one day
> I will have enough money and enough time to choose and to buy
> these things but er I think for me just now ... I think it's just a dream,
> yeah it's a dream. (interview 1)

These two — use and dream — come together in a "dream" (the word appears
in almost all the interviews) of the future which is characterised by
independence, career success — and a focus on appearance. It will be above
all different from their mothers' lives, which are seen as defined by sacrifice,
but the very choices that mark it as new and exciting are also *experienced*
as a form of gender regulation. This is "B" explaining the attraction of a
particular image:

> Because my head is not very high and I'm a little fat [laughs] so I
> want myself to lose weight so I always mm and when I read these

magazines I will see so many models, so beautiful and have so, so great build. (interview 1)

The "dream", then, is of an ideal — an absolute — beauty: these models are quite simply "beautiful", "perfect" (C, interview 5: "They have perfect face, perfect figure"). They are perfect static *images*. But it is also a dream of activity, success, *control*:

> And why I say it is the dream because sometimes you know when we read we will think "Wow, the model is so slim and I want to become her" and sometimes in the magazine I read, it often tells us about the life of the model and what will they do in their spare time and what books they read and I think this will let me feel er when I read about their lives I want to become the active one in my life. I want to be active in my life like models. (A, interview 3)

For "B", the dream of a fantasised self transformation shades into a dream of independence — and both are acknowledged to be fragile, and experienced self-consciously *as* dream:

> Yeah I will have my dream. If I lose my dream and I just want, I just want to be housewife I think I will lose my, I will lose my self. For the economics I will depend on my husband, it's so terrible, you know, if your economic is not very is not independent you will depend on him so no, a short time is OK but after a long time he will lose er *** [*translator*: look down upon] look down on me so I think it's so horrible, but I, so I still have my dream. (interview 1)

Similarly, these images are seen to be wholly constructed (D, interview 5: "I think the figure of the model we see from the magazine is not her real figure") and yet there is a repeated insistence that they *are* also *real*:

> I mean in the, at first they just use a model, they just use girls that didn't exist in the real world but in recent years I think these magazines just find some real girls on the street, they just, they are the same as us ... so the magazine just give us a clue that you can do that, you can achieve it. (D, interview 5)

And third, and most difficult to address, these ideal images are both *white* or *whitened* and absolutely, the students insist, *Chinese*. White, Western(ised) faces, and tall, thin Western bodies dominate, both in the images themselves and in the students' characterisations of what for them is the ideal appear-ance. Ads for skin whiteners are the single most frequently occurring type of advertisement, and a comparison of the skin tones of the models in the Chinese magazines with those of blonde models in UK magazines reveals that those of the Chinese models are usually lighter. The students' definitions of beauty emphasised thinness and white or fair skin (A. 3: p. 8), "very

Magazine stand, Guangzhou March 2007

世界時裝
MARCH 2007
25+
春夏潮流
备新品
瘦身误区:
三公斤
症候群
染发:
21个
IDEAS
轻易就优雅
THE COLOURS
OF FASHION
南方
人物
你有股份吗
瑞丽
饰美容
健康之
Woman's Day

big eyes, ... very good skin, very small lips, and very small and straight noses" (L.7: p. 6). Models or actresses whose eyes are "small ... slant", they said, "fit the Western imagination, but not our evaluation" (ibid.). Many of the students talked about the popularity of cosmetic surgery both among the Chinese models and amongst their own acquaintances. But all insisted that this makes the women not only more beautiful but also more *Chinese*:

> B: ... there is a Chinese model who became very popular in the Western world now because they think she's beautiful but in Chinese eyes she's very ugly. ....

> A: I think in China what we think beauty is different from the old days but in Western it's the same, and they think Chinese people *** [*translator*: Yes, the single eyelid] and their eyes are like this and small mouth. They think Chinese are like that, that is the beautiful Chinese woman, but in China I don't think so. Many girls like the eyes and higher nose so that is the reason why they go to do some operation on their face. (interview 3)

Conclusions: unavowable loss?

So how can we begin to understand this? Angela McRobbie (2007) writes that the fashion image "visualises the disturbance which accrues from the interplay of desire with constraint", producing what she calls "unavowable loss". She's talking about the postfeminist images of today's Western magazines and their readers, and the losses she identifies are of, first (following Judith Butler), the same sex love object, and second, the feminism which would have made both possible and legitimate such object-desire. Reflecting on these *Chinese* magazines and some of their readers, it seems to me that first, the loss(es) here are just as palpable. Second, that McRobbie's explanation of that loss doesn't quite work here. But third, there *are* explanations that work across both sets of magazines, and the other makeovers I have described.

Chinese feminism is a complex subject. According to Tani Barlow (1994: p. 255), the general category of 'generic woman' does not appear in Chinese until the 1920s. Until then, the various positions which women could occupy are complexly coded by age, rank, familial or marital relationship as well as gender (*funu* = female kinsfolk; *xiannu* = virtuous unmarried female and so on). *Nüxing*, as a term for a generic 'woman' (as in man/woman, woman as subject, woman as agent etc), is a neologism which appears in the 1920s, the outcome of the May Fourth revolutionary movement of 1919. It was replaced in the Mao era by *funü*, a state generated term which described (or produced) a social or political category (like *gongren* = worker or *qingnian* = youth). Thus the Chinese Communist Party-led 'women's liberation' of the Mao era has been much criticised for its lack of recognition of sexual difference and corresponding imposition of a notion of gender-equality which was in fact a gender-sameness based on men — what Dai Jinhua calls "the liberated woman as defined by revolutionary (male) norms" (2002: p. 119). But *funu* has in turn been replaced in post-Mao popular discourse with a return to *nüxing*— and this is the term that is used in the magazines I saw. What this means is that the notion of the 'strong' or 'liberated' woman is hopelessly compromised in contemporary Chinese discourse: linked with notions of revolution, state control and refusal of difference. *Nüxing*, on the other hand, promises a return to 'femininity' construed as 'female essence' in which sexual difference can be co-opted for a (Western) consumerism which places women as both consumers and objects of consumption.

'Feminism' itself can be translated by two terms, *nüquán zhuyì*, literally "theory/doctrine of women's power", or *nüxing zhuyì*, literally "theory/doctrine of the female gender". Significantly, the first is now less popular than the second, indicating just how problematic the Mao years have rendered any notions of a women's social or political identity or movement.

There is a loss here, then, which the students' constant sliding between a dream of the perfect appearance (and the commodified Western nature of that appearance), and a dream of autonomy and control, both gestures towards and cannot quite grasp. Chinese women, they recognise, are discriminated against as a group, but the individualised and individualising strategies which authorize them as subjects provide no explanation and no solution. Indeed, asked to look further forward, to how they see their futures, the conflicts seem insuperable. This is "B" again:

> Maybe after you get married you will, I will, you will have children yeah, you will have a family and your husband's family and my family. My family and my husband's family is 2 families and I think er his parents and my parents have to be looked after and to take care of them so I think this is so, many many things have to do with and then er, for me I think, when I was little I want to be a career woman but I think after I get married there is *so* many things [M: housework] and housework to do and then after I do these I have to do the, my job and now I think maybe the housework er can, my husband can do the half and I can do the half of it. This will be better but I think just now I think it's just a dream. You know in our culture it says the women to do the housework. You say "I'm a feminist" but it's just [laughter] *** [*translator*: slogan] just a slogan. In real life you can't do this, just a slogan yeah. (interview 1)

For these young women, continuity with an older feminism is impossible, because that lies behind the impassable barrier of 1976, but the new (imported, Western) feminism is not only "just a dream", as "B" says, but also hopelessly entangled with individualism and consumerism. The impossibility of even *thinking* that older moment (and hence the present) as political is captured in this student's account of her relationship with her mother:

> A: Because your skin, if your skin is very good and when your age is getting old but you don't look very old it will make you be happier. And I will send my mom some skin care things and sometimes she thinks that is unnecessary, but this time when I talk to her again and again now she cares about herself more. And I think it's very important for one woman. ...
>
> Interviewer: So she wasn't as interested in fashion as you then, when she was young?
>
> A: No. They have their fashion at that time, for example the trousers like this and when, in China at that time they will *** [*translator*: the Red Guard, you know, the Red Guard are young people] yeah they wear those very clothes and in that time they think that is fashion. Although everybody seems the same, but they think it's very fashionable. (interview 3)

History, here, is interpreted as makeover.

Despite this complex and different history, then, I want to argue that there *are* important connections here with the stories I was trying to tell earlier. Cut off, co-opted or made-over, all feature a feminism that has been rendered inaccessible. The loss, I think, is not so much that of an object of desire, as McRobbie in part suggests, as of a historical and political space, and the subject position that might inhabit it. Indeed, to call it a 'loss' is to risk obscuring the very active processes — of global capitalism, its media and cultural industries, its political cultures, and of our own active complicities — that produce it. The conclusion I would draw from the comparisons I've tried to make, then, is that we do our analysis a great disservice if, looking at forms of Western popular culture, we see the makeovers which constitute the cultural space of postfeminism as part of a historical shift specific only to us — evidence, perhaps, of a shift in the West to 'late modernity' — or worse still, as a kind of postfeminist liberation. My last interview in China was with a group of journalists who work as writers or editors of women's magazines which are locally produced, but mostly transnationally owned. They were wary of me, and divided about the prospects for change. In the magazine industry, one said,

> We always see men at the positions such as General Director of Editors, or Director of editorial department. But women are found to be the principal editor. Women have the title but no power, and they are supposed to work more. (A, interview 8)

They saw the problems as complex:

> I was doing reading on breast augmentation some days ago, which
> pains me. The big breast is absolutely not Chinese, but a pure
> outcome of consumerism. We have to fight against both the
> discrimination against women from the Chinese tradition and the
> new discrimination of women's bodies from the western capitalism.
> (J, interview 8)

And they were defensive about their own complicity. This is the editor of
Chic explaining why she doesn't try to change things:

> Nobody says you've got to read the women's magazines. The feminist
> thoughts may cause resentment. We must be very careful with them.
> (C, interview 8)

Nevertheless, a number of them had set up a Gender and Media Action
Group, to (I quote from its manifesto) "seek and create new culture and
new reality". It's a search which, in our own anxiety to embrace postfeminist
choice, we've rather forgotten.

Note

1   With thanks to Feng Pengpeng, Zhongshan University, Guangzhou,
      China.

2   The interviews were conducted with a Chinese research assistant,
      Feng Pengpeng, in a mixture of English and Chinese. Where the
      students spoke in English, their words are transcribed here. Where
      they spoke in Chinese, Feng provided a translation.

References

Aitkenhead, D. (2005) 'Most British women now expect to have cosmetic surgery
      in their lifetime. How did the ultimate feminist taboo become just another
      lifestyle choice?', *The Guardian* Wednesday September 14.
Barlow, T. E. (1994) 'Theorizing Woman: *Funü, Guojia, Jiating* (Chinese Woman,
      Chinese State, Chinese Family)', in Zito, Angela and Barlow, Tani E.
      (eds) *Body, subject and power in China.* Chicago and London: University
      of Chicago Press, pp. 255–289.
Baudrillard, J. (1990) *Seduction,* trans. Brian Singer. Basingstoke: Macmillan.
Brunsdon, C. (1978) 'It is well known that by nature women are inclined to
      be rather personal', in Women's Studies Group, CCCS, *Women Take Issue:
      Aspects of Women's Subordination.* London: Hutchinson, pp. 18–34.
—— (1997) *Screen tastes: Soap opera to satellite dishes.* London: Routledge.
—— (2000) *The feminist, the housewife, and the soap opera.* Oxford: Oxford
      University Press.

Cronin, A. M. (2000) *Advertising and Consumer Citizenship*. London and New York: Routledge.

Dai J. (2002) 'Gender and narration: Women in contemporary chinese film', trans. Jonathan Noble, in Dai, *Cinema and desire: Feminist Marxism and cultural politics in the work of Dai Jinhua*, ed. Jing Wang and Tani E. Barlow. London: Verso, pp. 99–150.

Grindstaff, L. (1997) 'Producing trash, class and the money shot: A behind-the-scenes account of daytime TV talk', in Lull, J. and Hinerman, S. (eds) *Media scandals*. Cambridge: Polity, pp. 164–202.

Hermes, J. (1995) *Reading women's magazines*. Oxford: Polity.

Hobson, D. (2003) *Soap opera*. Oxford: Polity.

Huyssen, A. (1986) 'Mass culture as woman: Modernism's other', in Huyssen, *After the Great Divide: Modernism, mass culture and postmodernism*. Basingstoke and London: Macmillan, pp. 44–62.

Kaplan, E. A. (1983) *Women and film: Both sides of the camera*. New York and London: Methuen.

McLaughlin, L. and Carter, C. (2001) 'Editors' introduction', *Feminist Media Studies* Vol. 1, No. 1: pp. 5–10.

McRobbie, A. (2004) 'Post feminism and popular culture', *Feminist Media Studies* Vol. 4, No. 3: pp. 255–64.

——— (2007) 'Illegible rage: Young women's post-feminist disorders'. Available at www.lse.ac.uk/collections/LSEPublicLecturesAndEvents/ events/ 2007/20061204t1746z001.htm

Mellencamp, P. (1992) *High anxiety: Catastrophe, scandal, age, & comedy*. Bloomington and Indianapolis: Indiana University Press.

Modleski, T. (1986) 'Femininity as mas(s)querade: A feminist approach to mass culture', in MacCabe, C. (ed) *High theory / low culture*. Manchester: Manchester University Press, pp. 37–52.

Phoca, S. and Wright, R. (1999) *Introducing postfeminism*. Cambridge: Icon Books.

Riley, D. (1988) *'Am I that name?' Feminism and the category of 'women' in history*. Basingstoke: Macmillan.

Shattuc, J. (1997) *The talking cure: TV, talk shows and women*. New York: Routledge.

Skeggs, B. (1997) *Formations of class and gender*. London: Sage.

Stuart, A. (1990) 'Feminism: Dead or alive?', in Rutherford, J. (ed) *Identity: Community, culture, difference*. London: Lawrence and Wishart, pp. 28–42.

Ware, C. (1970) *Woman power: The movement for women's liberation. New York*: Tower Publications.

Williams, L. (1990) *Hard core*. London: Pandora.

——— (1991) 'Film bodies: Gender, genre and excess', *Film Quarterly* Vol. 44, No. 4: pp. 2–13.

Women and Film (1972) 'Overview', *Women and Film* No. 1: pp. 3–6.

Women's Studies Group, CCCS (1978) 'Women's Studies Group: Trying to do feminist intellectual work', in Women's Studies Group, *Women take issue: Aspects of women's subordination. London*: Hutchinson, pp. 7–17.

Zhong, X. (2006) 'Who is a feminist? Understanding the ambivalence towards *Shanghai Baby*, 'body writing' and feminism in post-women's liberation China', *Gender & History* Vol. 18, No.3: pp. 636–661.

WOMEN'S IDENTITY AND CONSUMPTION OF HEALTH DISCOURSES ON THE INTERNET

Lesley Fishwick*, Elizabeth Sillence*, Pamela Briggs* and Peter Harris**

*School of Psychology and Sport, Northumbria University, UK
**Sheffield University, UK

Introduction

In this postmodern age the Internet is an important source of information and knowledge for an increasing number of consumers. For this growing population of Internet users it is information related to health that has attracted over sixty-two percent of users and influenced over 21 million people (Pew, 2000). This high level of engagement with health information corresponds to societal trends whereby individuals take personal responsibility for the 'duty to be well' (Greco, 1993). The shift to a knowledge economy has also been accompanied by a 20th century shift from collective care and treatment to more individual health care culture (Ingham, 1985). In this way, health promotion has become an important aspect of illness prevention; and moreover, keeping healthy is seen as primarily the responsibility of individuals. This shift of emphasis from state provision of medical care to an emphasis on individual consumerism of medical information has implications for health choices made by individuals. Several scholars have voiced concern and skepticism about the encroachment of medical authority into daily life (Crawford, 1980; Ingham, 1985; Lupton, 1995). As Wheatley (2005) highlights, a preoccupation with lifestyle and health risks combined with an emphasis on individual responsibility supports the assumption that individuals control their own health destinies. The concern is that health information on the Internet has become yet another source of disciplinary surveillance of one's own body. Such surveillance would be part of a consumer lifestyle of the middle classes identified by Featherstone (1991) in which the body is an enterprise, a project resource to be managed and developed. In this way, the health roles in contemporary society have moved beyond the boundaries of medical clinical encounters between physicians and patients. As Bunton and Burrows (1995) note, the contemporary citizen is expected to take into account recommendations

21

of a whole range of 'experts' and 'advisors' located in a range of institutional and cultural sites. The current study examines the cultural site of the Internet and in particular how women position their bodies within the biomedical and cultural discourses of the emerging industry of health advice on-line.

The Internet has a vital role as it provides up-to-date, current medical research that is accessible to the lay person. As Parr (2002) stresses, this diffusion of medical and health information encourages a different kind of medical gaze facilitated by virtual space. Physical bodies are discursively constructed in virtual space within sites focusing on health information and promotion. In this sense, bodies can be seen as healthy projects inscribed by medicalised information from a plethora of virtual resources. Citizens are urged to turn the medical gaze on themselves to monitor their own bodies and health states (Lupton, 1995). However, as Budgeon (2003) notes, the literature from the sociology of the body has been primarily concerned with the question of what bodies mean. Answers to this question have relied primarily on social constructionist strategies which, as Budgeon (2003) critiques too often posit the dominant relation that women have with their bodies as being discursively mediated and significantly over-determined. There is a need to redress the balance and focus on what participants 'do' with the information and examine how individuals work on their own bodies, enacting and embodying their newly acquired healthy knowledges, as suggested by Parr (2002).

The current study moves beyond a discursive constitution of the body by bringing back into focus the materiality of the body. The selection of hormone replacement therapy (HRT) as the health issue places "disrupted" bodies under scrutiny, focusing on menopausal women and how the materiality of their bodies influences their identity and their engagement with health information on the Internet. The analysis focuses on the women not as consumers who merely passively receive health information but as active subjects who generate meanings attached to their own embodied identities. In this way the potentially empowering and transformative capacities of electronic information flows, with their attendant social and cultural changes within the present virtual information society, are also considered (Parr, 2002). Questions revolving around the degree of passivity of receiving information versus engaging in a more active process are crucial as individuals are opening themselves up to new and more specialized medical discourse which serves as a resource for self-maintenance, discipline and control. Parr (2002) clarifies some of the consequences of the type of engagement. On the one hand an active engagement with medical discourses has the potential for emancipatory disruption of the traditional canons of medical power; but on the other hand a passive process could lead patients to increasingly objectify their own bodies through the effects of the power of medical inscriptions. This has implications for women's agency over their health choices in this age of individual health consumerism.

The key purpose of the present study is to explore how health information is communicated, consumed and embodied by women using the Internet. The study focuses on menopausal women whose physically lived-in bodies are the focus or cause of their travels into virtual space. The rationale is that during menopause the materiality of the body is disrupted in some way and is not so straightforward or stable, thus emphasizing daily negotiations of embodiment for these women. The research question is to determine to what extent the web offers critical opportunities for women to take control over their health choices? Do the women actively engage in the process of consuming health information? What impact does the Internet information have on how the women deal with their health issues? The significance of the current study is that it traces the interactions and reactions of women interested in searching for health information on the Internet.

Research design

The current study is part of larger scale project examining trust online in terms of health advice (Sillence *et al.*, 2004). Four longitudinal studies examined groups of people facing health decisions (the specific health issues were menopause and hormone replacement therapy [HRT], hypertension, MMR [measles, mumps and rubella vaccination] and healthy living). The focus of the current paper is on the issue facing menopausal women and their health dilemmas concerning HRT and alternate therapies. The methodological procedures were the same in each study and allowed for the examination of people's decision-making processes from the first few seconds of interaction with a Web site to one year of engagement.

The protocol for each study was as follows:

Week	1st hour	Concurrent	Break 10 min	2nd hour
1	Free web search	Verbal protocol	Break	Group discussion
2	Directed search	Verbal protocol	Break	Group discussion
3	Directed search	Verbal protocol	Break	Group discussion
4	Free web search	Verbal protocol	Break	Group discussion
Year (1)	Diary	Tel. Interviews	—	—

Fifteen women at various stages of the menopause participated in the study (Sillence *et al.*, 2004). The women were aged between 41 and 60 (X=41); all used the Internet at least once a week and were interested in finding out more about the menopause. Each participant attended a total of four 2–hour sessions and used the Internet to search for information and advice on the menopause, followed by a group discussion with a facilitator. The participants freely surfed the web in sessions 1 and 4 and were directed to specific web sites in sessions 2 and 3. The participants recorded their perceptions of each site visited in a logbook and were asked to "speak aloud" as they searched the sites. All verbal protocols and discussions were transcribed verbatim. After these sessions the participants were asked to keep a diary of their Internet usage for health-related issues in a 6 month follow-up period. They were asked to record any sites they had visited and make a note of what prompted them to go on-line. Participants were also asked to note any 'off-line' interactions concerning the health topic with health professionals, friends and family. After one year from the original study participants were interviewed by telephone (N=10) and these interviews were transcribed verbatim. All names have been changed to protect the anonymity of the participants.

The transcripts were then read through several times to identify key emerging areas of interest and to become familiar with the data. These emerging areas included material body, individual responsibility, GP-patient hierarchy, trust and empowerment. Of these emerging areas the relationship between use of the Internet and empowerment for women clearly emerged as a key theme from the data and as a focus for the current analysis. The researcher then returned to the transcripts and began an independent process of selecting, describing and coding pieces of text that reflected the women's experiences of searching for menopausal information on the Internet. Initial descriptive codes of positive and negative evaluation of websites were then compared and amalgamated into larger categories, moving from descriptive to analytical coding labels through a process involving a combination of hermeneutics and a grounded theory approach similar to that of Strauss and Corbin (1991). In particular, attention was paid both to the variation within each category, and the extent to which there might be commonality or difference between participants with different menopausal symptoms.

Results and discussion

The women very quickly devised a way of navigating through the virtual health sites as a very distinctive pattern of rejecting and selecting health sites became clear from the data. The women developed routines to navigate through this virtual library as they surfed and sorted their way through the medical information available on the Internet. During the sessions the women's on-line HRT searches involved gathering, sorting and learning about the menopause and involved making choices from, as Pitts (2004) describes it, "the Web's seemingly endless possibilities" (p. 43). What became abundantly clear were features that led to sites being rejected. In general, the women disliked many American sites as they did not relate to the jargon and indicated that, with their culture of litigation, these sites were often scaremongering. They noticed headlines such as "six million American women are adversely affected", and bristled at instructions such as "if you are on HRT contact your doctor IMMEDIATELY". Some of the participants evaluated such information as characterizing an anti-HRT bias and voiced this in terms of creating feelings that "the HRT police will be out to get you".

In general the women preferred more balanced sites and in this vein they were just as likely to reject sites that showed a bias towards HRT. Often such sites were sponsored by drug companies and many of the women expressed alarm and a degree of wariness and responded by rapidly rejecting sites that had visible signs of commercialism. Sponsorship by drug companies led the women to query the impartiality and credibility of the information: "all paths led to HRT and that was the one backed by drug companies, it was a bit disappointing" (Julia). Pop-up adverts also led to the women rejecting the site. As Mo states: " ... when they are just trying to sell you something or click down here for your free whatever, you just get turned off".

This finding corroborates Pitts (2004) assertion that cyberspace itself is not neutral and it is hardly free from corporate, media and other consumer influences. Search engines are often owned by major media companies, as health along with other industries is a big business and health sites often are saturated with advertising. The participants in the current study actively rejected blatantly commercial sites and brought into question the impartiality of the information presented. A similar level of active engagement was clear in terms of selecting preferred sites. The women stated a clear preference for health sites that had clear menus, from a recognised source that were "not selling anything". They positively evaluated "factual" sites that "aren't biased, they give you the facts and allow you to make up your mind". Moreover, the women praised informative sites with an index that were easy to navigate through and allowed searching within them. The women specifically mentioned features such as lists of symptoms, lists of categories of pills, as well as the risks and benefits outlined of HRT as positive features of some of the sites. Moreover, the search for voices from "experts" became a focus for many of the women as they stressed a desire to find comprehensive information written by medical doctors, gynecologists or experts on the menopause.

Another factor that emerged from the pattern of selection and rejection of particular sites was the impact of the women's material bodies. Even in cyberspace, the symptoms and risks for their own bodies were a key determinant in the overall self-reflexive process. The searches conducted by the women were led in part by their own materiality. Sites were quickly rejected if the women perceived that the content had little relevance to their specific set of circumstances. As Joanne indicated:

> "I think with the risks you know about them but it depends on your own personal interpretation in terms of how desperate you are because if you have terrible symptoms of hot flushes or flashes or whatever you might just think well I know about the breast cancer risk but the benefits for me are worth it I am just at my wits end."

Or as Linda noted, "I can't take HRT, that's my thing, that's the angle like you, everybody comes at it from their own angle". Moreover, as well as influencing the types of sites selected, the materiality of their body also influenced how the women evaluated the information on the health sites. Throughout verbal protocols and facilitated discussions it became evident that searches often revealed information that "confirmed what I thought" and cemented the participant's views whether this was pro-HRT or pro-alternative therapies. As Eliza indicated, "I think I was only looking for what I wanted to see anyway. I am fairly negative towards HRT and I found loads of stuff that reinforced my ideas tonight, so that was good, it put me off even more". Individuals quickly pinpointed their own specific areas of interest as their material body influenced their searches. Only one of the women was taking HRT. The remainder of the women were not taking HRT and there was a mixture of symptoms and medical conditions that influenced this health-related decision. One participant had a blood disorder, another had had cancer and another had a family history with breast cancer, so HRT was not an option for them. Their searches focused on alternative therapies linked to specific symptoms. Also, the level of menopausal symptoms influenced the perceptions of their willingness to take medication. Mild symptoms would not lead to taking HRT and several women indicated they would have to be "desperate" with hot flushes before resorting to taking HRT. In this respect, that feeling of "just putting up with it" came through and the notion that menopause was not an illness. Several of the women mentioned feeling guilty taking up doctor's time, or even doubting that anyone would listen. Julia suggested that she "couldn't imagine anyone on the NHS direct listening to you if you ring up with a symptom about the menopause". Several of the women viewed the menopause as a condition rather than an illness and as such not worth bothering the medical profession with their worries. For some, reading the symptoms from the websites appeared to affirm concerns about their physical bodies they had previously dismissed. In this sense, the information consumed through the health-sites gave women a greater voice in terms of acknowledging their symptoms.

An added benefit of searching some of the sites was that for several of the women reading about the experiences and views of other menopausal women gave them a sense of not being alone. Several women talked in terms of "being less isolated" by reading messages from "women worldwide". Similar to a study by Pitts (2004), the participants found that reading other women's stories ameliorated a sense of loneliness and normalized a process that had felt alienating and isolating. An unexpected finding in the current study was that there was a sense of belonging and commonality that clearly emerged in terms of being British women. Often the use of American terms led to sites being immediately rejected and in the free searching sessions the women selected the UK-only restriction on the search engines. The expression of citizenship also came through strongly in their discussions and the verbal protocols. As Joanne notes in her negative evaluation of American sites, "it is so alien to us, all the talk about suing people. I mean British people don't do that do they, and all the jargonism and American talk...". Similarly, Justine notes that the "menopause matters" site is very British, and Justine adds that this is "a bit like British Airways, it makes you feel safe doesn't it".

Overall there is a sense that the material body both in terms of level of symptoms and cultural factors very much impacted on the way the women searched and interpreted on-line health advice about menopause. This captures Giddens's (1991) arguments about the self-reflexivity of body projects within modernity. Turner (1992) critiques Giddens by suggesting that an over-emphasis on the process of reflexivity produces as individual as a reflexive self but not an embodied self. However, with the current group of menopausal women, their disrupted bodies very much make the link between self and the body — a process that develops an embodied consciousness.

Given this process of self-reflexivity, the women's evaluation of the health website information is an active process. There is very much a sense that the participants were able to arm themselves with information so as to be able to "ask the right questions", as Mandy commented:

> "Yes I think it's very good in that way because you then are armed with maybe how to ask questions; because you've got this back up information from the different sites, you also know the meanings of the different terminology "

In the interviews a year after the study, the majority of women indicated that it had reinforced their viewpoints. Very few of the women had re-visited the sites but several had recommended specific sites to friends and family. Overall, the sense from the women in this study is that taking responsibility and searching for health-related information had been a positive experience. This sense contradicts literature in which theorists argue that the pressures in modern society to be more knowledgeable and responsible for health choices could constrain and objectify women's bodies even more. Many studies interpreting health discourses within websites focus on this aspect. For the actual consumers in this study, however, there is an acceptance of the individual responsibility for awareness in terms of health choices, but it did not result in a passive acceptance of information about their bodies. The information-sorting process was an active process in conjunction with an acceptance of the materiality of their own bodies. There is a sense that women's attitudes reflect a subtle societal change in terms of a willingness to speak out. As Amy noted, "not enough people question;it's like we don't question, we don't complain". Yet with the information from the Internet the participants talked in terms of having "the right to have the information presented to them ... so they can make an informed choice".

The participants maintained that this choice was a very individual experience: "there are a lot of other women who've gone through it" and "it was good to see other people's experiences ... but I do think as people we are all very different". In this respect, there is a limit to the level of inter-subjectivity felt by the women. None had been tempted to post information on the chat rooms of sites or even leave their personal details. The majority indicated they found the letters posted interesting but felt leaving an address on a site left them susceptible to being inundated with junk mail. Several indicated that they are "not that type of person" and immediately rejected a site if you needed to register. Overall, the women took on the individual responsibility for their health choices but their interaction on the Internet was very much on their own terms. The women were able to negotiate discursive constructions of a menopausal body and its effects in a way that allowed for strategies of resistance. This supports Budgeon's (2003: p. 43) assertion that "the relationship between self and the body is about a process more complex than that which involves the inscription of the text upon the surface of the body".

The women in this study made very strategic choices when surfing the net for health information in terms of what sites to visit, evaluation of the evidence, relevance to them and their decisions in terms of taking or refusing medication. There was a healthy amount of skepticism about some of the information on the Web and participants reiterated their preference for unbiased sites, written by medical experts that allowed the individual to make her own choice. The sense of being involved in their own decision-making also moved beyond consuming the health information on the Internet. Several of the women talked in terms of gaining more confidence when they talk to the consultant or general practitioner (GP). There was a sense of gaining more control over their health decisions. This sense of control, however, did not detract from their belief and trust in traditional approaches to health care. When asked in the post-study interview who was their trusted source of information, all of the women still indicated it was their GP. The majority of the women indicated that their research on-line had not changed their interaction with GPs but had made them more willing to investigate and find out more information. When asked during the facilitated sessions several of the women felt that the GPs wanted to put them on HRT and often cited the benefits not the negatives of taking it. Others felt the GP did not have the time to answer all their questions and several indicated that it was difficult for GPs to keep up to date with the most recent research. In this respect, the participants felt their on-line research on the menopause complimented the information from the GP. Several women stated they had excellent advice from the GP and valued the professional one-to-one contact as a chance to say "what about this and what about the other". Key issues of the GP contact were "the trust thing ... as you trust them implicitly" because "they know your own case history", and this was contrasted to "some anonymous doctor" on the Net. As Linda explicitly states:

> I'd rather go to him prepared and say 'right I've done some research, and what do you think, this is what I'm thinking?'. And ask his advice, rather than just present problems.

Several women noted that when they have gone to the GP after looking material up on the Internet they have had a better reaction as the GPs "talk to you in a more intelligent way". These findings support Parr's (2002) suggestion that a revolution in patient medical knowledge is taking place that has powerful implications for doctor-patient relationships.

In conclusion, the present study demonstrates how the Internet as a relatively new form of medical technology contributes to the cultural dialogue surrounding women's bodies. In particular, the current study revealed the impact of the Internet on how a group of menopausal women 'see themselves' in relation to available health information. The findings suggest that consumers do not uncritically consume medicalised health information: the menopausal women in this study do not just inscribe their body with Internet medical discourse. Rather, embodied experiences informed the women's health choices. In this way, women's bodies are situated in culture rather than determined by it. As Budgeon (2003) indicates, reflexive monitoring of the body by knowledgeable agents is of central importance and a necessary condition for action. The women in this study demonstrate acts of negotiation of medical care and establish their own credibility in terms of defining meanings of menopause and the health choices regarding treatment. This reveals aspects of the complex relationship that embodiment has with identity as the women actively cultivated the corporeal through the pursuit of specific body regimes chosen for a diverse range of options from HRT and alternative therapies.

References

Budgeon, S. (2003) 'Identity as an embodied event', *Body and Society* Vol. 9, No. 1: pp. 35–55.

Bunton, R. & Burrows, R. (1995) 'Consumption of health in the "epidemiological" clinic of late modern medicine', in R. Bunton, S. Nettleton and R. Burrows (eds) *The sociology of health promotion: Critical analyses of consumption, lifestyle and risk*. London, Routledge, pp: 206–222.

Crawford, R. (1980) 'Healthism and the medicalization of everyday life', *International Journal of Health Services* Vol. 7, No. 4: pp. 663–680.

Featherstone, M. (1991) *Consumer culture and postmodernism*. London, Sage.

Giddens, A. (1991) *Modernity and self-identity: Self and society in the late modern age*. London: Polity Press.

Greco, M. (1993) 'Psychosomatic subjects and the duty to be well: Personal agency within medical rationality', *Economy and Society* No. 22: pp. 357–372.

Ingham, A. (1985) 'From public issues to personal trouble: Well-being and the fiscal crisis of the state', *Sociology of Sport Journal*, No. 2: pp. 43–55.

Lupton, D. (1995) The imperative of health: *Public health and the regulated body*. Newbury Park, CA, Sage.

Parr, H. (2002) 'New body-geographics: The embodied spaces of health and medical information on the Internet', *Environmental and Planning D: Society and Space* No. 20: pp. 73–95.

Pew Research Center (2000) The online health care revolution: How the Web helps Americans take better care of themselves. Retreived from http://www.pewinternet.org

Pitts, V. (2004) 'Illness and Internet empowerment: Writing and reading breast cancer in cyberspace', *Health* Vol. 8, No. 1: pp. 33–59.

Sillence, E., Briggs, P., Fishwick, L. and Harris, P. (2004) 'Trust and mistrust of online health sites', in *Proceedings of CHI@ 2004*, April 24–29, Vienna Austria (pp. 663–670). ACM Press.

Turner, B.S. (1996) *The body and society* 2nd edn. London, Sage.

Wheatley, E.E. (2005) 'Disciplining bodies at risk: C'ardiac rehabilitation and the medicalization of fitness, *Journal of Sport and Social Issues* Vol. 29, No. 2: pp. 198–221.

SPORT AND NEW MEDIA LEISURE TECHNOLOGY

Donna Wong

University of Edinburgh, UK

Introduction

OfCom's[1] (OfCom, 2006) latest research has shown that more people, especially young people aged 16–24, are turning away from television in favour of new[2] media for entertainment, as well as for information. Households across the UK are adopting new media services at a faster rate than before, subscribing to broadband, digital television, and are making more use of mobile phones and the Internet. As observed by Rowe (2004) and Whannel (2005), the growth of modern sport has always been supported and shaped by innovations in media technology. Given this link and the recent shifts in the use of media technology, an interesting question to ask is — is the advent of new media technology bringing about a new way of consuming sport and changing the way people interact with sport?

As newer forms of digital leisure technology continue to emerge, the mediated sport industry is undergoing a period of transition. New media sport now provides forms of viewing access previously non existent. The longer-term significance of these shifts is not yet apparent. This chapter sets out to examine this liminal phase of mediated sport. It considers this period of transition, which involves the move from delivery via 'old' media such as television and radio to current forms involving various digital platforms. The specific research that informs this chapter explores how sport is employed in new media and charts young people's involvement in sport via the use of digital leisure technology. The discussion focuses on the use of specific new media — digital television, the Internet, mobile telephony and video gaming — by people aged 11–35 years. This population is grouped into 3 cohorts of 11–15 (Cohort 1), 16–24 (Cohort 2) and 25–35 year olds (Cohort 3). In addition, analysis attempts to track the engagement with digital leisure technology and its relation to active sport participation.

The research questions

- *Access*. Who has access to which media? Which is the most popular new media form for sport content? How, where, when and why do people use new media to access sport?
- *The relationship between new media and sport*. How are new media transforming sport? How are people consuming sport via new media technologies? Do people use these new media technologies in isolation or in a social situation? Do new media technologies help to act as a driver for wider sport participation?
- *Displacement and engagement*. Do new media displace 'old' media? Do new media supplement 'old' media by providing another means to retrieve information and provide entertainment? Does increased availability and diversity of media mean more media use, and less physical activities? Does participation in 'virtual sport' displace the need for participation in physical sport? How does new media use affect participation in physical activities?

Sport and the media

The study of mediated sport is generally conducted with a theoretical model involving three components, those of production, text and audience (Crawford, 2004; Horne, 2006). Specific aspects of each component in the operation of the production, text and audience (PTA) media circuit have been studied. Those who are interested in the production context generally look into how production factors have affected both the output of the media and its reception by audiences and consumers. Researchers often look at other production influences, such as government regulations, commercial control, directors, producers, editors and commentators that are inserted between the live event and the audience.

At the same time, there are researchers who are more interested in the texts of mediated sport. They look at the reading of sports for their ideological meanings, focusing on the textual forms and patterns of mediated sports, which are important follow-ups to the focus on production. Here researchers are interested in the messages being sent and try to analyse texts through content analysis and/or semiology, investigating the production of spectacle, dramatisaton and personalisation (Horne, 2006; Whannel, 1998). There are generally two analytical points that are taken into consideration for those who focus on text. Firstly, the texts that audiences are given to interpret and 'decode'. The meaning of mediated sport is the "outcome of a complex articulation of technical, institutions, commercial, political, cultural and social factors" (Jhally, 1989: p. 84). Researchers explore these complexities and the approach suggests that interpretations are constrained by these production elements and texts are open to more than one interpretation. Relating to this first approach, the second considers the dispositional and situational factors which influence audience readings. It looks into the effect the surrounding conditions have on the nature of watching. Questions such as why audiences are watching in sports bars rather than doing some other activities are asked, emphasising that "reading" takes place in certain social conditions within the context of our daily lives. Audience readings of text cannot be divorced from the wider questions of social context, as texts are encountered in different ways depending on the particular social situation and spatial location (see for instance Sapolsky and Zillman, 1978).

No doubt the study of texts is important, as formal analysis can impart knowledge about the structure and content of the message; however, audience readings cannot be simply inferred from researchers' readings alone. With sports as a realm of popular pleasure, there is a need to focus on why media sport is popular, what the audience do with and what they make of mediated sport. Existing research on mediated sport tends to concentrate on the production and text, focusing mainly on the production practices, patterns of ownership and control, and, textual form and pattern. Audience, as the third of the PTA component, has not received the same scrutiny. Audiences have frequently been viewed as the end-point or even as a by-product of processes of media production within many media studies, and hence largely irrelevant compared with the central importance of these processes (Crawford, 2004). The focus here is to see audiences not as an end product created by the text and its processes of production, but rather as active agents. An example of the active audience is identified as the fan audience, who animatedly participate in the creation of new content such as fanzines and fansites. These groups contribute to a broader set of 'satellite' works around a primary text of sports programme, sport team or athlete (Cover, 2004; Crawford, 2004).

The focus on the audiences has been explored, to some extent, by those writing on the consumption of sport and the sports consumer. The increasing commercialisation of sport has led to a "massification" of sport (Jhally, 1989: p. 81). Expanding television coverage means that "the real product of sport is the television audience, which is produced by televised sport performance" (Horne *et al.*, 1999: p. 276). Researchers such as Scherer (2007) investigate audience's consumption patterns and look into the ways audiences could be and are 'sold' to advertisers. Electronic and cyber sporting spaces have progressively become important battlegrounds for corporations and media conglomerates to reach and interact with consumers and sports fans (Scherer, 2007). These existing media sports studies tell us what audiences get from the corporately-controlled consumption of sport, but they do not tell us what audiences do with it. However, some researchers are interested in the pleasure audiences obtain through the use of media sport. These researchers concentrate on the study of how needs are gratified through different forms of media. After all, different audiences use the media in different ways in order to obtain different pleasures. It is with this background that this audience research takes place.

Defining new media

Western capitalist societies at the start of the twenty-first century are surrounded by new media technologies which are rapidly permeating society and becoming an integral part of how we live. The leisure developments usually associated with new media are plenty and include such technologies as cable/digital/satellite television and computer networks, gaming consoles, (3G) mobile telephones, computer-mediated communication developments (for example, e-mail, blogs, newsgroups, and real-time chat services) as well as new forms of presentation by traditional newspaper and broadcasters. All these new media leisure developments raise the issue of what actually is meant by 'new media'. The phrase itself suggests a development in media that marks both a new stage of evolution and some sort of break from the past. Sociologists and psychologists Lievrouw and Livingstone (2002: p. 7) defined the parameters within which they place new media:
The artefacts or devices that enable and extend our ability to communicate; the communication activities or practices we engage in to develop and use these devices; and the social arrangements or organisations that form around the devices and practices.

They suggested that new media technologies have contributed to the changing social environment. For the purpose of this chapter, the characteristics of new media outlined by McQuail (2000: p. 127) serve as a useful delineation of the term. New media, he suggests, generally involve decentralisation of channels for the distribution of messages; an increase in the capacity available for the transferral of messages — satellites, cable and computer networks; an increase in the options available for audience members to become involved in the communication process, often entailing an interactive form of communication; and an increase in the degree of flexibility for determining the form and content through the digitisation of messages. McQuail (2000: p. 127) defined the four main categories of 'new media' as: interpersonal communication media, such as the mobile telephone; interactive play media, such as computer based and video games; information search media, such as Internet search engines; participatory media, such as Internet chat rooms and MSN messenger.

To summarise from the numerous attempts to characterise new media (for example, Lievrouw and Livingstone 2002; McQuail, 2000; Rice, 1984), new media can generally be distinguished by the key processes of digitisation, interactivity and convergence.

Digitisation — Arguably the most fundamental aspect that underpins new media technology is digitisation, hence new media are also referred to as digital media. Digitisation has been characterised by Negroponte (1995) as the movement from 'atoms' to 'bits'. Where 'old' media were produced and distributed in a physical form or via analogue waves, digital media are broken down into intangible 'bits' of information for manipulation, distribution and reproduction via computer-mediated communication. Digital technology has enabled new forms and patterns of communication to emerge. As described by Negroponte (1995: p. 84), "[b]eing digital will change the nature of mass media from a process of pushing bits at people to one of allowing people to pull at them". For instance, digitised broadcasting is time-shiftable and need not be received in the same order or at the same rate as they will be consumed. With very little real-time broadcasting involved, digitisation has liberated sport audiences by allowing off-line processing and time shifting of sports broadcasts.

Interactivity — Digitisation has extended the capacities of the global media industries by adding interactivity to mediatised leisure. Traditional media were about one-way flows of information. New media incorporate the ability to interact with the medium in a two-way or multilateral communication without the control of intermediaries. These interactive functions of new media offer users a significant increase in opportunities to manipulate and intervene in media. McQuail (2000: p. 128) suggests that "new media when compared with 'old' media have a capacity to be more interactive and have a greater capacity for playfulness, in so far as play is interactive either with people or machines". The interactive aspect of new media technologies affords users more selectivity in their information choices and communication with others. It provides users with choices to generate, seek and share content selectively and to interact with other individuals and groups. It potentially provides audiences with more opportunities to create their own schedules from services available on demand. That said, there are debates on these interactive spectacles being a "monitored, branded consumption experience" (Scherer, 2007: p. 490) with the corporate colonisation of electronic space. Audiences are reported to be under the illusion that they still enjoy the autonomy to interpret the increasingly commercialised interactive mediatised leisure.

Convergence — The third most widely noted feature of the new media is the increasing integration of mass communication, telecommunication and data communication in the delivery of media content. Digitised data can be transmitted, stored and retrieved without regard for its content or its forms of output. The previously separate industries of telecommunications, broadcasting and computing are merging, which suggests the increasing convergence of information services. The convergence of technologies is also creating an overlap of function for content as well as for hardware. There is an alleged diminishing popularity of 'traditional' leisure under the impact of new forms of electronic entertainment as competition for leisure time is now taking place against the background of an ever-widening range of mediatised leisure activities. New media can therefore be characterised by the key processes of digitization, interactivity and convergence. The arrival of the new media has brought about new distribution channels and services for sport content. The following section seeks to exemplify how these key processes are embodied in the new media services for the delivery of sport content, thereby creating new avenues for experience and access sport.

Sport and new media technology

Advances in digital technology have introduced new opportunities for the presentation of sports information. New media, particularly the Internet, digital television, mobile telephone and digital gaming, have provided new distribution platforms and services for the delivery of sport. Sport has always been seen as crucial to the development of new broadcast services and to converging telecommunications and computing services as it provides ready-made audiences for digital technology. Sport and media have been dubbed the "dream team" (Wilson, 2007); virtually every new communication technology and service seeks a sporting application as sport is often viewed as a key driver for their uptake. The importance of sport content to media development can be demonstrated through the development of home videocassette recorders (VCRs). Betamax was one of the initial formats for VCRs introduced in 1975 by Sony Corporations. A similar format, the video home system (VHS) was introduced by Japan Victor Company (commonly known as JVC) in 1976. Despite being the market leader initially, the Beta format was lagging behind in the VCR market towards the end of 1970s. A decade later, Sony's Beta models ceased production. It was acknowledged that the most vulnerable aspect of the Betamax was its limited playing time (Cusamano *et al.*, 1992). A market test conducted by the Radio Corporation of America (RCA) in 1974 concluded that a minimum two-hour playing time was necessary for commercial success of VCR. A successful machine would have to offer at least two hours of playing time to record an American football game, which could usually take up to two to three hours in real time. JVC's VHS was able to do this and the playing time, linked to mediating sport events, became a significant factor for consumers. In this way, JVC successfully established a foothold in the American market (Cusamano *et al.*, 1992).

The affiliation between sport and the media has since strengthened with the advent of digital media technology. These new media developments have brought about a plethora of means of access to sport content; there is now a greater volume of sport available than ever — via the Internet, digital television, mobile telephone and video gaming. Obviously there is a proliferation of media sport platforms, and with this in mind, the Uses and Gratifications (U&G) approach is employed here to help understand the specific reasons that bring audiences to new media sport. The U&G tradition considers audience needs, motives and circumstances as the starting point and places emphasis on the explanation of audience experience. Audiences are viewed as active interpreters and choice-makers, rather than passive receivers of media messages. The approach stresses that different people use the media in different ways in order to obtain different pleasures or meet different needs.

The uses and gratification approach

The uses and gratification (U&G) theory is utilized here to provide the theoretical basis for examining audience activity and behaviour. The approach assumes that media use is motivated by needs and specific gratification-seeking motives. It takes the perspective of the audience who are seen as actively selecting media use and access for gratification. Since the 1980s, the U&G approach has been used to analyse the origin, nature and degree of the motives for media sport choices and the perceived gratifications and uses of mediated sport. Studies include research into the motives of watching televised sports (for example, Wann, 1995; Wenner and Gantz, 1989), spectating pleasures in televised sports (for example, Duncan and Brummett, 1989) as well as selection patterns of mediated sport audiences (for example, Bryant *et al.*, 1981).

Although U&G is a well-established perspective, the concept of a self-motivated audience actively seeking gratifications is not without criticism. McQuail (1997) commented that there has been little successful prediction or causal explanation of media choice and use as a result of research based on the U&G approach. This is because of methodological weakness in the approach. Typologies of "motives" often fail to match patterns of actual selection or use (McQuail, 2000). In general, U&G overestimates the rationality and activity of audience use behaviour. Most audiences turn out to be respondents who had "varied, overlapping, and not always consistent expectations", needs and motives (McQuail, 1997: p. 73). The main problem associated with the approach is that 'needs', which supposedly underlie particular patterns of gratification, can only be inferred from the audience's explanation about the gratifications themselves. For example, if an audience member claims to like basketball matches on television because she or he finds the close finishes exciting, it can be inferred that she or he have has a 'need' for excitement and therefore it is this 'need' that has lead them to search for excitement in televised basketball matches. Murdock (1974) claimed that this is clearly a circular argument.

Despite the criticisms, the U&G approach has continued to be utilised to explore the impact of new technologies on the audience. The U&G perspective becomes more valid with the advent of new media technology, which has allowed audiences to be more in control of the media. The assumption of an active audience is a unique aspect of the U&G approach. It proposes that the audience member, by his/her use of media, obtains a reward in the form of needs gratifications, suggesting that audiences are psychologically active in choosing the media that interest them. The current digitised media environment affords audiences with interactivity — they are given the opportunity to be active and selective. Hence the U&G approach is a time-honoured media research tradition which many theorists believe to be eminently suitable for the study of new media (see Johnson and Kay, 2003; Lin, 1999; Newhagen and Rafaeli, 1996; Stafford, 2000; Weiser, 2001).

Despite its shortcomings, the U&G approach has empirical support in substantiating the behavioural motives for and satisfaction with media use activity (Blumler and Katz, 1974; Lin, 1996; Rosengren *et al.*, 1985). The broad theoretical framework and flexibility offered by the approach make it a popular technique for researchers interested in all forms of media content. In recent years the U&G tradition has been fundamentally rethought and revived. This means there is now a combination and interaction of empirical and interpretive research method, which probe more dimensions and offer more comprehensive analysis and compelling conclusions. The U&G perspective has since been applied to scenarios ranging from cable and digital TV (for example, Livaditi *et al.*, 2003), mobile phones (for example, Leung and Wei, 2000) as well as the Internet (for example, Ruggiero, 2000; Stafford *et al.*, 2004).

As the advent of media technology allowed the audience to be more in control of the media, it has arguably rendered the U&G approach more useful. The U&G approach is generally characterized by a quantitative research methodology. Hence in this chapter, questionnaire-based surveys are used as the main source of data. The next section describes the design of the study and the data analysed.

Methodology

Defining sport participation

The term 'active sport participation' is used here interchangeably with 'physical activity'. The definition of what constitutes sport participation and what does not has always been a subject of much debate (Sportscotland, 2001). In recognition of the recreational nature of some of the activities young people participate in, there are certainly some activities which could be regarded as physical activity (such as walking [2+ miles], dancing, hill walking, yoga). Likewise, other moderate intensity activities are carried out as part of transportation, physical education, games, sport, recreation, work or structured exercise. Sports participation data collected for this research was also based on these physical activities. Examples of other physical activities that constitute active sport participation for young people also include brisk walking, cycling, swimming, most sports and dance. That said, it is worth bearing in mind that it is acknowledged that the amount of physical activity for young people cannot be precisely defined (Biddle *et al.*, 1998; Marshall *et al.*, 2006). To measure sport participation in this research, respondents were asked how often they take part in sport or physical activities.

Research design

To attempt to obtain an account of the access, uses and gratifications of new media leisure technology, an approach was devised involving a combination of qualitative and quantitative research methodologies, developed in two cumulative phases. Survey methods were first used to chart and examine the audience experience of new media sports. These were followed by case studies of individual cohorts to investigate motives for media choice and the perceived gratifications of new media sport technology. It is research findings from the first phase of the research that are discussed in this chapter.

The first phase of research was a questionnaire survey, conducted from November 2005 to May 2006, spanning late autumn to early summer to even out any seasonal effect that might influence the outcome of the survey. The survey format was designed to enable researchers to capture broad social impacts of new media (Coget *et al.*, 2002). The survey questionnaire charted the following: which media people use to access sport content; the duration of use; with whom they use media; and what relationships, if any, exist between their use of various media and their demographic groups. The survey results helped to determine these cohorts' exposure to sports via each medium, to establish the context of use for each medium and to assess how new technologies influence their involvement in sports.

Sample

The first task was to generate data to document three age cohorts (11–15, 16–24 and 24–35) of young people's access to the range of new media (specifically mobile phones, video games, the Internet and digital television) and how they are using them to access sports content. Participant surveys were local to an area of Midlothian in Scotland. For Cohort 1 (n = 352), the questionnaire was distributed to participants from Secondary Schools; for cohort 2 (n = 228), to undergraduates from a university; for Cohort 3 (n = 258), to working adults in offices and leisure centres. Overall, the breakdown of gender was even across the cohorts (Male = 50.5%, Female = 49.5%). Questionnaire responses were collated and results displayed in figures and tables. A summary of the raw data and brief descriptions are included here.

Findings

Access

Studies of media preferences among children and adults have shown that sports programmes have remained one of the most preferred genres across all media platforms among children and adults (Comstock *et al.*, 1978; Fromme, 2003; Livingstone, 2002). It is clear from the data that the majority of young people had accessed media sport via one or more platforms (**Table 1**), with the mean hours of accessing mediated sport per week for Cohort 1 = 6.1 hours; Cohort 2 = 4.4 hours and Cohort 3 = 5.0 hours (**Table 2**). Comparatively more hours are spent in physical activities than in sport-related media use, with the mean hours of exercising per week for Cohort 1 = 11.9 hours; Cohort 2 = 7.8 hours and Cohort 3 = 6.5 hours (**Table 3**).

Table 1   Number of media platforms used to access sport

Cohort %	11–15	16–24	25–35
1 Platform Only	25.6	19.7	25.6
2 Platforms	23.0	21.9	17.4
3 Platforms	23.6	27.2	30.2
4 Platforms	13.9	17.5	14.3
5 Platforms	6.8	7.0	–
None	6.5	6.1	12.4
Missing	0.6	0.4	–
Total	100.0	100.0	100.0

Table 2   Mean number of hours spent per week on mediated sport

Cohort	No. of Hours
11–15	6.1
16–24	4.4
25–35	5.0

Table 3   Mean number of hours spent per week on sport

Cohort	No. of Hours
11–15	11.9
16–24	7.8
25–35	6.5

The data reveal that although the Internet is the most proliferated media among young people (**Table 4**), a majority of young people have still chosen digital television as their favourite platform to access media sports (**Table 5**), with 58.5% of Cohort 1, 65.3% of Cohort 2, and 58.9% of Cohort 3 watching sport on TV at least 2–3 times a week (**Table 6**).

Table 4   Access to media platforms

Cohort %	11–15	16–24	25–35
Digital TV	86.4	75.4	75.2
Internet	86.9	97.8	94.2
Videogame	77.0	61.0	34.5
Mobile Phone	79.5	92.5	89.9
3G Mobile Phone	13.1	14.5	18.6

Table 5   Media preference to access sport

Cohort %	11–15	16–24	25–35
Digital TV	59.4	66.2	59.7
Internet	22.7	23.7	29.1
Mobile Phones	4.8	1.3	–
Videogames	6.5	2.6	–
Missing	6.5	6.1	11.2
Total	100.0	100.0	100.0

Table 6   Frequency of Platforms (Sport-Related)

Cohort 1

Frequency %	Digital TV	Internet	Mobile phones	Video games
Everyday	18.2	10.5	6.0	9.4
5–6 times a week	12.2	4.0	2.6	6.0
3–4 times a week	16.5	8.8	3.4	12.8
2–3 times a week	11.9	15.1	7.7	9.1
2–3 times in 4 week	8.5	9.7	3.7	6.5
1–2 times in 4 weeks	6.8	8.0	8.0	8.5
Less Often	10.5	40.1	64.2	46.8
Missing	15.3	4.0	4.5	0.9
Total	100.0	100.0	100.0	100.0

Cohort 2

Frequency %	Digital TV	Internet	Mobile phones	Video games
Everyday	8.3	11.4	1.8	3.9
5–6 times a week	9.2	4.4	0.4	4.8
3–4 times a week	29.8	16.2	3.1	6.6
2–3 times a week	18.0	18.0	9.2	9.2
2–3 times in 4 week	5.3	6.6	0.4	11.4
1–2 times in 4 weeks	4.8	8.3	6.1	3.1
Less Often	20.6	33.3	69.3	61.0
Missing	3.9	1.8	9.6	–
Total	100.0	100.0	100.0	100.0

Cohort 3

Frequency %	Digital TV	Internet	Mobile phones	Video games
Everyday	12.4	10.9	0.4	–
5–6 times a week	3.1	7.4	1.9	0.4
3–4 times a week	22.1	11.6	8.9	3.1
2–3 times a week	21.3	23.3	6.6	8.9
2–3 times in 4 week	7.0	3.1	–	1.2
1–2 times in 4 weeks	6.6	2.3	1.9	1.6
Less Often	26.0	40.3	79.4	84.8
Missing	1.5	1.1	0.9	–
Total	100.0	100.0	100.0	100.0

The relationship between new media and sport

With increasing availability and ease of access to new technologies and media forms, public media discourses suggest that these new media technologies have gained a dominant position in people's leisure time. Along with each decade's technological change came the recurrent concerns about the impact of new media on people's lives (Critcher, 2006). Each new communication technology and genre brought with it "concerns about supposedly unprecedented and unholy new risks that reference earlier panics" (Miller, 2006: p. 7). Concerns are raised among academicians, teachers, parents and media groups, namely that increased time spent on new media technologies affects social interaction and displaces leisure activities, specifically active participation in sports. Discourses are mainly concerned with the possible declines in certain aspects of social life such as interpersonal communication and social networking. In other words, does time spent on the new media devour leisure time and social life?

The survey results suggest that, contrary to popular belief, time spent on mediated sport might not have affected social interaction. Only one-tenth of the participants (Cohort 1 = 11.6%, Cohort 2 = 4.8% and Cohort 3 = 13.6%) indicated that they watch sports on TV alone. Likewise, less than 10% of participants from Cohort 2 (8.8%) and Cohort 3 (4.7%) were found to play sport related videogames alone. However, Cohort 1 differ in this aspect. Most of the school children were found to be playing videogames alone (Cohort 1 = 23.0%). Although there is a slight variation in patterns with whom participants play videogames (**Table 7**), watching sport on TV and playing sport related videogames can prove to be a popular source of conversation as well as inform general conversations on sports (Crawford, 2005; Fromme, 2003). The results from this research reveal the use of Internet for sport-related purpose is mainly conducted alone (Cohort 1 = 46.0%, Cohort 2 = 55.3%, Cohort 3 = 53.9%).

Table 7   With whom they use sport-related media

Cohort 1

%	Digital TV	Internet	Video game
Alone	11.6	46.0	23.0
Friends	7.4	9.1	18.5
Family/Relatives	47.7	7.7	6.3
Family & Friends	7.4	1.1	2.0
Alone & Friends	2.6	6.5	10.2
Alone & Family	4.3	1.7	1.1
Alone, Friends & Family	3.4	–	1.4
Missing*	15.6	27.8	37.5
TOTAL	100.0	100.0	100.0

* *Missing includes those who do not use the selected platform*

Cohort 2

%	Digital TV	Internet	Video game
Alone	4.8	55.3	8.8
Friends	37.7	3.9	25.4
Family/Relatives	16.7	2.6	2.2
Family & Friends	14.0	0.4	1.3
Alone & Friends	13.2	7.9	3.5
Alone & Family	2.2	0.4	0.4
Alone, Friends & Family	7.5	–	0.4
Missing	3.9	29.4	57.9
TOTAL	100.0	100.0	100.0

Cohort 3

%	Digital TV	Internet	Video game
Alone	13.6	53.9	4.7
Friends	41.1	3.1	17.1
Family/Relatives	30.6	0.8	0.4
Family & Friends	1.9	–	–
Alone & Friends	3.9	4.7	4.3
Alone & Family	5.8	0.4	–
Alone, Friends & Family	1.6	–	0.4
Missing	1.6	37.2	73.3
TOTAL	100.0	100.0	100.0

In investigating the interactive functions of new media sport, the "Press the red button" function (Cohort 1 = 32.4%, Cohort 2 = 25.0%, Cohort 3 = 34.1%), followed by visit to programme website (Cohort 1 = 25.6%, Cohort 2 = 26.8%, Cohort 3 = 16.7%), were found to be the two most frequent interactive TV functions used by the majority of the participants while watching sport programmes (**Table 8.1**). The reason for use is mainly indicated as the need to find more information (**Table 8.2**). Similarly, the same reason is given for using the Internet to access sport (**Table 9**).

Table 8.1   Functions used while watching sport programme on digital TV

Cohort %	11–15	16–24	25–35
Sent Text Message	11.4	2.6	11.6
Made Phone Call	7.1	2.2	6.6
Sent Email	6.5	3.1	5.4
Visited Prog Website	25.6	26.8	16.7
Press Red Button	32.4	25.0	34.1
Sent Letter	2.8	–	3.9
Other	–	–	–
None	35.2	36.4	2 2 . 1

Table 8.2   Reasons for use

Cohort %	11–15	16–24	25–35
Enter Competition	11.9	5.7	9.3
Take Part in Quiz	8.0	2.2	3.9
Place Bet	N.A.	1.8	0.4
Vote/Nominate	13.9	2.2	4.3
Respond to Features	5.1	5.3	3.9
Speak On Air	2.6	–	–
Purchase Items	5.1	0.9	–
Find Out More	22.7	28.1	18.6
Other	2.6	4.8	14.7
Can't Remember	4.3	0.9	5.4

Table 9   Reason for surfing net for sport content

Cohort %	11–15	16–24	25–35
Engage in Online Gaming	13.9	5.3	1.2
Find Out More Info	37.5	56.6	48.1
Place Bet	N.A.	7.9	6.6
Book Tickets	6.8	11.4	6.6
Watch Live Streaming	8.8	16.2	14.0
Purchase Items	6.5	9.2	2.7
Find Out More From TV	15.3	18.9	22.1
Engage in Online Discussion	15.1	10.1	4.7
Other	0.3	2.6	1.2
Can't Remember	5.7	0.4	1.2

However, the purpose of using mobile phones for sport differs between cohorts. Playing sport games is cited as the most common use of mobiles for Cohort 1 and 3, whereas getting sport/team/score alerts is most frequently used for Cohort 2 (**Table 10**).

Table 10   Reason for using mobile phones for sport content

Cohort %	11–15	16–24	25–35
Play Sport Games	24.1	6.1	15.5
Live Betting	N.A.	2.2	0.4
Access Internet Browser	13.4	7.0	5.8
Watch Live Streaming	9.9	3.5	0.4
Receive Sport News Alert	17.3	10.5	4.7
Get Sport/Team/Score Alerts	19.0	14.0	4.7
Receive Post-match Highlights	14.8	4.4	3.9
Other	2.3	-	2.7
None	40.9	64.9	72.1

Displacement and engagement

It appears that with the proliferation of new media technology, mediated leisure begins to occupy a bigger portion of leisure time. As with the concern of 'older' media, the central issue here is whether new media use has transformed the way people spend time on other daily activities. As in many other fields of inquiry, two schools of thought have emerged: one which claims that new media use impacts on daily activities and communication activities in particular and that alternative activities have been displaced; and the other, that there are no apparent deleterious effects of new media on sociability and leisure. It might be that the introduction of media does not displace but rather supplements the diversity of leisure activities available. However, since every one of us has exactly 168 hours each week, these extra minutes spent consuming new media must come from somewhere. Displacement is used here to refer to the substitution of one activity for another that must have taken place given the finite time available.

The Pearson Correlation result revealed that there is a significant positive relationship between the time spent on new media sport use and the time spent on physical activities (r=.39, n=788, p<.0005). This finding is further supported by an independent sample t-test conducted to compare the number of hours spent on using new media sport between those who do and those who do not participate in physical activities. There was a significant difference in results for those who participate in physical activities (M=9.74, S.D.=10.36) and those who do not (M=3.27, S.D.=9.20; t(815)=5.70, p=.000). The magnitude of the differences in the means was moderate (eta squared=0.037).

With regard to the relationship between the frequency of exercise and tendency to use new media sport (digital television, the Internet, mobile phones and videogames), chi-squared test results suggested that all correlations are significant. (Digital TV: n=769, c^2=121.6, p<.005; Internet: n=815, c^2=90.0, p<.005, Mobile: n=796, c^2=70.1, p<.005; Videogames: n=833, c^2=79.7, p<.005). This is also supported by the statistically significant difference found in the frequency participants take part in physical activities and the number of hours they use new media sport (n=802, c^2=79.6, p<.005).

Discussion

As Newhagen and Rafaeli (1996: p. 10) note, "the evolution of mediated communication rarely leads to extinction. We have had conversation, lecture, letter writing, storytelling, playing, acting, exhorting, defaming, creating — and we still have them. The Net will no doubt become one more place where these occur". It appears that new media rarely replace or even displace older media. Rather, new media add to the available options, to some extent prompting new, more specialised, uses for books, television and radio, to name a few. The results gathered from this questionnaire survey indicate that (digital) television remains one of the most popular platforms for accessing mediated sport in spite of the extent of the Internet in homes and workplaces. Despite the considerable 'hype' regarding new forms of media, television remains the media widely used by children and young people on a daily basis (Table 4). The amount of time devoted to newer media sport (videogames, mobile phones, Internet) is relatively smaller compared to overall media use, suggesting that while they add to the repertoire of leisure activities of young people, they are only beginning to find a slot in the regular routine of leisure/daily use.

The survey further reveals that in the overall list of activities, television sport is still most commonly shared among family/relatives, friends and children. This is despite the advent of other newer forms of media. Sport-related videogaming is the second most shared media device. Contrary to popular fears that video games have an isolating effect on young people, it is possible that there is a positive socialisation impact of these new media leisure technologies. As Bryce and Rutter (2001) and Fromme (2003) have suggested, video gaming can prove to be a very sociable activity: gamers frequently come together and interact via the Internet, chat rooms, fan sites, at gaming conventions and workshops, from locations around the world. The findings of this research also suggest that new media sport users are not a generation of passive 'couch potatoes' or 'mouse potatoes' (I return to this point below). Media sport users are actively making use of the interactive nature of new media to select which elements to display or which paths to follow according to their own needs. Users are also able to attend to, perceive and retain information selectively according to their needs.

The primary reason indicated for making use of such interactive functions of new media is mainly to obtain more information.

The possibility that time spent with new media in particular directly displaces other leisure activities has long been a concern among the public, policy-makers and academics alike. With each new decade, potentially displacing new media are introduced, giving rise to the same questions yet again. Today, one may ask whether sport-related video games displace healthy activities such as exercising, or whether the widening range of media options detracts from time for physical leisure activities.

Overall, the data collected from this research survey so far reinforces Fromme's (2003) and Crawford's (2005) assertions that participation in video gaming had no negative effect on levels of sports participation. In fact, Crawford (2005) suggests digital gaming may increase interest in and knowledge of sport, and can prove for many a popular source of conversation that can crosscut and inform conversations on sport.

The research for this chapter also considered whether there was a reciprocal relationship between participation in sport and interest in sport related leisure technologies. The data suggest that participation in physical activities can (for some) generate an interest in the use of new media leisure technology. In fact, in support of Livingstone's (2002) research, the results gathered here confirm the argument that the introduction of media does not displace but rather supplements the diversity of sports activities. These data challenge the view that use of new media is often linked with the creation of a generation of 'couch potatoes' and media reports which convey the misleading impression of a 'time bomb' of obesity due to sedentary pursuits of video gaming and TV viewing (see Smith and Green, 2005). In fact, these data support previous findings by Schoenbach and Becker (1989) who surveyed the impact of media on households for media introduced in the 1980s (particularly VCR and cable/satellite television) across a variety of Western countries. They found little evidence of a reduction of time spent on non-media leisure. Instead, there was consistent evidence for increasing specialisation in uses of all media, not just new ones. They concluded that while there is little evidence that new media create new audience interests, they might provide new means of satisfying existing interests.

A look at other similar studies investigating the situations in which young people tend to play computer games revealed that they did it when there was nothing else to do, when the weather was bad or when they could not go outside and when there was nobody there to do something else with (Fromme, 2003; Livingstone, 2002). This may indicate that new media leisure technologies are important media to pass time between other activities and to fill empty parts of the day. Young people choose this option especially when other attractive options are not available or accessible. Studies have shown that video and computer games tend to be 'second choice media' for most young people (Fromme, 2003; Livingstone, 2002).

Conclusions

With consumption of new media technologies growing at a steady rate, today's mediated sports are being recognised as a powerful and unique entertainment force. Hence the aims of this research are to chart the patterns of participation in new media technology, and to consider the relationship between sport and interests in new media leisure technologies. Research results indicate that a link and relationship exists between the use of sport-related new media and taking part in physical activities. It appears that interest in the digital version of sport can encourage participation in sport itself. However, the direction of the causal effect is not determined in this research. There is also evidence to support the argument that the introduction of media does not displace but rather supplements the sport activities, reinforcing several studies conducted earlier (Franzen 2000; Kestnbaum *et al.*, 2002; Livingstone, 2002. These studies have also supported the argument that new media use does not impact on other daily activities, including socializing.

Although these data have provided support to challenge the common notion that use of new media leisure technologies are anti-social or deter participation in sport, existing empirical evidence on the impact of new media is still controversial. As in many other fields of inquiry, two schools of thought dominate: one which claims that new media use impacts on daily activities and communication activities in particular and that alternative activities have been displaced, and the other, that there are no apparent deleterious effects of new media on sociability and leisure. In order to diffuse public anxieties about user isolation, addiction, or even sedentary lifestyles attributed to use of new media leisure technologies, further attempts to contextualise new media use in relation to leisure activities might help. An informed account of the nature of children's and adults' new media use and gratifications is crucial in order to counter the concerns and confusion stimulated by moral panics over the supposed dramatic consequences of new media leisure technology options. This research only provides data on a small sample: more extensive research is needed into the relationship between sport and new media use. [3]

Notes

[1]   Office of Communications (OfCom) is the independent regulator and competition authority for the UK communications industries, with responsibilities across television, radio, telecommunications and wireless communications services.

[2]   The term 'new' media is used here as a social rather than purely technical term. The media referred to in this paper are still relatively novel. They are not in widespread use as 'traditional' media and are

still awaiting established practices of use. At the same time, new media is sometimes referred to as digital media.

3   The second phase of this research project will look into the gratifications derived from and the reasons participants bring to the use of new media technologies. Case studies from each of these cohorts will be examined to provide an in-depth analysis of motives for media choice and gratifications offered by new media sports. Information gathered from interviews will help to paint a better picture of new media sport users and the needs new media sport fulfills. This will provide the basis for explanations how and why new media use could impact on daily life.

References

Biddle, S., Sallis, J.F. and Cavill, N. (1998) *Young and active? Young people and health-enhancing physical activity: Evidence and implications.* London, England: Health Education Authority.

Blumler, J. G. and Katz, E. (1974) *The uses of communications.* Beverly Hills, CA: Sage.

Bryant, J., Comisky, P. and Zillman, D. (1981) 'The appeal of rough-and-tumble play in televised professional football', *Communication Quarterly* Vol. 29: pp. 256–26.

Bryce, J. and Rutter, J. (2001) *In the game — In the flow: Presence in public computer gaming.* Paper presented at the Computer Games and Digital Textualities Conference, Copenhagen.

Coget, J. F., Yamauchi, Y. and Suman, M. (2002) 'The Internet, social networks and loneliness', *IT & Society* Vol. 1, No. 1: pp. 180–201.

Comstock, G., Chaffee, S., Katzman, N., McCombs, M. and Roberts, D. (1978) *Television and human behavior.* New York: Columbia University Press.

Cover, R. (2004) 'New media theory: Electronic games, democracy and reconfiguring the author-audience relationship', *Social Semiotics* Vol. 14, No. 2: pp. 173–191.

Crawford, G. (2004) *Consuming sport: Fans, sport, and culture.* London: Routledge.

——— (2005) 'Digital gaming, sport and gender', *Leisure Studies* Vol. 24, No. 3: pp. 259–270.

Critcher, C. (2006) 'Just kidding', *Leisure Studies Association Newsletter* Vol. 73: pp. 26–28.

Cusumano, M.A., Mylonadis, Y. and Rosenbloom, R.S. (1992) 'Strategic maneuvring and mass-market dynamics: The triumph of VHS over Beta', *Business History Review* Vol. 66, No. 1: pp. 81–94.

Duncan, M. C. and Brummet, B. (1989) 'Types and sources of pleasure in televised sports', *Sociology of Sport Journal* Vol. 6: pp. 195–211.

Franzen, A. (2000) 'Does the Internet make us lonely?', *European Sociological Review, 16*(4), 427–438.

Fromme, J. (2003) 'Computer games as a part of children's culture', *Game Studies* Vol. 3, No. 1. Retrieved 15 March, 2006, from http://www.game studies.org/0301/fromme/

Jhally, S. (1989) 'Media sports, culture and power: Critical issues in the communication of sport', in L.A. Wenner (ed) *Media, sports, and society: Research on the communication of sport.* California: Sage, pp. 70.

Johnson, T. J. and Kaye, B. K. (2003) 'Around the World Wide Web in 80 ways', *Social Science Computer Review* Vol. 21, No. 3: 304–325.

Horne, J. (2006) *Sport in consumer culture.* Houndmills, London and New York, N.Y.: Palgrave Macmillan.

Horne, J., Tomlinson, A. and Whannel, G. (1999) *Understanding sport: An introduction to the sociological and cultural analysis of sport.* London: Spon.

Kestnbaum, M., Robinson, J. P., Neustadtl, A. and Alvarez, A. (2002) 'IT and social time displacement', *IT & Society* Vol. 1, No. 1: 21–37.

Leung, L. and Wei, R. (2000) 'More than just talk on the move: Uses and gratifications of the cellular phone', *Journalism and Mass Communication Quarterly* Vol. 77: pp. 308–320.

Lievrouw, L. L. and Livingstone, S. (2002) 'The social shaping and consequences of ICTs', in L. L. Lievrouw and S. Livingstone (eds) *Handbook of new media.* London: Sage, pp. 1.

Lin, C. (1996) 'Looking back: The contribution of Blumbler and Katz's uses of communication to communication research', *Journal of Broadcasting and Electronic Media* Vol. 40: pp. 574–581.

—— (1999) 'Online service adoption likelihood', *Journal of Advertising Research* Vol. 39: pp. 79–89.

Livaditi, J., Vassilopoulou, K., Lougos, C. and Chorianopoulos, K. (2003) *Needs and gratifications for interactive TV applications: Implications for designers.* Paper presented at the 36th Hawaii International Conference on System Sciences, Hawaii.

Livingstone, S. M. (2002) *Young people and new media: Childhood and the changing media environment.* London: SAGE.

McQuail, D. (1997) *Audience analysis.* Thousand Oaks, Calif.; London: Sage Publications.

—— (2000) *McQuail's mass communication theory* (4th ed). London: Sage.

Marshall, S.J., Gorely, T. and Biddle, S.J.H. (2006) 'A descriptive epidemiology of screen-based media use in youth: A review and critique', *Journal of Adolescence* Vol. 29: pp. 333–349.

Murdock, G. (1974) 'Mass communication and the construction of meaning', in N. Armistead (Ed) *Reconstructing social psychology.* Harmondsworth: Penguine, pp. 205.

Negroponte, N. (1995) *Being digital.* London: Hodder and Stoughton.

Newhagen, J. E. and Rafaeli, S. (1996) 'Why communication researchers should study the Internet', *Journal of Communication* Vol. 46, No. 1: pp. 39–50.

OfCom (2006) The communcations market 2006. Office of Communications, UK. Retrieved 11 August, 2006, from http://www.ofcom.org.uk/research/cm/cm06/

Rice, R. E. (1984) *The new media: Communication, research, and technology*. Beverly Hills: Sage Publications.

Rosengren, K. E., Wenner, L. A. and Palmgreen, P. (1985) *Media gratifications research: Current perspectives*. Beverly Hills, CA: Sage.

Rowe, D. (2004) *Sport, culture and the media: The unruly trinity* (2nd ed). Maidenhead: Open University Press.

Ruggiero, T. E. (2000) 'Uses and gratifications theory in the 21st century', *Mass Communication and Society* Vol. 3, No. 1: pp. 3–37.

Sapolsky, B. and Zillmann, D. (1978) 'Enjoyment of a televised sport contest under different social conditions of viewing', *Perceptual & Motor Skills* Vol. 46, No. 1: pp. 29–30.

Scherer, J. (2007) 'Globalization, promotional culture and the production/ consumption of online games: Engaging Adidas's 'beat rugby' campaign', *New Media & Society* Vol. 9, No. 3: pp. 475–496.

Schoenbach, K. and Becker, L. B. (1989) 'The audience copes with plenty: Patterns of reactions to media changes', in L. B. Becker and K. Schoenbach (eds) *Audience responses to media diversification: Coping with plenty*. Hillsdale, NJ: Lawrence Erlbaum Associates, pp. 353.

Smith, A. and Green, K. (2005) 'The place of sport and physical activity in young people's lives and its implications for health: Some sociological comments',*Journal of Youth Studies* Vol. 8, No. 2: pp. 241–253. SportScotland. (2002).

Sportscotland (2000) *Sports participation in Scotland 2000*. Edinburgh, UK: Sportscotland.

Stafford, T. F., Stafford, M. R. and Schkade, L. L. (2004) 'Determining uses and gratifications for the Internet', *Decision Sciences* Vol. 35, No. 2: pp. 259–288.

Wann, D. L. (1995) 'Preliminary validation of the sport fan motivation scale', *Journal of Sport & Social Issues* Vol. 19, No. 4: pp. 377–396.

Weiser, E. B. (2001) 'The functions of Internet use and their social and psychological consequence', *CyberPyschology and Behavior* Vol. 14: pp. 30–39.

Wenner, L. A., and Gantz, W. (1989) 'The audience experience with sports on television', in L. A. Wenner (ed) *Media, sports and society*. Newbury, CA: Sage, pp. 241–269.

Whannel, G. (1998) 'Reading the sports media audience', in L. A. Wenner (ed) *Mediasport*. London: Routledge, pp. 221–251.

Whannel, G. (2005) 'Pregnant with anticipation: The pre-history of television sport and the politics of recycling and preservation', *International Journal of Cultural Studies* Vol. 8, No. 4: pp. 405–426.

Wilson, B. (2007) *Sport and mobile seek 'dream team'*. BBC. Retrieved 15 August, 2007, from http://news.bbc.co.uk/1/hi/business/6944139.stm

II

LEISURE AND THE COMPLEXITIES
OF CONSUMPTION

EXPLAINING THE VICIOUS CIRCLE OF OVERWORK AND OVER CONSUMPTION

Tim Robinson

School of Economics and Finance,
Queensland University of Technology, Brisbane, Australia

> It is to be noted that the willingness to submit to 'work', in the true sense, is an acquired capacity which the human race has taken on, with vast advantage to the mass, within the last ten thousand years or so. Some of us have not got it yet. ... But the rest of us, along with the horse, the ox, the jackass and the elephant, are long since broken into 'work', to the idea of submitting to the imposition of labour by the hour, often very meaningless in itself, as a condition living, a sort of compromise between freedom and slavery. (Leacock, 1944: p. 14)

Introduction

At no time in the recent past has there been more interest in the issue of work-life balance than there is today. A subset of the recent literature dealing with this issue looks specifically for explanations of a perceived tendency for individuals to engage in overwork (for example, Bunting, 2004; Schor, 1992). Implicit in the work-life balance issue is the idea that the balance between work and 'life' involves two forces working in opposite directions. This is precisely the position taken by mainstream economists in trying to understand people's decisions about how much time they should commit to work; that is, how they should deal with the trade off between work and leisure (or 'life'). From the economist's perspective, resolution of this battle between the two opposing forces boils down to a decision as to the extent to which paid work (Leacock's slavery) with its benefit of disposable income should substitute for the more pleasurable activity of engaging in leisure (Leacock's freedom).

Although good economists will be aware of the cultural and institutional factors that bear upon the making of this decision in a social democracy, they will also assert that, with a given set of these cultural and institutional factors, the outcome ought to largely reflect the preferences of workers.

Thus the enormous decline in lifetime waking hours devoted to work as opposed to leisure that has occurred in democratic nations over the past century or more is viewed as evidence of an increased preference for leisure over work. As an example of this decline, it is estimated that over the past 150 years in the UK the percentage of lifetime disposable hours allocated to work has declined from approximately 50 per cent to just 20 per cent (Nordhaus, 2000). This increased preference for leisure is typically explained as being fuelled by continual increases in real remuneration for work that have occurred, almost without exception, over the whole of this period. The argument is that, in spite of the tendency for increased remuneration to encourage greater work effort in the short term, the capacity of this increased remuneration to enable us to work less hours for a given income dominates in the longer term, leading to a reduction in work hours. So, if the long term tendency over the past century has been for us to substitute leisure for work, why is there such current concern with work-life imbalance?

One of the most important reasons for this concern is the increasing evidence that individuals are, during that part of their lifetime when they engage in full-time work, working longer hours than previously. **Table 1** gives an example of the manifestation of this phenomenon.

Table 1   **Percentage of workforce working long hours (>50 per week), selected countries**
(Source: Relationships Forum 2007)

Country	%working > 50 hours per week
Japan	28
Australia	22
New Zealand	21
USA	20
UK	15
Canada	14
Greece	6
Ireland	6
Spain	6
France	6
Portugal	5
Germany	5
Denmark	5
Finland	5
Italy	4
Belgium	4
Sweden	2

While the idea that there has been a recent increase in work hours is undoubtedly true for many countries, there may be good reasons — some of which will be examined shortly — for such an increase. Nonetheless, *regardless of whether work effort has increased or decreased in recent times*, it will be shown that in modern economies individuals engage in excessive work effort as compared to the optimal or 'right' level of work.

It will be argued that this outcome stems from a 'fundamental flaw' in market economies which causes us to unknowingly work excessively. That is, although there have been very large reductions in the proportion of waking hours spent at work in developed countries over the past century or more, these reductions have been less than would be required to maximize well-being. In short, although we work much less than we did a century ago we still work more than we should.

The fundamental flaw

The fundamental flaw in market economies that causes use us to work excessively is caused by environmental disamenity (including congestion) which is the consequence of the productive activities we engage in at work and the consumption activities that are funded by the income we earn at work. The environmental disamenity caused by aggregate work and consumption in the economy constitute costs of work which we do not take into account when deciding the amount of work we will undertake. Rather, in deciding what the level of work effort should be (either collectively or individually), we make a comparison only between the displeasure directly caused by work effort and the consequent pleasure experienced when work-based income is spent for consumption.

If, however, our comparison were between the pleasure experienced from consumption and the displeasure caused by work effort *plus* the cost of the environmental disamenity caused by that work effort and by the consumption it enables, the outcome, in terms of hours worked, would be very different. We would be setting the benefits of a given level of consumption against a higher level of costs. And how would the level of work effort change in these circumstances? There are two aspects of this question that need to be considered.

The effects of acknowledgement of the increased costs of work effort

The first aspect of the consequences of increased costs of work effort to be considered is associated with the short term. Recall that it has already been argued that over the past century rising real incomes have had a long term and a short term effect. In the short term, rising real incomes have encouraged an increase in work effort as the better-remunerated work is substituted for leisure. Using an extension of this logic, it would be expected that, for any given level of real income, recognition of the increased costs of work effort caused by environmental disamenity would encourage a short term substitution of leisure for work. Unfortunately, when assessing the trade off between work and leisure we do not directly attribute these economy-wide costs to our work effort and so, on this count, we work excessively. And even if we did take these costs into account there is nothing we could do about them: a unilateral decision on our part to reduce work effort in order to reduce the extent of environmental disamenity would make no difference to the amount of disamenity we would experience since our individual contribution to it is miniscule. When individuals are the unintended beneficiaries of the actions of others we say that they are *free riding*; in the case being discussed here, where individuals are the unintended victims of the actions of others, we could say they are *forced riders*.

The second aspect of the consequences of increased costs of work effort is associated with the longer term. Recall that it was earlier argued that in the long term rising real incomes have the effect of reducing work effort because a given level of consumption can be funded by working fewer hours — more leisure can be afforded. This tendency has clearly dominated the short term effect during the past century, with the result that the overall effect of rising real incomes has been for work effort to decrease. If, however, we look at the past 30 years or so we see that this decrease in work time has halted or even been reversed in many English speaking countries in spite of continuing increases in real incomes. It is this tendency that has given rise to concerns about *The Overworked American* and Britain's *Willing Slaves*. So, what is it about the past 30 years that has caused work effort to increase or stabilize rather than fall?

Fortunately, the relatively recent phenomenon of measuring and tracking quality of life — as opposed to income — gives us some important insights as to what is going on. If we look at this quality of life data it can be seen that the effect on well-being of increases in real income or gross domestic product (GDP) per capita over the past 30 years have been largely negated by a range of factors, the most important of which are growing environmental disamenity, congestion and resource depletion. This is illustrated in **Figure 1** which shows that, since the mid 1970s, the Genuine Progress Indicator (GPI) — the most comprehensive alternative measure of well-being per capita constructed to date — has declined in spite of large increases in GDP per capita. This contrasts strongly with the 1950s and 60s when GPI rose in concert with GDP per capita. While the GPI is calculated only for the US, other indices of well-being per capita indicate that falls in quality of life have also occurred in a number of Western European countries (see, for example, Douthwaite, 1998).

Not only is there cost-based evidence of declining quality of life but there is also anecdotal evidence. For example, commenting on English jour-nalist Jeanne MacKenzie's contemporaneous account of the Australia she

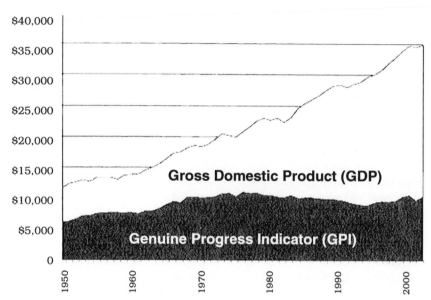

Figure 1   **U.S. GDP versus GPI 1950–2002 ($ per capita)**
(Source: Redefining Progress 2004)

visited in 1959–60, travel writer Bill Bryson remarks that what strikes him
about comparisons between then and now is "… not how much better off
Australians are today, but how much worse they feel" (Bryson, 2001: p.
172). In a photographic history of a renowned Australian beach resort, Bryson
observes that the holiday makers of the 1940s and 50s were not "happy";
they were "*happy*". He goes on to say: "I wouldn't suggest for an instant
that Australians are unhappy people now — anything but, in fact — but
they don't have that happiness in their faces any more. I don't think anybody
does" (Bryson, p.165).

Or consider the call from British Conservative leader David Cameron
in his 2006 general well-being speech (http://www.conservatives.com/
tile.do?def=news.story.page&obj_id=131047&speeches=1):

> Well-Being can't be measured by money or traded in markets. It's
> about the beauty of our surroundings, the quality of our culture,
> and above all the strength of our relationships. Improving our
> society's sense of well-being is, I believe, the central political challenge
> of our times.

Although its conservative source may be novel, such a call is, of course,
not new. Witness the following from Democrat Robert Kennedy's 1968 speech
on the shortcomings of national income or, as he terms it, Gross National
Product (GNP) as a measure of well-being:

> [GNP] does not include the beauty of our poetry or the strength
> of our marriages or the intelligence of our public debate or the
> integrity of our public officials... GNP measures neither our wit
> nor our courage, neither our wisdom nor our learning, neither our
> compassion nor our devotion to our country. It measures everything,
> in short, except that which makes life worthwhile. (Kennedy, 1968)

When, over time, rising real incomes are linked with rising quality of life, as occurred in the 1950s and 60s, it is to be expected that individuals will reduce their work effort because a given quality of life can be obtained with less work effort — leisure is more affordable. If, on the other hand, rising real incomes are associated with falling quality of life, as has been the case over the past 30 years, individuals will tend to work harder to earn more income to compensate for this fall in quality of life — leisure has become less affordable. (For those yet to be convinced a simple example may suffice: imagine a worker with a given annual income who lives and works in a benign environment and who has no need to spend any of her annual income to pay for home heating or cooling. If such a person were to now move to a harsh, cold environment where they lived and worked for the same income but where large heating costs were incurred, their quality of life would be lower and, having much less income at their disposal after incurring their heating costs, they would be likely to increase their work effort. The person with whom they might have traded places would find themselves in the opposite situation: quality of life has risen, no longer does a large portion of income need to be spent for heating, work effort will decrease.) This environmentally based incentive to work more has some similarities with Glaeser *et al.*'s social multiplier that sees, inter alia, the benefits of leisure increasing as positive externalities of partaking of leisure grow with increases in the amount of leisure undertaken by individuals in a society — a sort of social network externality (see Alesina, *et al.*, 2005). In this case, however, it is the loss of social networks that occurs as work effort increases — the reduction in the level of positive externalities of partaking of leisure as work effort increases — which is reducing quality of life and encouraging increased compensatory work effort. Nonetheless, unlike the adverse environmental costs of increased work effort, this loss of positive externalities is much more likely to be understood to be related to work effort and to be acted upon by individuals. This paper thus looks only at the environmental incentives to increase work effort.

The hypothesis being put forward here, then, is that, all other factors remaining constant, declining quality of life over time encourages increased work effort. Unfortunately, there is a double whammy here: this additional work effort occurs on top of the already excessive level of work effort brought about in the short term because of workers' ignorance of, or refusal to act upon, the environmental costs of their work and consumption. Furthermore, and more importantly, these longer hours of work aggravate environmental damage and congestion resulting in further increases in compensatory work effort. Thus there is a vicious circle of overwork and over consumption. This vicious circle has important implications both at home and abroad.

Implications of the vicious circle

The most important implications of the vicious circle are known to us all: they may include, but are certainly not limited to, crime, stress, family breakdown, loss of community, environmental degradation, and congestion. In this analysis emphasis is given to environmental degradation and congestion which can be shown to be significantly contributed to by increases in output that accompany increased work effort (see the impact, population, affluence, technology [IPAT] model in York, *et al.*, 2003). In the context of work-life balance, what are the implications of this increased environmental degradation? Apart from the already explained tendency for exacerbation of the problem as a result of further increases in work effort, there are important implications for the distribution of income both within and between nations. There are also implications for future generations. Finally, there may be implications for the way in which we structure the composition of our national and global output.

It has been explained above that the fundamental flaw in market economies which causes us to work excessively can be attributed to a range of economy-wide environmental costs of work and consumption that do not enter into the calculus when we decide the extent of work effort to undertake. The greater are these costs, the greater is the excess of actual work hours over optimal work hours. This is so because the greater are these costs, the smaller are the net benefits of engaging in work and consumption. As a corollary to this it can be seen that, in the case of an individual worker, the lower the level of real income, the higher these given economy-wide environmental costs will be in relation to that income, and the greater will be the extent to which work is excessive. In short, acknowledgement of the fundamental flaw would require that low-income workers reduce their work effort (increase their leisure time) by more than high-income workers: the net benefits of work effort (real income minus environmental cost) are higher for high income workers than for low income workers. Unpalatable though this may be, the reality is that if all workers were to decrease work hours to the extent necessary to take account of the fundamental flaw, an increase in inequality measured by the dispersion of real incomes would result. This would be, of course, an outcome that most governments and captains of industry would abhor — governments on account of the effects of the increased inequality of incomes and reduced GDP, captains of industry on account of the reduced supply of less skilled labour. Nonetheless, there would be a distinct improvement in environmental outcomes and a rise in quality of life for all.

The principles that apply to differences in income within nations apply equally, if not more so, to differences between nations. Put simply, application of the principles put forward here would require that, if the costs of environmental disamenity were the same in every country, workers in developing countries where incomes are lower should reduce work effort by more than workers in developed countries where incomes are higher. This would clearly have the effect of widening the income gap between many developing and developing nations. Furthermore, and this is the rub, the practice of exporting dirty industries from developed to developing nations — to what are sometimes described as offshore havens — means that environmental disamenity is often far greater in developing that in developed countries. This, of course, means that the extent to which work effort should be reduced in these highly polluted developing countries is even greater than differences in income alone might suggest. Again, if work hours were to be adjusted globally to account for the costs of environmental degradation, the outcome would be a significant increase in inequality in terms of the distribution of real incomes (but a likely improvement in equality in terms of leisure time enjoyed). There would also be a distinct improvement in environmental outcomes and a rise in quality of life in both developed and developing countries. Furthermore, a decision to work fewer hours in developing countries would likely raise the price of imports from these countries to the developed world with the result that 'dirty' industries may re-migrate from their offshore havens to developed countries. This would be likely to result in a reduction in the inequality of adverse environmental incomes between developed and developing nations.

There is a caveat to the conclusion that work effort should decrease for lower income workers. This revolves around the perception of the costs of environmental disamenity which are said to be lower amongst the poor who have primary needs for basic food and shelter that are further up the hierarchy. While this phenomenon of discounting the environmental costs might be thought to be revealed by the willingness of the poor to accept far higher levels of environmental disamenity than the rich, it does raise the question of whether the poor are generally as well informed as are the rich concerning the benefits of a clean environment as compared to the benefits of consumer goods.

So much for the implications of the fundamental flaw for the distribution of income within and between nations; we now turn to the implications for future generations.

Excessive work and future generations

Excessive levels of work effort over time result in an accumulation of environmental problems and their associated costs. Thus today we bear the costs of a level of environmental degradation, including species loss, site contamination, destruction of habitat and global warming, that is the result of the accretion of environmental problems that has been occurring year in and year out since the commencement of the industrial revolution at least. Calculations undertaken by the author and reported elsewhere indicate that current GDP per capita in the developed world would be up to one quarter less than its current environment-sapping level if workers had chosen to reduce their work hours in recognition of the adverse environmental and congestion costs that accompany their work effort and consumption. (Robinson, 2006: pp. 81–85). Unless something is done about it, future generations will suffer from an even greater accumulation of these costs; and, what is more, these increased costs will lower quality of life further and encourage further increases in compensatory work effort. The vicious circle will become even more vicious. In the context of the leisure society, this means that over time its realization is less and less likely to occur in spite of ever increasing levels of real GDP per capita. Indeed, the aspirations for a leisure society that were held in the 1970s will never be realized so long as the pursuit of economic growth results in declining quality of life.

What is to be done?

The extent of environmental regulation designed to reduce the ill-effects of environmental degradation and so increase quality of life grows exponentially. If such regulation were sufficient to actually turn around the decline in quality of life that has accompanied real GDP growth in recent decades so that both were on an upward path (like they were in the 1950s and 60s) an increase in leisure could be expected. Unfortunately, the track record is not good: the increased regulation since that time has been inadequate to the task of actually raising quality of life. Furthermore, if the future adverse effects of global warming are as devastating as an increasing number of commentators expect them to be, the future situation can only worsen: increased pressure will be placed on our leisure time as we work harder and harder in an endeavour to compensate for ever declining quality of life.

If regulation designed to improve environmental outcomes is inadequate to the task, what can be done? Certainly the attempts to improve environmental amenity through regulation must continue and be strengthened. However, limits to their efficacy suggest that more draconian (at least in economists' eyes) measures must be pursued. One solution is to mandate decreases in work hours. If such a policy could be successfully implemented it would, as already explained, require a concomitant decrease in real remuneration. Nonetheless, the net effect of such a solution would be for increased environmental amenity to more than compensate for the fall in income with the result that there would be a net increase in quality of life. This is a straightforward solution that would extend the existing regulation of the labour market. Mandated decreases in work hours occurred throughout the first three quarters of the twentieth century in most developed countries; there is every reason for this process to continue in the twenty first. If workers will not agitate for reductions in work hours because they do not see the connection between work effort and adverse environmental incomes, governments may have to go it alone. Nonetheless, there is likely to be a significant contribution that could be made by government engagement in public education campaigns that explain the wisdom of a policy of reducing work hours. Finally, it is important to ensure that policies designed to reduce work effort have a long-term focus and are implemented slowly over time to allow the economy to adjust smoothly to lower, but sustainable, levels of production and consumption

Another way of tackling the problem is for society to embark on projects that improve environmental outcomes — positive externality generators. Typically, because the benefits of such projects are shared by all rather than being captured by the producer, these activities would need to be subsidized by the state: they have a strong public good element. An increase in work effort channelled into these activities would, because they have side effects that benefit the whole community, result in workers collectively receiving a supplement to their work-related income (see Boyce, 2002). Because these are side effects that constitute benefits of work which are not taken into account when making decisions about the amount of work effort to engage in, we would be undertaking less work than we should in these types of employment. The net effect of increasing the scope of these activities would be a reduction in the economy-wide level of excess work effort and an improvement in environmental amenity. Already governments are engaging in a limited range of these activities which include, for example, restoration of wetlands, restocking of fisheries, and environmental education. That said, there is a political limit to the degree to which governments can extend their involvement in these activities since any such extension would involve higher levels of taxation and government expenditure.

The economies of the developed world are increasingly becoming centred on service industries. The world's richest nations typically have service sectors that constitute more than 60% of GDP. An oft noted characteristic of service industries is that they are generally less environmentally malignant than the goods-producing (manufacturing) industries which they have progressively replaced in the West over the past half century (see, for example, Panatayou quoted in Galeotti, 2003). Indeed, Rosenblum, *et al.* have estimated that the adverse environmental impact of service industries in the US is typically one third to one half of the effect of manufacturing (Rosenblum, 2000). This may help explain why pollution per dollar of GDP has been declining in developed countries but increasing in developing countries where manufacturing has increased as a proportion of GDP. An obvious way of reducing the adverse side effects of work effort would be to increase employment in the service industries at the expense of manufacturing. This could be achieved through a system of taxes and/or subsidies that advantage the service industries in relation to manufacturing. A disadvantage of pure-form value added tax systems, which are now widespread and which are from time to time mooted for the US, is that they treat all industries alike. Any move to use taxes or subsidies to advantage service industries over manufacturing would involve differential taxes and would be part of the wider 'green tax' agenda involving an increase in taxes on, and revenues from, polluting activities which is compensated by a fall in taxes on, and revenues from, 'clean' activities.

Clearly, there are many ways in which current environmental problems can be tackled; a holistic approach involving less work and more leisure should be an integral part of the policy approach. Not only would it improve the natural environment but it would also bring the added benefit of realization of the leisure society that was foreshadowed three and more decades ago.

Conclusion

A rigorous explanation of the reason for overwork in contemporary society has hitherto eluded researchers. The explanation offered here by the application of economic theory to market failure in the form of misinformation about key variables that determine the work, leisure trade trade-off is a novel one that has not previously been promulgated. It provides a basis for policies that would not only give rise to a significant reduction in environmental deterioration but that would also make the realization of the leisure society more likely.

Bibliography

Alesina, A., Glaeser, G. and Sacerdote, B. (2005) 'Work and leisure in the U.S. and Europe why so different?', Harvard Institute of Economic Research, Discussion paper 2068, April.

Boyce, James K. (2002) *The political economy of the environment*. Cheltenham, UK and Northampton, MA, USA: Edward Elgar.

Bryson, Bill (2001) *Down under*. London: Black Swan.

Bunting, Madeleine (2004) *Willing slaves*. London: HarperCollins.

Cameron, David (2006) General well-being speech; at http://www.conservatives.com/tile.do?def=news.story.page&obj_id=131047& speeches=1 accessed 15 June 2007.

Douthwaite, R. (1999) *The growth illusion*. Gabriola Island: New Society Publishers.

Galeotti, M. (2003) 'Economic development and environmental protection', Fondazione Eni Enrico Mattei, Working paper No. 89.

Kennedy, John F. (1963) Speech at Amherst College, Massachusetts to praise American poet Robert Frost, 27 October; at http://www.cc.gatech.edu/people/home/idris/Speeches/kennedy_frost.htm accessed 16 July 2004.

Leacock, S. (1944) *How to write*. London: John Lane the Bodley Head.

Nordhaus, W.D. (2000) 'New directions in national economic accounting', *American Economic Review* Vol. 90, No. 2: pp. 259–263.

Relationships Forum (2007) 'An unexpected tragedy: Evidence for the connection between working patterns and family breakdown in Australia', Sydney.

Robinson, T. (2006) *Work, leisure and the environment*. Cheltenham: Edward Elgar.

Rosenblum, J., Horvath, A., Hendrikson, C. (2000) 'Environmental implications of service industries', *Environmental Science and Technology* Vol. 34, No. 22: pp. 4669–4676.

Schor, J. (1992) *The overworked American*. New York: Basic Books.

York, R., Rosa, E. A. and Dietz, T. (2003) 'STIRPAT, IPAT and ImPACT: Analytic tools for unpacking the driving forces of environmental impacts', *Ecological Economics* No. 46: pp. 351–365.

LEISURE AND CONSUMPTION: NOT ALWAYS THE SAME

Robert A. Stebbins

Department of Sociology, University of Calgary, Canada

Consumption, says Russell Belk (2007: p. 737), "consists of activities potentially leading to and actually following from the acquisition of a good or service by those engaging in such activities". *Acquisition* is defined in this paper as buying (includes renting) a good or service with money (bartering, borrowing, stealing, begging, and other forms of nonmonetary acquisition are not considered). More particularly the social scientific study of consumption has been primarily concerned with a celebrated variety of this process, namely mass consumption, or the wide spread acquisition of popular goods and services (with these two sometimes referred to as mass culture). Moreover there is in the literature on mass consumption a tendency to say little about leisure other than to relate it to such consumption, thereby creating the impression that mass leisure is the only leisure there is. This tendency has a long history, dating at least to the influential anthology assembled by Larrabee and Meyerson (1958).

In the present paper, however, I argue, following Roberts (1999: p. 179) and Kiewa (2003: p. 80), that in no way can all of leisure can be equated with mass consumption, indeed with consumption of any kind. That is, leisure and consumption are not always an identity. And this, even though as Cook (2006: p. 304) writes, leisure "is often seen as having been taken over by money and the money economy". My goal here is to clarify where consumption and taking leisure are separate processes, where they are similar if not the same, and in such overlap, what that looks like.

It should be clear that I will not, for the most part, be considering the first part of Belk's definition — "the activities potentially leading to acquisition of a good or service". This, the first phase of consumption, compared with the second phase, has been well examined, both conceptually and empirically, under the banner of "shopping" (e.g., Bowlby, 1997; Falk and Campbell, 1997; Prus and Dawson, 1991; Stebbins, 2006a). Whereas what follows after the act of acquiring a good or service, the second phase of consumption, has, from the angle of leisure, been comparatively unexplored. My general model is that the act of monetary acquisition (i.e., purchasing or renting) of a good or service stands between these two phases, demarcating them, in the old days often and figuratively by the sharp ring of a cash register, but today, more often than not, by the muted hiss of a bank card being swiped. Note that the informal, or non-monetary, borrowing of something, since no commodity is traded in this process, is not regarded here as a consumptive acquisition.

1. Distinguishing consumption and leisure

Let us start by observing that a substantial amount of consumption today has little or nothing to do with leisure, exemplified in buying toothpaste, life insurance, accounting services, natural gas for home heating, transit tickets for getting to work, and the like. Such consumption, call it *obligatory consumption*, however important for consumers, lies beyond the scope of this paper. As for the other areas of consumption the relationship of this process with leisure is often complicated.

In these other areas — in *leisure-based consumption* — a critical distinction to make is whether the leisure component of a particular activity is directly and solely dependent on the acquisition of a thing or service (e.g., buying a CD, concert ticket, or a session of massage) or whether purchase of something is but a prerequisite to a set of conditions that, much more centrally, shapes the activity as a leisure experience. In other words is consumption an initiator of a leisure experience or a facilitator of such experience. In *initiatory, leisure-based consumption* a person buys, for instance, a ticket enabling entrance to a cinema, a CD enabling listening to recorded music, a new sporty car enabling pleasurable motoring, or a club membership enabling fine drinking and dining with valued members. In such consumption the purchaser proceeds more or less directly to use of the purchased item. Here leisure and consumption do seem to be inextricably linked — an identity — even while sense of the initial consumption may fade as the owner replays for the tenth time the CD or drives six months later the flashy new automobile.

Not so with *facilitative, leisure-based consumption*. Here the acquired item only sets in motion a set of activities, which when completed, enable the purchaser to use the item in a satisfying or fulfilling leisure experience. As an example note that amateur violinists, if they are to play at all, must first rent or purchase a violin — an act of acquisition. Yet their most profound leisure experience is competently and artistically playing music and, earlier, practicing to accomplish this, all of which costs nothing, though, obviously, it is certainly facilitated by using the acquired instrument (a consumer product). Moreover this profound leisure experience might be further facilitated by buying music lessons and paying for public transit tickets to get to a teacher's studio.

In this last example, one or more consumer purchases or rentals are necessary steps to experiencing the leisure being sought. Still leisure activities exist for which no facilitative consumption whatsoever is needed for participation in them. There are areas in free time where consumption and leisure are clearly separate spheres. It is in the free-time sphere that we find *non-consumptive leisure* (examples presented later). As a basis exploring this complicated relationship between leisure and consumption, let us review some concepts in leisure studies, which together, can show in detail how leisure and consumption are not always the same.

2. The serious leisure perspective

Consumption as initiator of leisure or as a facilitator of it varies across the three forms of the serious leisure perspective. This perspective (Stebbins, 2006b) may be described, in simplest terms, as the theoretic framework that synthesizes three main forms of leisure showing, at once, their distinctive features, similarities, and interrelationships. The three forms — serious leisure, casual leisure, and project-based leisure — may be briefly defined as follows:

- Serious leisure: systematic pursuit of an amateur, hobbyist, or volunteer activity sufficiently substantial, interesting, and fulfilling for the participant to find a (leisure) career there acquiring and expressing a combination of its special skills, knowledge, and experience;

- Casual leisure: immediately, intrinsically rewarding, relatively short-lived pleasurable activity, requiring little or no special training to enjoy it;

- Project-based leisure: short-term, reasonably complicated, one-off or occasional, though infrequent, creative undertaking carried out in free time, or time free of disagreeable obligation (Stebbins, 2005b).

The idea of core activity is a further conceptual tool of use in our effort to explore the relationship between leisure and consumption. A *core activity* is a distinctive set of interrelated actions or steps that must be followed to achieve the outcome or product the participant finds attractive (e.g., enjoyable, satisfying, fulfilling). This activity carries with it a substantial, positive emotional component. It lies at the center of what Dubin (1992) calls a "central life interest". In the preceding example, playing the violin is a core activity for the amateur, whereas buying music and rosin, arranging for instrumental repairs, traveling to music lessons, and even purchasing the violin are, by comparison, peripheral activities.

3. Casual leisure

Much of casual leisure may be qualified as initiatory consumption, even while some kinds of play, relaxation, and sensual stimulation, for instance, are not at all consumptive. The examples presented earlier about buying a CD, a cinema ticket, and the like open the door to casual leisure activities. Considering the eight types of casual leisure allows us to see where initiatory consumption is most likely to occur in this form (Stebbins, 2006b: pp. 38–39):

- play (including dabbling, dilettantism);
- relaxation (e.g., sitting, napping, strolling);
- passive entertainment (e.g., through TV, books, recorded music);
- active entertainment (e.g., games of chance, party games);
- sociable conversation (e.g. gossip, "idle chatter");
- sensory stimulation (e.g., sex, eating, drinking, sight seeing);
- casual volunteering (e.g., handing out leaflets, stuffing envelops);
- pleasurable aerobic activity.

The first six types are more fully discussed in Stebbins (1997), while casual volunteering is considered further in Stebbins (2003). The last and newest addition to this typology — pleasurable aerobic activity — refers to physical activities that require effort sufficient to cause marked increase in respiration and heart rate. Here I am referring to "aerobic activity" in the broad sense, to all activity that calls for such effort, which to be sure, includes the routines pursued collectively in (narrowly conceived of) aerobics classes and those pursued individually by way of televised or video-taped programs of aerobics (Stebbins, 2004). Yet, as with its passive and active cousins in entertainment, pleasurable aerobic activity is, at bottom, casual leisure. That is, to do such activity requires little more than minimal skill, knowledge, or experience. Examples include the game of the Hash House Harriers (a type of treasure hunt held in the outdoors), kickball (described in *The Economist*, 2005, as a cross between soccer and baseball), and such children's games as hide-and-seek.

People consume on an initiatory basis mainly in passive and active entertainment and to a lesser extent in relaxation and sensual stimulation. Much of our entertainment is commercial; it is bought, for example, with subscriptions to cable television and tickets to shows as well as with instruments of entertainment such as board games, iPods, and DVDs. We may relax after paying the fee for a session at a spa or the price for a drink at a bar. Additionally some sensory stimulation may only be experienced with the purchase of something: a bag of marijuana, the services of an illegal bookmaker, or a ticket, say, to ride a tour bus, take a scenic cruise on a lake, or go by cable car up the side of a mountain.

Elsewhere in the vast realm of casual leisure, non-consumptive leisure reigns. Some people can relax, without financial outlay, while sitting on their front porch, strolling in a nearby park, or taking a nap. Consensual sexual relations, unless purchased through prostitution or in-kind favors, are free of charge. And so is all of casual volunteering. The same may be said for some of the pleasurable aerobic activities (e.g., kickball, the treasure hunts of the Hash House Harriers).

4. Serious leisure

Many serious leisure pursuits require one or more prerequisite purchases, but here participants accent the highly appealing core activities of their leisure. This was illustrated above in the vignette about purchasing a violin and then learning to play it. Moreover here, too, there are pursuits, including much, if not all, of volunteering, where consumption is negligible, if nonexistent. Here there is no need to acquire something, to buy it or rent it. The same is true for a variety of hobbies, among them, the liberal arts reading hobbies (e.g., reading a kind of history or science), some collecting hobbies (e.g., leaves, seashells, insects), and some outdoor sport and activities (e.g., playing soccer or touch football, walking in nature, swimming in a lake).

Moreover some interesting exceptions come to mind. Sometimes consumption, though peripheral to the core activity of the serious leisure in question, may nevertheless be quite a momentous act. Thus, buying an expensive, fine violin is a memorable event for the committed amateur violinist, as would be the purchase of a pure bred dog for a hobbyist dog breeder or a top-class sailboat for a hobbyist sailor.

In fact the complex relationship between consumption and leisure becomes still more complex when the act of acquisition is itself complicated. This complexity, among the serious leisure activities, appears to be most common in the hobby of collecting. Consider the efforts a coin collector has to make to locate and buy a rare specimen. This person must learn where to look for the item, travel to this place to acquire it, and perhaps bargain with its owner for an affordable price. This is, in fact, a core activity of all collecting — acquisition of collectibles — though there are typically other such activities, among them, cataloguing the collectibles acquired and preserving them. Collectors of fine art, old cars, and antique furniture, and possibly other objects, also commonly experience in these complex terms acquisition of their collectibles. Furthermore the violinist and dog breeder exemplified in the preceding paragraph, even though they are not collectors, they, too, may undertake acquisitions at this level of complexity. Given that, in these instances, consumption is itself a core leisure activity, I will refer to such activities as *core facilitative consumption*. They occur during the first phase of consumption, culminating in one or more purchases.

5. Project-based leisure

Before discussing the relationship of project-based leisure and consumption, let us look at a typology of the first. Whereas systematic exploration may reveal others, two types have so far been identified: one-off projects and occasional projects. These are presented next using a classificatory framework for amateur, hobbyist, and volunteer activities developed earlier (see Stebbins, 1998: chaps. 2–4).

One-off projects

In all these projects people generally use the talents and knowledge they have at hand, even though for some projects they may seek certain instructions beforehand, including reading a book or taking a short course. And some projects resembling hobbyist activity participation may require a modicum of preliminary conditioning. Always, the goal is to undertake successfully the one-off project and nothing more, and sometimes a small amount of background preparation is necessary for this. It is possible that a survey would show that most project-based leisure is hobbyist in character and next most common, a kind of volunteering. First, the following hobbyist-like projects have so far been identified:
* Making and tinkering:
  - Interlacing, interlocking, and knot-making from kits;
  - Other kit assembly projects (e.g., stereo tuner, craft store projects);
  - Do-it-yourself projects done primarily for fulfillment, some of which may even be undertaken with minimal skill and knowledge (e.g., build a rock wall or a fence, finish a room in the basement, plant a special garden). This could turn into an irregular series of such projects, spread over many years, possibly even transforming the participant into a hobbyist.
* Liberal arts:
  - Genealogy (not as ongoing hobby);
  - Tourism: special trip, not as part of an extensive personal tour program, to visit different parts of a region, a continent, or much of the world.
* Activity participation: long back-packing trip, canoe trip; one-off mountain ascent (e.g., Fuji, Rainier, Kilimanjaro).

One-off volunteering projects are also common, though possibly somewhat less so than hobbyist-like projects. And less common than either are the amateur-like projects, which seem to concentrate in the sphere of theater.
* Volunteering
  - Volunteer at a convention or conference, whether local, national, or international in scope.

- Volunteer at a sporting competition, whether local, national, or international in scope.
- Volunteer at an arts festival or special exhibition mounted in a museum.
- Volunteer to help restore human life or wildlife after a natural or human-made disaster caused by, for instance, a hurricane, earthquake, oil spill, or industrial accident.
• Entertainment Theater: produce a skit (a form of sketch) or one-off community pageant; create a puppet show; prepare a home film or a set of videos, slides, or photos; prepare a public talk.

Occasional projects

The occasional projects seem more likely to originate in or be motivated by agreeable obligation than their one-off cousins. Examples of occasional projects include the sum of the culinary, decorative, or other creative activities undertaken, for example, at home or at work for a religious occasion or someone's birthday. Likewise, national holidays and similar celebrations sometimes inspire individuals to mount occasional projects consisting of an ensemble of inventive elements.

Project-based leisure may be consumer based. Thus most, if not all, one-off projects require preliminary purchases, though not however, of the momentous variety, as seen in the example about the expensive violin given earlier. The same may be said for the liberal arts projects, with the possible exception of constructing a genealogy. Although computer programs may be bought for this purpose, some people prepare their genealogies by writing and telephoning relatives and writing up by hand their results (Lambert, 1996). Finally activity participation seems to invariably involve purchase of equipment and travel services. Indeed getting to some of these activities, itself often a major commercial undertaking, may be quite involved and not especially pleasant (e.g., international travel to the base of Mt. Everest). But this is still not a core activity of the sort described above in acquiring certain collectibles.

By contrast one-off volunteering projects, with one possible exception, can be qualified as non-consumptive leisure. That is unless we count as acquisitions the costs of transportation, clothing, and food borne by the volunteer while engaging in the altruistic activity and the festival, museum, or sporting organization does not reimburse these. Nonetheless some disaster volunteers may have to spend a great deal of money on transportation, lodging, and meals to help at the site of a hurricane or oil spill.

Occasional projects seem, much of the time, to require buying something to make the project possible. Holding a surprise birthday party will have its costs, as will decorating the house and yard for the Christmas season.

Here, too, there are exceptions, among them, the research some people conduct to buy a new car, which they carry out on the Internet and at certain dealers (this example assumes they are not coerced to make this purchase). Another exception is evident in those who plan a major holiday in a faraway place, which they do by consulting the Internet, certain print media, and possibly, knowledgeable friends and relatives. Here they engage in a sort of core facilitative consumption.

6. Conclusion

Much of what has been said here may be summarized in the generalization that consumption in relation to leisure, to the extent the first is either initiatory or facilitative, is, in part, a practical process: to be able to engage in the leisure, depending on its nature, the participant will have to buy a particular thing or service. A second generalization follows, namely, that the heart of the consumption-based leisure experience, which is found in participating in the core activity or activities, lies outside this practical expenditure. This was discussed earlier as the second phase of consumption. Furthermore, for some kinds of leisure, such monetary outlays, I have argued, are more or less flatly unnecessary; they are non-consumptive leisure.

Two exceptions to the first generalization are, however, also highly important. One of them has already been treated of earlier, namely, core facilitative consumption in Phase One. The other, to be discussed here for the first time in this paper, is the role of conspicuous consumption in leisure (Veblen, 1899). Conspicuous consumption elevates significantly the importance for the consumer of the commercial side of this person's leisure. Purchasing expensive, dazzling goods and services earns the buyer a special cachet in the eyes of the other people in his or her circle. As Veblen (1899: p. 64) put it: "conspicuous consumption of valuable goods is a means of reputability to the gentleman of leisure".

Still such commercial activity seems to be the wealthy person's version of initiatory consumption, as suggested by the word "means" in the preceding quotation. An expensive gift, a lavish feast (for friends, associates), an extravagant holiday somewhere must first be bought before they can be enjoyed. The principal difference, and an important one it is, is that these acquisitions have an unusual layer of meaning, namely that of demonstrating the social standing of the buyer as expressed in a flashy display of wealth. In conspicuous consumption the actual leisure appears, most often, to follow the purchase of a good or service such as just described, leading, commonly, to a casual or project-based leisure experience.

Nonetheless some types of serious leisure, gained through facilitative consumption, can also be conspicuous. For example someone with the money might purchase season tickets for the best seats in the house for the opera or a major league sport. This would be conspicuous casual leisure were the buyer a mere consumer of the art or sport, but would be conspicuous serious leisure were this person a buff. *Consumers, or fans,* more or less uncritically consume, for instance, restaurant fare, sports events, or displays of art (concerts, shows, exhibitions) as pure entertainment and sensory stimulation, whereas *buffs* participate in these same situations as more or less knowledgeable, albeit nonprofessional, experts (Stebbins, 2005a: p. 6). The latter have been classified as a kind of liberal arts hobbyist (Stebbins, 2006b: pp. 28–29).

In sum, it seems that, whereas economists see the act of purchasing a good or service as lying at the heart of consumption, a leisure studies-based understanding of the consumptive process places the accent elsewhere. The latter stresses the first and second phases of consumption, minimizing, in doing this, the demarcating act of acquiring something. To be sure, purchases relate in major ways to the economy, as felt in wages earned, businesses sustained, taxes collected, to mention a few. But the motivational and socio-cultural context behind these ways is lost in this kind of analysis. In this respect a leisure studies perspective sheds important new light on modern-day acquisition and consumption.

References

Belk, R. (2007) 'Consumption, mass consumption, and consumer culture', in G. Ritzer (ed) *The Blackwell encyclopedia of the social sciences*. Cambridge, MA: Blackwell, pp. 737–746.

Bowlby, R. (1997) 'Supermarket futures', in P. Falk and C. Campbell (eds) *The shopping experience*. London: Sage, pp. 92–110.

Cook, D.T. (2006) 'Leisure and consumption', in C. Rojek, S.M. Shaw and A.J. Veal (eds) *A handbook of leisure studies*. New York: Palgrave Macmillan, pp. 304–316.

Dubin, R. (1992) *Central life interests: Creative individualism in a complex world*. New Brunswick, NJ: Transaction.

The Economist. (2005) 'Up off the couch', 22 October: p. 35.

Falk, P. and Campbell, C. (1997) 'Introduction', in P. Falk and C. Campbell (eds) *The shopping experience*. London: Sage, pp. 1–14.

Kiewa, J. (2003) 'Consumption', in J.M. Jenkins and J.J. Pigram (eds) *Encyclopedia of leisure and outdoor recreation*. New York: Routledge, pp. 79–91.

Lambert, R.D. (1996) 'Doing family history', *Families* Vol. 35: pp. 11–25.

Larrabee, E. and Meyerson, R.B. (eds) (1958) *Mass leisure*. Glencoe, IL: Free Press.

Prus, R. and Dawson, L. (1991) 'Shop 'til you drop: Shopping as recreational and laborious activity', *Canadian Journal of Sociology* Vol. 16: 145–164.

Roberts, K. (1999) *Leisure in contemporary society.* Wallingford, Oxon: CABI Publishing.

Stebbins, R.A. (1997) 'Casual leisure: A conceptual statement', *Leisure Studies* Vol. 16: 17–25.

—— (1998) *After work: The search for an optimal leisure lifestyle.* Calgary, AB: Detselig.

—— (2003) 'Casual leisure', in J.M. Jenkins and J.J. Pigram (eds) *Encyclopedia of leisure and outdoor recreation.* London: Routledge, pp. 44–46.

—— (2005a) 'The role of leisure in arts administration', *Occasional Paper Series*, Paper No. 1. Eugene, OR: Center for Community Arts and Public Policy, University of Oregon Arts (published online at: http://aad.uoregon.edu/icas/documents/stebbins0305.pdf).

—— (2005b) 'Project-based leisure: Theoretical neglect of a common use of free time', *Leisure Studies* Vol. 24: 1–11.

——. (2006a) 'Shopping as leisure, obligation, and community', *Leisure/Loisir* Vol. 30: 475–486.

—— (2006b) *Serious leisure: A perspective for our time.* New Brunswick, NJ: Transaction.

Veblen, T. (1899) *The theory of the leisure class: An economic study of institutions.* New York: Macmillan.

TRAVELLING LIGHT IN HOSTILE COUNTRY: MOUNTAINEERING, COMMITMENT AND THE LEISURE LIFESTYLE

Lee Davidson

Museum and Heritage Studies,
Victoria University of Wellington, New Zealand

Introduction

Dedicated mountaineers sustain a commitment to a demanding activity, voluntarily chosen and unremunerated. In this respect mountaineering falls within the realm of activities identified by Stebbins (1992: p. 3; 2001) as serious leisure; that is, "the systematic pursuit of an amateur, hobbyist, or volunteer activity that participants find so substantial and interesting that, in the typical case, they launch themselves on a career centred on acquiring and expressing its special skills, knowledge, and experience". Indeed, Stebbins' (2005) most recent study in this area scrutinises what he terms 'nature-challenge' hobbies, which include mountaineering. Nature-challenge hobbies, like all serious leisure, can be considered 'central life interests'.

A central life interest "is that portion of an individual's life space in which [a major] affective investment has been made" (Dubin, 1979: p. 419). Through aspects of lifestyle, the extent of one's investment in a serious leisure pursuit may be identified. Stebbins (2005: p. 24) labels as 'devotees' those hobbyists who demonstrate a high level of dedication to their chosen activity, and differentiates these from "the more ordinary 'participant'", who invests less significantly and commits less time to their hobby. The mountaineers in this study are 'devotees', in that they have made substantial investments of time and affect in mountaineering; they have chosen lifestyles that allow them to participate as much as possible in the core activity and associated activities (for example, training, staying fit, reading about and socialising with other mountaineers); and it is central to their sense of who they are. Importantly, also, they have sustained this level of investment over a long period of time. The mountaineers included in this study represent a range of age groups, therefore the time during which they have been committed to their leisure activity varies from five years to more than fifty years. Nevertheless, they all expressed an intention to continue mountain-eering in some capacity for the duration of their life time, and all had m-ade important life choices in order to facilitate this. This is what I understand as *commitment* for the purposes of this study.

According to Bauman (2000; 2001), modernity and its aftermath have been particularly inhospitable to a sense of coherence and enduring commitment throughout our lifetimes. 'Moderns' lived their lives as pilgrims: their trajectory towards a fixed destination was established at an early stage — both because it could be and because it had to be — and they could head off with reasonable confidence that the end-point would not shift, nor would their path deviate unexpectedly (Bauman, 1995). But the world of liquid modernity in which we now live is no longer conducive to such pilgrimages, and we have a resulting "horror of being bound and fixed":

> the life of men and women of our times is more like that of tourists-through-time: they cannot and would not decide in advance what places they will visit and what the sequence of stations will be; what they know for sure is just that they will keep on the move, never sure whether the place they have reached is their final destination. (Bauman, 1995: pp. 268–269)

Rojek (1993: pp. 212–216) describes the implications of this shift for our leisure lives:

> We shrink from deep commitments and cast our energies in leisure out toward reassuring, consumerist experience which requires passive involvement or transitory relationships which avoid putting ourselves on the line. ... Dedicated leisure activity is quite rare, which is why the compulsive hill-walker, the serious amateur musician, or even the serious reader of fiction, stand out so starkly. ... The ephemeral, the fugitive and the contingent describe our experience of leisure just as they are at the heart of the phenomen-ology of Modernity.

If Bauman and Rojek are correct, then committed mountaineers are something of an anomaly and certain questions immediately present themselves: how do they sustain their commitment to a leisure activity with an intensity and durability that elude others? Have they found for themselves some 'fixed points of orientation' from which they can navigate towards a 'predictable destination'? I investigated these questions using a biographical narrative approach (Denzin, 1989; Wengraf, 2001). The primary method was the in-depth biographical interview, based on the structure proposed by Wengraf (2001). Twenty-two New Zealand mountaineers, representing a range of ages, gender, length of climbing career and family/relationship situations, were interviewed. The empirical material gathered by this method was interpreted using a combination of the concepts and techniques recommended by Denzin (1989; 2001), Wengraf (2001) and Pamphilon (1999). A number of supplementary materials were used to *contextualise* (Denzin, 1989) the interviews. These included additional personal records volunteered by participants, supporting literature and other media including films, videos and climbing magazines and journals, and a number of key informants.

Mountaineering virtues, commitment and the leisure lifestyle

Mountaineers are sustained in their commitment to a lifestyle centred around a leisure pursuit by a moral framework, encapsulating certain "ordinary virtues" (Gordon, 2001), that has grown-up around the practice of mountaineering as it has evolved historically. MacIntyre (1981: p. 119) suggests that morality is invariably and to a greater or lesser extent linked to the "socially local and particular", not to universality as modernity would have us believe. In addition, we possess virtues only to the extent that they are passed on to us through a tradition, associated with certain *practices*, and the *goods* (that is, what is valued) and *virtues* (that is, the special qualities required to excel) associated with these practices. Mountaineering fits the requirements of such a practice, as MacIntyre (1981) describes it, with its own "living tradition" delineating a certain *telos*, or notion of what constitutes the 'good' life (a life that is "higher or better" as Frank (2002) puts it), and the virtues required for its attainment. This places it among the subcultures maintaining "versions of the traditional scheme of the virtues" and destined, consequently, to exist on the periphery of a dominant culture which is inhospitable to such conceptions of morality (MacIntyre, 1981: p. 210).

Orienting one's life towards "things that matter" requires, according to Frank (2002: p. 10), "on-going dialogical recognition from others that one's life expresses values they share". And it is through stories that the "local and contingent solutions" to the question of how best to live one's life are expressed (Frank, 2002). Thus, within the mountaineering community in New Zealand, the 'central bond is a shared vision of and understanding of goods' (MacIntyre, 1981: p. 240) and these goods, or values, are embodied in the narrative theme of the 'true' mountaineer. With respect to a leisure lifestyle, the 'true' mountaineer possesses two important virtues: *enduring commitment* to mountaineering as a way of life; and *non-materialism*.

Enduring commitment

> Climbing mountains is a way of life. Yeah, climbing mountains has got to be your soul ... being, in the mountains, walking, tramping, sitting down looking, listening to birds, getting high, in the snow, that's, you know, a way of life ... you've got to live it. *(Terry)* [1]

The single most important virtue that marks out a 'true' (as opposed to 'great') mountaineer, is not the height of one's achievements but the durability of one's commitment to mountaineering as a way of life; and an enduring commitment is underpinned by a deep love of the mountains. As Thomas says, "just being in the mountains" is the most important thing:

> It's the being there and love for the, yeah for the country, for the mountains and all, and that makes us mountaineers. ... I don't think you're better mountaineers if you climb grade 20 or 30. I think that has nothing to do with it, it's in what we bring to it and what we get back from it and we can do it in our own stages. *(Thomas)*

In emphasising the importance of how they feel about the mountains, the mountaineers differentiate themselves from others who climb but who are, as Pip puts it, "often, not really focused on the environment they're in; they're really focused on, ah, the technical side of the climb and achievement". Adam says, "you do come across people whose attitude to the environment is, sort of not related to ... how I envisage climbers to be". For 'true' mountaineers, the mountains must be central. Pete feels that, for him, the mountains are "the real essence of your being" and that "just doesn't go away". Even though he hasn't been climbing as much recently as he used to, "in my mind I haven't left it". Simon has a similar feeling:

> I don't know what life would be like without, appreciating the mountains, whether your climbing them or, or viewing them or, enjoying them in some way or another. I mean that's the essence of mountaineering really you don't always have to be climbing, to enjoy it. You know you can do trans-alpine trips and, take in the views and, carry a light pack and, eat good food. *(Pete)*

This aspect of their commitment to the mountains allows for its durability over a life-time. As mountaineers grow older, Thomas says, "we adjust our ambitions to our capabilities". If someone gives up because they can no longer "keep up", or do what they used to do, according to Thomas "that has nothing to do with mountaineering". The commitment can be, and must be, for life:

> Mountaineers keep trooping away, keep, you know, keep ticking away at you know, the odd tramp, the odd walk ... right until he drops dead, he will. *(Terry)*

Those who are not sustained by a fundamental love of the mountains will burn out after a few years and drop out; or people will try it because it is fashionable and then give it up and try the next thing when that comes along. For Thomas, the "real mountaineers" are those who are still doing it after fifty years, not those who give up once they can no longer perform the most difficult feats.

Two of those I interviewed were no longer climbing. While Bob swapped climbing for flying as he grew older, his life is still intimately connected to the mountains as he lives in them and runs his business of ski-planes and scenic flights. Bob feels that he is "a very lucky man ... to still be able to get around the hills" even though he's older now and less fit. When he sees climbers from the air, he feels a "strong bond" with them: "I know exactly why they're there and what it's about". As for Mark, a climbing accident left him with debilitating and permanent injuries. While he will never climb again, and has great trouble even getting back in and around mountains, the way in which he describes them in his interview suggests a strong and enduring connection. In telling his story he takes great care to vividly describe experiences and intense emotions, pausing at times and closing his eyes. One thing is clear: deprived of the practice, Mark still embodies the tradition and the mountains remain pivotal to his life.

A mountaineer's commitment must not only infuse the length of her or his life, but also its breadth. For Terry, a mountaineer is someone who "lives, eats, sleeps thinking, you know, mountains". It is an indivisible part of his life, "you've got to live it", constantly. For Thomas too:

> it's part of my life. It's one activity which sometimes I have been doing more and sometimes less. And I've been fanatical about it at times, and more relaxed about it ... I can't single it out of part of my life. *(Thomas)*

A love of the mountains renders comprehensible the capacity to persevere and overcome obstacles in the pursuit of climbing mountains, in a way that such exploits are not always comprehensible to outsiders. His "mountain feeling", as Dave calls it, allows him to suffer, and mountaineering would be a "weird experience" (that is, an incomprehensible thing to do) without it. To explain this Dave tells a story about an expedition during which he had to spend a lot of time walking up and down a glacier. To begin with, it was a grind and he "didn't really get it [laughs], didn't feel anything for the place", until he stopped to watch the light changing across the landscape:

> I just sat there for ages and I felt that, that feeling and felt really good about the place and, got my mountain feeling back, and ... I mean that's one of the lasting memories I've had of that trip, is of the light changing and me sitting there in the middle of the glacier with all these big mountains around, and feeling really nice. Feeling really sort of, well at home I suppose and grounded with, with the place. ... If you can't go into the mountains and feel, get something from them, like that, amazing feeling then, it'd be a fairly weird experience going mountaineering. ... that's kind of what, allows you to suffer a little bit and put yourself through quite a lot of, ah, angst and suffering, pain and, all the rest of it. *(Dave)*

A love for the mountains, therefore, provides a source of 'narrative unity' in the lives of these climbers. This renders their enduring commitment to a life of mountaineering — including not just the technical feat of climbing mountains, but also a passion for "just being in the mountains" — meaningful. Having such a unity, according to MacIntyre (1981), runs contrary to the forces of individualism and bureaucracy which dominate in modernity, and tend to compartmentalise our lives. Indeed, the rise of modernity so eroded the potential to conceive of a life as a unified whole, MacIntyre (1981) argues, that by the eighteenth century it could no longer be taken for granted. As evidence, he cites the novels of Jane Austen, in which constancy (in actions and not just words) emerges as a central virtue, essentially in response to the necessity of continually demonstrating what can no more be considered a given.

Constancy is so crucial to a stable moral life because in the absence of narrative unity, which bestows a telos at the level of a human life in its entirety, individual virtues lose their context, without which they cannot be fully understood. This leaves us vulnerable to "a certain subversive arbitrariness" in our moral lives (MacIntyre, 1981: p. 189). In mountaineering, as in Jane Austen's novels, constancy — or an enduring commitment as I have called it here — underpinned by deep feeling, is a central virtue.

Non-materialism

> [Mountaineers are] not as interested in acquiring stuff as feeling feelings. That's more important, to have experiences than to have chattels, and crap. The mountains are a very unencumbered place. ... you can't buy the feelings of achievement and, of self-reliance.
> *(Mark)*

Another virtue which is seen by many to distinguish 'true' mountaineers is that they "don't aspire to great wealth". "Most mountaineers are satisfied with their lot. They're very satisfied with their existence, most mountaineers", says Terry. It is about being able to live, according to Bob, "in a relatively uncomplicated way". Dan suggests that 'making do' is part of "the Kiwi mentality", and is critical of the consumerism among some climbers that he met overseas. So mountaineers' lives, like the mountains, should be "unencumbered". Not only is this a matter of priorising climbing over the pursuit of wealth and the accumulation of consumer goods, but it is also a virtue that is seen to spring from experiences in the mountains. Pete feels that having mountaineering as a central focus of his life "keeps it all in perspective" and lies behind many of the important decisions he has made. For example, he recently gave up a well-paid professional job:

I wanted to make the lifestyle change, this job got advertised and I could see it gave me the opportunity to [spend time in] the mountains ... and that's really attractive, you know, and the salary doesn't really matter too much. So, um, that's a big attraction, yeah, and I feel like 'ah, this is good, and I'm going back into the old hills again for a bit'. *(Pete)*

Sue too feels that the satisfaction she finds in climbing has led her to place less emphasis on the material side of life:

I've found that as I climb less the material side of life grows more around me and if I go climbing I can shed that more and get away from it. Because you just realise you don't need so much stuff and you can live at a much more basic level than most of us do. So I like that. *(Sue)*

Non-materialism also has a practical advantage in terms of maintaining the leisure lifestyle in a materialistic, consumption-driven world. The employment situations of the mountaineers were diverse, but the majority fell into two broad groups: those with professional careers or skilled work, which require a relatively high degree of commitment in terms of time, and possibly "occupational devotion" (Stebbins, 2005); and those with "throwaway jobs" (Stebbins, 2005: p. 130), which give a much greater degree of flexibility as they are "relatively easily acquired and abandoned", including seasonal and casual work. Eight of the interviewees were in the first category. Six supported themselves predominantly through a variety of seasonal forms of employment, and fitted the second category. The remainder fell somewhere between these two ends of the spectrum. Four were involved in skilled work, but were essentially self-employed, which allowed them a high degree of flexibility. A further two had previously been engaged in professional careers, and had "downshifted" (Breakspear and Hamilton, 2004) — as illustrated above by Pete — to part-time and/or less skilled work in order to suit their mountaineering lifestyles. This work nevertheless still provided a degree of satisfaction and was on-going in nature. One was retired and another a part-time student.

Trading income for time and flexibility to go climbing means that most mountaineers do not have high disposable incomes, and what they have is often spent facilitating their leisure pursuit. *Pleonexia*, or "acquisitiveness", may well now be the "driving force of modern productive work", but Aristotle considered it a vice (MacIntyre, 1981: p. 211). Mountaineers too consider it a vice because it is not conducive to a lifestyle centred on mountaineering and because the world of consumption is seen to stand in opposition to life "in the hills".

The leisure lifestyle in an inhospitable world

It is characteristic of ordinary virtues, Gordon (2001: pp. 28–29) argues, that they "acknowledge their limits and know their impermanence"; "they are open to unseating". In a number of the narratives the mountaineers grappled with difficulties that arose from trying to be the kind of mountaineer that they aspired to be, while living in a world not always conducive to their aspirations. These struggles were evident when the moral imperatives of mountaineering clashed with responsibilities and norms in other aspects of their lives. Especially problematic for the mountaineers was the question of divided commitments, between the world of mountaineering and the 'outside'; and the "false values" of the outside world, which appear to impinge upon the tradition of mountaineering and compromise the values it espouses.

Divided commitments

Commitment to one's life as a mountaineer is, as I have argued, highly admired within the mountaineering community, but inevitably draws people away from their co-existing commitments outside that world. Selfhood, Bruner (2002: p. 69) tells us, "involves a commitment to others as well as being 'true to oneself'", and this is a "balancing act" in which the mountaineers are frequently engaged. Steph seems to feel she has little choice but to be 'true to herself', though she does not suggest that this is easy:

> It's always, drawing me away from, from my family and, and my friends and, and the things that I feel like people would like [me] to be doing as well. Like my parents would really like me to finish my degree and, get a proper job and stuff, but, it's just not really within me to settle down in, in one place and not have the freedom to, go climbing, so, yeah it sometimes, it does feel like it's, it's an impact that it's making on me. Sometimes it just feels like, well, that's the way I am. *(Steph)*

Guilt over the cost that their commitment to mountaineering can have for partners and families was strongly evident in a number of the narratives. Bill, Terry and Jan all feel that their mountaineering has conflicted with their family responsibilities and are very wary of being considered selfish. Pip also feels that since she has had children, "I'm really caught, between, my responsibilities as a mother, and, my desire to go and climb. ... I've tried not to feel it. But it's definitely there". Sue had never originally wanted to have children:

> ... then I met Geoff and Geoff wanted to have kids and I thought 'oh well if I'm going to have him, I've got to agree to have kids. So okay yeah that's alright'. That was an easy decision to make. But

not for a while, you know that was the idea. So I was 28 when we got married and I was 29 when we had our first child so that was a bit too quick ... but yeah I found it very difficult to cope with the restriction of being a parent. Very difficult. Yeah I guess it took years and years to accept it. *(Sue)*

Dave has experienced similar conflicts. Commitment is a word he uses often in his narrative, but with some ambivalence. He is aware that much of the "magic" of climbing and the ability to perform at a high level, requires a capacity to detach oneself from the everyday world and to value the challenge — and all that it represents — more highly than survival, or the fear of dying. At the same time, he wants to live to be an old man, he finds being married "fantastic", and does not want to be portrayed as being selfish. The levels of commitment he reached when he was young and living the life of the "climbing bum", on the dole and with no girlfriend, set a benchmark for his life, and when he talked about commitment he tended to return to a particular year (a date he describes as being etched more deeply in his memory than his wife's birthday), and a trip where the stakes were extremely high, and he realised just what was to be gained, if everything else was put on the line. He and his climbing partner did a major climb in the middle of winter, at a time that was particularly cold and had high snowfall:

> We hadn't done anything like it before, nobody had, and we didn't know what we were in for and we did a few things wrong and stuff. But we ... we were totally committed to what we were doing. ... three or four days into the trip we lost our tent in a big snow storm. ... we were lucky to sort of get out of the storm alive ... we dug a snow hole and we cowered in that for two days ... but then it cleared up and we dug most of our gear out ... I don't remember discussing whether or not we would bail — like we were so committed and so into it that, umm, we carried on, but with minus the tent, so we had to bivvy. And bivvying in the middle of winter, back then, when we didn't have any bivvy bags, we just had our sleeping bags and stuff was full on, I mean, we, sort of, were starting to push the boat out. But ... it didn't really matter because we were ... committed, you know, it's like when you get to a level, that level of commitment in mountaineering it ... becomes magic and sort of magic happens, you know, you sort of don't really care whether you live or die kind of thing and it's really really cool. *(Dave)*

When I asked Dave if he has had any disappointments in his climbing, he described experiences when, for one reason or another, the level of commitment did not match the level he had achieved on the trip he describes above. On one recent trip, he says, there were "funny group dynamics", where two of them were "really committed" and the other two in the group were "kind of easy-osy 'oh, this is a good holiday' kind of thing, you know, 'we're having a good time but, we've gotta get home for our jobs'". But, he continues:

> You can't approach a peak like that. You've gotta have lots of time and you've gotta, release yourself from society. You can't have any ties, otherwise ... you'll rap off quite quickly. So that was a, that was a pretty big disappointment. *(Dave)*

So it seems that sometimes mountaineers may not just be in a double-bind (self versus others), but indeed a triple-bind (self versus others versus others). If the self is "oriented towards 'reference groups' and 'significant others' who set the cultural standard by which it judges itself" (Bruner, 2002: p. 71), then the mountaineers potentially have two opposing groups of others to which they must refer: those on the mountain, and those 'back home'. Dave admits that he struggles with the ties that bind him to the world outside of his climbing trips. He likes the fact that the job he has requires "no commitment": "if [my boss] suddenly went down the gurgler and, couldn't afford to have me then I'd [say], 'see you John', 'see you Dave', you know, no love lost sort of thing, no redundancy". But things have changed since his early carefree days, and his frame of reference has shifted. He says that now he is married, there is a bit more "give and take", although his wife "understands" that because mountaineering is "part of my, being you know, I have to go every now and then". He does not want to have children and, he says, "I definitely don't want three weeks holiday a year". So while his "need to go climbing" has been tempered over time, "every now and then ... you just get this, 'oh yeah, here it comes, I've got to go' [laughs] ... It's amazing that we actually have steady relationships really, sometimes [laughs]".

But internal conflict over the all-consuming nature of mountaineering is not limited to those with family responsibilities. For Dan, a devotion to climbing clashes with his sense that he should be making a more significant contribution to society. He says he "struggled for a long time thinking that ... climbing was quite a selfish activity". Dan reconciled his inner struggle by deciding that he could contribute through climbing by becoming an outdoor instructor and working with young people, as well as just feeling more fulfilled in himself:

> I've kind of, been realising that, that just by doing what you want to do and what you love to do that, you're going to be a lot happier and, more inspired in yourself all the time and, that just by living like that, you know, you are giving and helping people around you. *(Dan)*

Some of the mountaineers simply express regret that climbing is such an all-consuming activity that it leaves them insufficient time to do other things that they have an urge to do. Sometimes Jess feels regret that climbing "takes up every spare minute of your life", because "there's so many other things I want to do as well". Tim does not think he "could be a climbing bum any more". These days he likes to be able to "switch off from climbing" at times, and to have "things to put in the gaps between climbing", such as kayaking. This means thinking of himself as more than "just a climber". Simon has become more aware of and attempted to ameliorate the "selfish" aspects of mountaineering as he has grown older.

> I think mountaineering is quite a selfish sport actually. Like as much as it can enrich your own life, and, it doesn't necessarily mean it might enrich those around you, like partners and, friends. ... if you're hanging out with a core of friends who are into the mountains then, it's great. ... [but] I haven't enjoyed some of the other, things that there are to enjoy in life. ... [because] it's a sport that requires, commitment ... Yeah I'm definitely more well rounded about that now though. *(Tim)*

If assessments of the postmodern condition are anything to go by, it is no wonder that, particularly for the younger climbers, they can feel pulled in many directions. Due to a process he calls "social saturation", Gergen (1991: p. 80, p. 219) argues that people today are afflicted by multiphrenia, which splits them into "myriad, fractional relationships" and exposes them to "manifold and competing potentials". In a world of limitless, technology-assisted possibilities, our daily lives he says, have "become a sea of drowning demands, and there is no shore in sight" (Gergen, 1991: p. 75). Wolfe (2001: p. 95) describes the effect of confronting so many choices as a kind of "moral vertigo". Subjected to such forces, commitment — to anyone, to anything — is seen as the exception rather than the rule, although option-overload can, according to Gergen (1991) lead to a renewed desire for the conflict-free simplicity of a single-focus life. As we have seen above, however, this is more likely to be an ideal than the reality, and a heavy-duty pair of blinkers would be required not to see all the other temptations and responsibilities that surround us on every front.

"False values" of the outside world

Implicit in what mountaineers hold as being important values or virtues, are their opposites: the "false values" ('Wendy Butler', 1967) or vices, of the outside world. In the narratives these include 'the easy life', competition and technical specialisation, reliance on technology, the commercialisation and regulation of the mountains, instant gratification and self-centredness. The opposition between "two worlds", embodying two very different and seemingly incompatible sets of values, each impinging on the other, is illustrated by the following story, published in the New Zealand Alpine Journal (NZAJ), about a climbing expedition to Antarctica:

Opening the door in bleary-eyed sleepiness one morning, I discovered to my horror not the usual calm of lapping water, snow and lazy penguins, but a hundred red-coated tourists walking in a line towards us. Bizarre scenes like this continued to surprise me. ... I felt caught on the border of two worlds. I had expected a world of adventure, exposure and isolation, but this was juxtaposed against sudden alarming influxes of people, catering and loud speakers. It was a struggle to maintain the feeling of adventure ... we were constantly being confronted with invitations onto superyachts for French wine and cheeses. The passengers on board took some effort over their personal appearance and in contrast we were conspicuously smelly, uncouth and scruffy.

When offered a passage back to South America on a super-yacht, this climber felt that "[a]gain I was being confronted with decadence. It seemed people everywhere were conspiring to smooth my trip with luxuries" (Goddard, 2002).

So the world of adventure and mountains is threatened from without by "luxuries" and "decadence": the easy life. It takes a force of will, as Tim suggests, not to take the "easy" option:

Climbing's always like going on a quest or something. I just, I guess life would be really simple, life would be quite easy if you didn't challenge yourself and so you know set these great feats to go and climb these mountains and stuff and suddenly life becomes really hard and you get hungry and sore and tired and yeah so you know it certainly hardens you up a bit because yeah life could be far too easy if you wanted it to be. So — you get a bit tougher. *(Tim)*

The alternative, Tim told me, would be to "live in a glass jar". Instead, you have to "try and suck it all up, yeah". It seems, however, that there are fewer people willing to inhale life in this way. Both Dave and Chris observe that there are fewer "hard core climbers" in New Zealand than there used to be. Dave's theory is that people are not prepared to put themselves through the "hardship" that is required to get good at mountaineering, when so many "quick thrills" can be had more easily:

You can go, hang gliding, you can go body boarding, you can go surfing ... there's so much variety of things you can do. You don't need to go and suffer on a glacier, you know, and scare yourself senseless trying to grind your way up a mountain. *(Dave)*

Similarly, Pip is "disheartened" by what she sees as a more conservative and less self-reliant attitude among others in the mountains: "the number of little rules and regulations", and the way in which "our New Zealand wilderness has just become so commercial". The prevalence of commercial guiding, in particular, Pip sees as the antithesis of "real adventures" in the "good old kiwi fashion". Commercialisation and consumerism — buying increasingly technical equipment and clothing — are mentioned by others as changes they have noticed in climbing over the years they have been involved. A lot more people, Pete says, are "paying to go into the mountains", using guides and other 'aids' like helicopters to streamline the experience and bring about a greater chance of success: "people want a package almost … [the] actual true sort of alpine climbing, there's not as much of it getting done I don't reckon". Bob thinks that mountaineering has become more competitive and there is less of a "feeling of craft": "it's the appearance thing and the instant aspect, and it's crept into the world of mountains and mountaineering".

It is important to the mountaineers that the practice of mountaineering should not be confused with "extreme sports" or adventure tourism, although sometimes it is promoted this way, which Adam thinks is done just to "draw a bigger crowd". Jess is scornful of sports such as bungee-jumping, which she sees as "an utterly ridiculous concept. It's just totally adrenaline buzz for no reason and it's like well, so what's the point of that. To prove that you can be stupid enough to jump off a bridge, okay". For Bob, those who consume the products of the 'adventure industry' are "people who want their creature comforts, and who aren't prepared to go on nature's terms":

> I'm quite sure that a lot of people engaging in this adventure tourism will do these things once and that's it, and boast about that until it sort of gets boring. It probably won't have any … major meaningful change or effect on their, on their character, on their strength, on their self reliance. On their ability to be a good human being, to understand other people. … I do see a lot of, you know, really beautifully, physically, fit young people doing this stuff and yet they haven't got a clue really about what it's all about. *(Bob)*

What is being rejected here is what Bauman (1995) sees as our postmodern leaning towards becoming 'sensations-gatherers'. The postmodern body is, he says, "first and foremost a receiver of sensations; it imbibes and digests experiences; the capacity of being stimulated renders it an instrument of pleasure" (Bauman, 1995: p. 116). What we end up with is a succession of episodic thrills, periods of high excitement interspersed with periods of boredom, and no "meaningful change", except that each successive thrill will need to be more thrilling than the last, due to our ever increasing tolerance for the intensity of these sensations. Such an attitude is clearly anathema to the mountaineers' singular commitment, and their willingness to strive and suffer for their passion, for a life-time, though to outsiders they may sometimes seem indistinguishable from the sensations-gatherers.

You can laugh, Dan says, about "climbing bums, bumming around and drinking coffee and, running around in the hills", but he sees the virtues of mountaineering "as a way to ... hold onto, some of the values and principles that are really important to people and life, and society" in a world which is "stepping away from those values". Climbing for Dan means that you are "present" and "aware of what you're doing and who you're with", which are things that we miss "in the fast track of modern life". And being in the mountains can make us "thankful and appreciative for ... the little things in life" and lead us to have "respect" for others.

Simple reliance on self, then, is best: approaching the mountains "on nature's terms"; not using too much "fancy", "artificial" equipment; not depending on guides for skill and judgment; and utilising kiwi ingenuity and resourcefulness. But the outside world impinges on the world of mountaineering. It threatens it with consumerism, commercialisation and superficiality, offering packages of instantly gratifying "quick thrills" and championing a technological, conquering attitude to the environment. The result, according to these mountaineers, is a reduction of our sense of responsibility and an increasingly seductive alternative of "a glass jar" of "decadence" and "luxury" and life-sapping ease.

Travelling light in hostile country

While climbers have the tradition and practice of mountaineering to help combat the 'harms, dangers, temptations and distractions' of this world, and keep them roughly on a single path leading to a relatively well-formed destination, this may not always be enough, as shown above. However, in addition to the well-defined moral framework of mountaineers, there emerged from the narratives certain other characteristics of the world of mountaineering that contribute to its 'solidity' in comparison to the everyday world. Firstly, there is a clarity and sense of control that differentiates mountaineering from everyday life; then there is the way in which the mountaineering lifestyle can provide direction and life-focus, which can lend the sense of a central purpose and meaning to life; and finally the values of the mountaineering tradition which I have been describing are seen as giving perspective to life away from the mountains, and providing a guide for acting in the everyday world.

A world of "clarity" and a "sense of control"

On a climbing trip, Dan says, you can become "just completely involved in what you're doing ... and it's so removed from anything else in normal life". Being required to focus on the immediate present and to block out distracting thoughts and emotions, simplifies the world of mountaineering and differentiates it from the world of the everyday. Compared with life beyond the mountains, then, there are less confusing and conflicting decisions to make when climbing. Relieved of the clouds of ambiguity and 'saturation', the focus can be on small, "intense moments", and these are "the things that really stand out" and become memorable in a way that 'normal' life is not. In addition to the clarity, focus and simplicity of life "in the hills", there is a kind of paradoxical sense of control in extreme environments: "being there in this most amazing place and being in control of it". Pete describes it as a sense of feeling "solid" in "nasty" conditions. Chris alludes to something similar when he says:

> I've done some amazing trips through some potentially quite hostile-looking country, with not too much drama. Just with running shoes and travelling light. *(Chris)*

Such a sense of control can be seen as paradoxical because, as Bob observes, part of the "fascination" is "that it is so out of our control, in any way shape or form, and with a, some rudimentary skills you can actually be part of that and experience all that stuff that is going on". Control lies, so to speak, within sight of what is 'out of control'. It is close enough to the border between order and disorder, chaos and calm to be able to clearly differentiate one from the other. As Jess says, what one is faced with is "black and white", not grey, not ambivalent, not a confusing array of barely distinguishable options. Even when things go wrong, it is generally in a clear and unequivocal way, and the sense of that possibility, and its very clear consequences, is always near.

Pip, for example, likes the fact that climbing requires "self control", sometimes "for days on end". Developing the ability to concentrate and control her fear has stood Pip in good stead for other life situations. Not surprisingly, having such a strong and well-defined sense of control appears to facilitate a profound sense of competence and efficacy in the world. Being able to focus on the task at hand, and block out the 'background noise' of everyday life is a welcome relief, a reprieve from the moral ambiguity and saturating technologies of liquid modernity. And being able to "travel light" through "hostile-looking country", as Chris puts it, not only gives the satisfaction of competence and control in the mountains, but is, by all accounts, a useful skill to have when traversing landscapes in which the postmodern condition is encountered.

Direction and life-focus

> I always see it as being a very significant part of my life, and I find myself, almost always thinking about climbing in some way or another, you know. *(Adam)*

I have argued that a deeply felt and enduring commitment to a life of mountaineering is considered one of the markers of a 'true' mountaineer. It is evident from the narratives that such a commitment to a demanding lifestyle gives direction and a life-focus: a point around which they can centre their lives. "It's totally and utterly with you, all the time".

Lyn's narrative is a particularly vivid example of how mountaineering can provide a focus and direction, without which she feels a loss of purpose and meaning. She had been deeply immersed in the development of her professional career, when a friend who is a rock climber introduced her to the activity she had barely heard of before. From her very first climbing experience Lyn was "hooked", and within a year or so she had completed a mountaineering course and joined an expedition to climb in Nepal: "since then, it's really changed my life. Yeah, since then it has been, the biggest passion". She describes her decision to go to Nepal as the desire to give herself something "different" to do. She was at a "crossroads" in her life, and "feeling unsettled":

> My job until then had given me, most of the satisfaction in my life. By that stage, you know, it no longer gave me the fulfilment it used to so I was quite restless. *(Lyn)*

On her return from success in Nepal, Lyn experienced "this renewed energy, and life felt, mm, you know [laughs], that energy, that aliveness". Since then, climbing has provided her with new goals to work towards and a "sense of direction", which has made her feel "a bit more settled". When she is attempting something challenging and technical, Lyn feels "energised" and "at my best":

> [The] most important thing is the fact that you've actually exerted yourself mentally and physically to get to where you are. It's not the same, driving to the top of a hill and looking down at fantastic views around. ... every time I struggle on a hard climb and I get to the top, and look down, that's, you know, it's memorable. ... That's why I climb you see, that feeling of 'wow I'm here, I've done it and it's beautiful'. *(Lyn)*

To live one's life as a "journey-to-a-destination" (Bauman, 1995: p. 268) is certainly no easy task, as the ground tends to shift beneath our feet. But, as Bruner (1990: p. 22) observes, and the stories of Lyn and others demonstrate, we are prepared to suffer in order to find "such fulfilment as we can in terms of these ways of life". And if we did not have to suffer, the view, as Lyn suggests, may not be as good.

Perspective: Determining the 'real' from the 'trivial'

Repeatedly throughout the narratives, the world of mountaineering was compared with the world of the everyday, as I have already touched on in the discussion of the "false values" of the outside world. These two worlds are not only different and in many respects oppositional, but it is the world of mountaineering that is seen to represent and lead one towards what is "real" and "important". That is, it provides a clearer, less ambiguous moral source — a kind of solidity that is lacking elsewhere. Familiarity with the "solid" mountains and the values of mountaineering made people "happier" and "nicer" and their lives "easier", "simpler" and "more sane", by changing their focus and putting things in "perspective". While the world of the everyday is "frivol[ous]", "silly", "trivial", "the trappings", "contrived", the world of mountaineering is "real", "down to earth", "basic" and, again, "simpler". Pete speaks expressly of solidity, a word and theme that recurs in his narrative. It is he who feels "solid" in "nasty" conditions:

> Nothing compared to putting your life out there on a bit of a line at times climbing so ... you'd go into the mountains and that was reality, back out, back at home, back at work or varsity, that was just living you know and that put, um, everything in perspective in a lot of ways, it made life quite easy I reckon. Um. Yeah and you didn't seem to get caught up in, it just seemed to focus you on, on what was real in life, what was important in life and what wasn't. ... you can look back through your life and there's key decisions you make that take you one way or another way. I think they're relatively easy to make. ... the living as opposed to the trappings ... you look at some people just totally focused on, on possessions. ... I think [mountains] make you quite solid ... *(Pete)*

Conclusion

The notion of the 'true' mountaineer embodies a sense of "what's important and what's not" among New Zealand mountaineers, and the primary virtue within this moral framework is commitment to a leisure lifestyle centred around mountaineering. Non-materialism is a complementary virtue, which priorises the pursuit of a leisure activity over the accumulation of wealth and consumer goods. While these values provide a basic moral code for the mountaineers which can help them negotiate many of the dilemmas of their lives, it is not always easy to live up to the ideals.

Working against them is the inhospitality of a world which casts the subculture of committed mountaineers out to the margins. There they battle divided commitments, the myriad distractions and contradictions of 'social saturation', and the 'temptations' of globalised consumer culture. In their favour though, are the "simple and clear-cut situations" of mountaineering, which give them a sense of "perspective" and "control". This, it can be said, helps to sustain mountaineers within the moral wasteland that modernity has become, and allows them to, in a sense, 'travel light' through 'hostile country'. Safe passage is not guaranteed of course, as life on the fringes is still life shot through with ambiguity and conflicting demands. Nevertheless it is a way of travelling, somewhere between the pilgrims and the tourists, which to mountaineers is preferable to most other modes on offer.

Notes

1   The original transcripts of the interviews included all hesitations and repetitions in order to maintain their integrity as spoken texts during interpretation. Later, when including quotes in the writing up of this research, the text was 'cleaned' (Elliott, 2005) to a certain extent: that is, enough to make the reader's task less arduous, but not so much as to lose the sense that these were oral accounts (Jennings, 2005).

References

Bauman, Z. (1995) *Life in fragments: Essays in postmodern morality*. Oxford, UK and Cambridge, USA: Blackwell.
——— (2000) *Liquid modernity*. Cambridge: Polity Press.
——— (2001) *The individualized society*. Cambridge: Polity Press.
Breakspear, C., & Hamilton, C. (2004). *Getting a life: Understanding the downshifting phenomenon in Australia*. Canberra: The Australia Institute.
Bruner, J. (1990) *Acts of meaning*. Cambridge, Mass.; London: Harvard University Press.
Bruner, J. (2002) *Making stories: Law, literature, life*. New York: Farrar, Straus and Giroux.
Denzin, N. K. (1989) *Interpretive biography*. Newbury Park: Sage.
——— (2001) *Interpretive interactionism* (Second ed). Thousand Oaks: Sage.
Dubin, R. (1979) 'Central life interests: Self-integrity in a complex world', *Pacific Sociological Review* Vol. 22, No. 4: pp. 405–426.
Elliott, J. (2005) *Using narrative in social research: Qualitative and quantitative approaches*. London; Thousand Oaks; New Delhi: Sage.
Frank, A. W. (2002) 'Why study people's stories? A dialogical ethics of narrative analysis', *International Journal of Qualitative Methods* Vol. 1, No. 1: Article 6. Retrieved March 31, 2006 from http://www.ualberta.ca/~ijqm/.
Gergen, K. J. (1991) *The saturated self: Dilemmas of identity in contemporary life*. New York: Basic Books.
Goddard, P. (2002) 'A green boat and big dreams', *New Zealand Alpine Journal* Vol. 54: pp. 56–60.
Gordon, R. S. C. (2001) *Primo Levi's ordinary virtues: From testimony to ethics*. Oxford: Oxford University Press.
Jennings, G. (2005) 'Caught in the irons: One of the lived experiences of long-term ocean cruising women', *Tourism Review International* Vol. 9, No. 2: pp. 195–211.
MacIntyre, A. (1981) *After virtue: A study in moral theory*. London: Duckworth.
Pamphilon, B. (1999) 'The zoom model: A dynamic framework for the analysis of life histories', *Qualitative Inquiry* Vol. 5, No. 3: pp. 393–410.

Rojek, C. (1993) *Ways of escape: Modern transformations in leisure and travel*. Basingstoke: Macmillan.

Stebbins, R. A. (1992) *Amateurs, professionals and serious leisure*. Montreal: McGill-Queen's University Press.

——— (2001) *New directions in the theory and research of serious leisure*. Lewiston: Edwin Mellen Press.

——— (2005) *Challenging mountain nature: Risk, motive and lifestyle in three hobbyist sports*. Calgary: Detselig Enterprises Ltd.

'Wendy Butler' (1967) *New Zealand Alpine Journal* Vol. 22, No. 1: pp. 227–229.

Wengraf, T. (2001) *Qualitative research interviewing: Biographical narrative and semi-structured methods*. London: Sage.

Wolfe, A. (2001) *Moral freedom: The impossible idea that defines the way we live now*. New York; London: W. W. Norton & Company.

THE CHANGING FACE OF GAMBLING: THE GAMBLING ACT (2005) AND WORKING-CLASS GAMBLING CULTURES

Carolyn Downs

Manchester Metropolitan University, UK

Introduction

The impetus for this paper is an ongoing research project into working-class gambling cultures. Research consistently indicates that people with higher levels of qualifications are less likely to gamble and that the manual social classes, IIIM, IV and V (or C2, D and E), are those most likely to gamble regularly, and especially on bingo, slot machines, off-course betting and the football pools (Sproston, Erens and Orford, 2000: p. 22). A striking feature of my research into the history of bingo was discovering a common set of understandings and beliefs related to the role of money and the nature of risk, luck and superstition amongst the working classes who gambled. This pattern was repeated over time, suggesting cultural transmission. Furthermore, it was accompanied by a sense that in the context of the lives of the poor who gambled this was a logical life-choice. Gambling offered excitement, made sense of risk, added colour and hope to routineised lives. In fact, it appeared that to the poor gambling could be more akin to an investment in hope for the future rather than evidence of dissipation. The weaknesses of moral arguments against gambling, when countered by the economic logic of the pastime, have been pointed out:

> Lotteries allow a large group to pool their resources, but [when] chance selects a beneficiary, this is described as irrational gambling. In insurance on the other hand a large group pool their resources, and chance decides which of those will lose and claim a share in the pool. (Skolnik, 1978: p. 16)

Indeed, Ross McKibbin (1979) noted a similar phenomenon as an aside in his important article on working-class gambling.

97

As the work on bingo did not allow thorough investigation of the possibility that different groups in society may have different cultural beliefs around gambling, a discrete project was established to examine the phenomenon. The current phase of this new research is concentrating on attempting to establish whether the possibility of culturally specific understandings of gambling had firm foundations in the past, using a range of primary sources including autobiography, parliamentary reports and enquiries, newspaper articles and various archives. The second part of the project is work-in-progress, and will assess, through questionnaire, observation and interview, whether the working classes who gamble in the twenty-first century continue to have culturally specific understandings about gambling that may be radically different to those of policymakers, gambling providers, support agencies and educators. The concluding section of the research project will consider how knowledge of culturally specific understandings of gambling, money, luck and risk can assist policymakers, industry, educators and support agencies in tailoring their services to fit these needs.[1] While the second stage of the research project continues, the completed opening section offers a survey of historical sources over four hundred years that consider whether the argument for a culturally specific and transmitted understanding of gambling, luck, risk and money amongst a section of the working classes, could be sustained over a lengthy period of time.[2]

Research based in several countries has illustrated that some social groups are consistently more vulnerable to the harms associated with gambling than the majority of the population.[3] Such research is so persuasive that the Economic and Social Sciences Research Council (ESRC) and Responsibility in Gambling Trust (RIGT) are currently funding a study among the British Chinese community that will evaluate whether culturally specific understandings about gambling cause increased vulnerability to gambling harms among this social group.[4] The particular concern is that if there are culturally specific understandings of gambling held by groups in society that are at odds with more general views about gambling, then liberalised gaming laws — that include making high-stakes high-jackpot gambling machines widely available, allow betting shops to stay open late into the evening, allow onshore betting exchanges, encourage the development of remote gambling where credit cards may be used as a source of funding and remove the need for membership of casinos and gambling clubs — may all add up to potential for significant harm to occur to culturally vulnerable social groups.[5]

Legalising vice

The main part of this paper is concerned with illustrating the historical likelihood of group-specific cultural understandings of gambling. It then considers the possible impacts of the full implementation of the Gambling Act (2005) on groups that may be culturally vulnerable to gambling harms.[6] This legislation is only the latest in a succession of Acts of Parliament directed towards the control, regulation and taxation of gambling. This paper will discuss developments in gambling legislation over the twentieth century and the role of gambling in working-class culture in the same period as a means of considering the potential impacts of the Gambling Act (2005) on working-class gambling behaviours. Whilst there was legislation to regulate gambling well before 1906, by the period 1906 to 1961 it was the case that off-course cash betting was completely illegal. This was the result of the Street Betting Act (1906). It is generally agreed that the Street Betting Act should be seen as the culmination of a tradition ranging from social concern to downright hostility towards working-class gambling that figured in most legislation about gambling until the Betting and Gaming Act (1960).[7]

The main impact of the Street Betting Act (1906) was to criminalise many working-class bettors for taking part in an activity legally available to the well-to-do. However there were considerable difficulties in enforcement: widespread police corruption; reluctance amongst the magistracy to convict or even try cases of people brought before them for cash betting, plus a widespread popular legitimacy of betting that made it impossible to stamp out.[8] When considered together these factors contributed to a number of attempts to change or modify the law.[9] In the years after World War II betting was still seen as an activity that should not be encouraged but most people viewed it as relatively harmless. In fact the majority of the country was found to have taken part in some form of betting or gaming when the first comprehensive survey of gambling in Britain was conducted in 1949 (Kemsley and Ginsberg, 1951). In effect, the impacts of the Street Betting Act on an important part of working-class popular leisure and culture can be seen as a slow fuse that led to the legalisation of off-course cash betting allowed by the Betting and Gaming Act (1960).

The Betting and Gaming Bill was broadly welcomed by the press and members of parliament on its publication in 1959. Nevertheless, it was a contentious piece of legislation and MPs were determined that if off-course cash betting were to be legalised then this was to be with the most stringent set of controls. Criminals must be prevented from entering the betting industry, people must not be encouraged to bet and the spectre of the street bookie and the social ills that many opponents of gambling perceived to be linked to this phenomenon should no longer exist. Whilst the committee considering the legislation spent more than eighty hours on the betting aspect of the new law, the gaming elements of the legislation received a scant three hours of consideration. It was hardly surprising therefore that a significant loophole existed within the section of the new Act dealing with gaming; part II subsection seven of the Betting and Gaming Act (1960) in its un-amended form allowed the easy establishment of casinos, gaming and bingo clubs. Within three days of the Betting and Gaming Act passing into law the first commercial gaming and bingo clubs opened their doors.

The government had not intended commercial gaming to develop as a result of their new approach to betting and there was some immediate concern at this unforeseen development.[10] However it rapidly became apparent that the police were not able to prevent clubs opening and operating. Matters rapidly worsened when gangs of organised criminals, including the notorious Kray family, moved into the gaming industry, making huge profits mainly though control of lucrative slot machines, as well as buying casinos and using gaming as a vehicle to launder the proceeds of crime. Amending legislation was passed in 1963 and case-law was beginning to make inroads into the gaping holes in the legislation but the impacts of unregulated commercial gaming were seen as an urgent social issue. The Labour government elected in 1964 acted swiftly to rein-in the excesses. This determination to limit access, regulate effectively and vet ownership of gaming venues led to the Gaming Act (1968) which established the Gaming Board of Great Britain as the means through which commercial gaming was regulated and controlled.

The Rothschild Commission of 1977 made further recommendations regarding gambling legislation, including that research into gambling impacts be funded on a regular basis, but these were not adopted. The arrival of the National Lottery in 1994 was accompanied by only minor changes to gambling laws. The Gaming Act (1968) was widely regarded as extremely successful in keeping gambling in Britain crime-free, ensuring it was fair to punters, restricting demand and protecting the vulnerable, and was the last major change to United Kingdom betting and gaming legislation during the twentieth century. The paternalistic approach to gambling legislation adopted before 1960 was patently unfair, particularly unpopular with working-class gamblers, compromised the police and judiciary and failed to protect the vulnerable. However, the legislative process after 1968, if judged by a complete absence of demand for further liberalisation, was ultimately successful at regulating a popular leisure activity in a way that was generally acceptable to the public.

As there had been no public demand for changes to the regulation of commercial gaming even after the popular success of the National Lottery, the announcement that the New Labour Government elected in 1997 were to liberalise gambling caused some surprise. The Budd Report was commissioned, and reported in July 2001, recommending significant changes. There was press concern at the notion of a "Casino in Every City" and condemnation of proposals to allow warehouses full of addictive jackpot machines (known in Australia as 'pokies') that could offer a potential £1 million jackpot. (*Daily Mail* and *Daily Express* 23rd July 2001; *Guardian* 22nd July 2001)

After a rocky ride through parliament the Gambling Act passed into law in 2005. However, after plans for a regional (super) casino in Manchester caused widespread public concern, Prime Minister Gordon Brown delayed this aspect of the new legislation.[11] However there has been far less media concern over the potentially more dangerous shift of gaming out of the specialist gaming environment and into the home via remote gaming or over the rapid increase in numbers and locations of Video Lottery Terminals (VLTs) and Fixed Odds Betting Terminals (FOBTs). These machines can now be located in a wider range of venues and offer rapid-play high-jackpot random-numbers gambling of the type known to be particularly addictive to certain social groups; research from Australia and New Zealand has illustrated potential cultural vulnerability to harm from this type of gambling.[12] Until the Gambling Act (2005) these machines were tightly controlled. The highest jackpots under the previous regulations were £500; jackpots of £4,000 are now offered in many locations, including all bookmakers' outlets, and could be as high as £1,000,000 if regional casinos eventually go ahead. [13]

Remote gambling is an increasing concern: portable technologies ('Web and Walk') allow people to take the Internet with them and opens the possibility of gambling anytime, anyplace, anywhere. The recent British Gambling Prevalence Survey (2007) gave headline figures for Internet gambling of only 6% (8% for the 25–34 age group) — a figure that is surprisingly low when other sources find Internet gambling accounting for up to 44% of all gambling (Gambling Prevalence Survey, 2007: p. 48). There may be methodological reasons for the low Internet gambling rates shown in the prevalence survey. The sample used was representative of the UK population as a whole, and research by National Statistics found only 54% of the population had Internet access in 2006, rising to 61% in 2007 (National Statistics, Internet Access 2007: p. 1). These access rates will be reflected in the sample used for the prevalence survey and could therefore be responsible for the low headline rate of Internet gambling. Other studies of Internet Gambling have used samples composed entirely of Internet users and found far higher rates of gambling. A further reason for considering that the prevalence survey may under-estimate Internet gambling is that the National Statistics study of Internet Access found that 48% use the Internet for playing games. The types of games being played are not broken down, and this research asks no questions about gambling, but the assumption must be that some of this game play includes gambling. The Gambling Act (2005) recognises the potential for harms caused by remote gambling and attempts to regulate this rapidly growing area.[14] However, it seems likely that offshore, unregulated Internet gambling sites will remain accessible from the UK. Internet gambling takes commercial gambling away from the specialist, regulated gambling environment that has to be sought by the punter and into the privacy of the home where individual behaviour

is virtually impossible to regulate, difficult to research and has the potential
to become an aspect of gambling that causes significant social harms in
the future.

Gambling and hope

Gambling is a pastime that is risky, and the risks can potentially cause
harm far beyond the gambler. It is for this reason that legislation controlling
gambling has been concerned with minimising harm. Poorer groups in
society, who might logically be supposed to have insufficient income to
spare for gambling, have long been noted as prolific, if small-stakes,
gamblers.[15] This has puzzled social reformers for more than two hundred
years. However, a potential key to this puzzle is the focus of this research.
Working-class life is risky: even with the welfare state safety net there is
often very little room for financial manoeuvre in working-class budgets;
it is always difficult to make ends meet and the slightest adverse event
can potentially tip a family over the edge from fiscal stability into the financial
abyss. Gambling offers a chance to control fate and manage uncertainty,
for the lucky to be favoured by whatever gods there are. In addition, poorer
groups in society may feel powerless, that their opinion is viewed as irrelevant
by wider society. "Betting offers ... the only possibility of making a decision,
of a choice between alternatives, in a life otherwise prescribed in every detail
by poverty and necessity, and always the object of other people's
decision"(Pilgrim Trust, 1938: p. 99). Placing scarce money on the outcome
of an event may help validate the opinion of a low-income gambler, and
thus increase self-esteem.

One of the key features of the various elements that people cite as a
reason for gambling is the hope of winning. A recent study of debt and
poverty found that "most people on low incomes dream of wining the pools
or the National Lottery" (Kempson, 1997: p. 8). This factor was also noted
in work by Emma Casey who found prizes and dreaming of prizes were
important features of the lottery for poorer women: almost 86% of her sample
regularly planned how a win would be spent whether they had won or not
(Casey, 2003: p. 260). "In particular they were motivated by the prizes that
they occasionally won" (Casey, 2003: p. 253). The centrality of the hope
of winning as a motivating factor for the gambling habits of the working
classes has been a recurrent but little-considered theme in social research
amongst the working classes for more than one hundred years. The hope
provided by gambling appears to be driven by a strong tradition of myth-
making about the role of luck: stories and songs about wins by "people
like us" in the popular press; almanacs; music hall and oral tradition. Effective
and persistent urban myths — by detailing not just the football pool or
lottery winner but also the lucky escape from poverty through a pretty face
and good marriage, the boxing ring, entrepreneurship or show business,

all ways out of poverty that could be achieved through good fortune and risk-taking — were and remain a staple element of the cheaper end of the popular press.

The dream of a way out of poverty through luck is not new. Eric Hobsbawm commented that football pools, the entertainment business and boxing were well-understood routes out of poverty for the working-class poor in inter-war Britain (Hobsbawn, 1992: p. 289), an opinion anthropologist Geoffrey Gorer concurred with: "Quite literally the only way a person without capital can acquire a substantial sum is in a gambling win" (*Time Magazine*, 20th April, 1970). Over the period under consideration here, the working classes' "dominant cultural institutions were ... the pub, the sporting paper, the race course and the music hall" (Stedman-Jones, 1974: p. 479), along with the cinema and popular press. There were many popular songs about winning the football pools that demonstrate the centrality of the hope of a gambling win in working-class popular culture, including this from the 1940s:

> Now it's very very difficult for working blokes like me
> What ain't been educated at posh schools
> To make a bit of dough unless they has a go
> At that institution wot they calls the pools.[16]

This is part of a wealth of evidence that illustrates that what the non-gambler or social reformer has tended to view as an irresponsible attitude towards money and irrational tendency to gamble among a significant element of the working-class poor may be grounded in an entirely different tradition. The working-class gambler may have established an understanding, based upon a combination of fact and belief that equates to knowledge, that the chance of a big win is worth the investment of scarce resources. The working-class gambler may 'know' that for 'working blokes' luck remains the only realistic method of escape from a life with little opportunity for improvement though thrift, hard work and education.

The original National Lottery advertisement, with its star-studded finger of fate and booming voice proclaiming "it could be you', develops from the traditional understanding that ordinary lives can be changed dramatically for the better by chance. The National Lottery was not the first British attempt at government-sponsored gambling. The State Lottery was drawn annually from 1710 to 1826 and although tickets were ten guineas, and well out of reach of the majority of the population, it was extremely popular amongst the working-classes. Small groups of people would get together and buy one sixteenth of a lottery ticket each. This purchase would be saved for over the course of a year and would not be relied upon as the sole source of a potential win. Alongside a lottery ticket lottery insurance would be purchased. This was an entirely illegal system of side-bets that was hugely prevalent. In general, people would bet sixpence or a shilling that their number would not be drawn; laying-off a small proportion of their original investment. A government enquiry among London servants in 1806 found that most spent twenty-five shillings a year on the State Lottery, illegal lotteries and insurances. They postulated that if all other wage-earning classes in the metropolis were spending similar amounts on such gambling then perhaps half a million pounds sterling was being placed by the poor on various numbers games in London each year (Select Committee on Laws Relating to Lotteries, 1809: pp. 29–30). What Keith Thomas said of the role of luck in the lives of the working-classes of the seventeenth century was surely also true in the eighteenth:

> Gambling diverted the attention of the labouring poor from the possibilities of self-help and political activism, by holding out the prospect that a lucky person would be able to better himself despite the inequalities of the social system. (Thomas, 1971: p. 20)

People had aspirations that they knew could not be met by honest toil; gambling seemed a positive way of making an effort to escape from poverty, and even if a big win failed to materialise making the bet offered a temporary glimmer of hope. In large part the determination of the poor to obtain at least a share in a lottery ticket was because they knew that people like them did win significant prizes as a result of widespread publicity whenever a poor person won:

> The £20,000 prize, drawn on Friday, is divided amongst a number of poor persons; a female servant in Brook Street, Holborn, had a sixteenth; a woman who keeps a fruit stall in Greys Inn Lane another. (*The Times*, 19th March 1798)[17]

In the closely-packed slum areas of London news spread rapidly, papers were read in the houses of the wealthy by servants who spread the news amongst family and friends. The poor did not only gamble for life-changing wins. Penny lotteries, known as 'little goes' were also popular, the prize in such a lottery was generally around five shillings for a stake of four pence, at a time of extreme poverty this was a significant addition to the budgets of the poor (*The Times*, 6th October, 1806). The poor law guardians of Mary-le-Bone were concerned that most of the widows they supported on outdoor relief were spending 4d each week on an illegal lottery ticket in the "hope of winning five shillings" (*The Times*, 6th October, 1806). This scenario is extraordinarily similar to the findings of Emma Casey's study of women's lottery play in the twenty-first century. Casey described women juggling financial responsibilities alongside:

> The appeal of purchasing National Lottery tickets which the women believed offered a possible means of alleviating some of their financial concerns. (Casey, 2003: p. 251)

Like the gentlemen bringing evidence to the magistrates in 1806 Casey's subjects were also very much aware that the lottery was a risk and that "they were in danger of jeopardising the money intended for 'essentials' for the family" (Casey, 2003: p. 251). The Poor Law Guardians certainly felt that the lack of the 4d gambled on the lottery was causing women to be "literally in a state of starvation" (*The Times*, 6th October, 1806). Such court cases were a familiar feature of life, often attracting a full public gallery supporting the organiser of the illegal lottery, and were reported in the popular Newgate Calendar as well as the daily press and became an additional source for the mythology of gambling wins.

Although the last State Lottery was drawn in 1826 many of the working classes remained keen on the chance of a win and racing sweeps became the favoured and widely reported means of both gambling and winning a significant amount. Despite government concern little effort was made to stamp out racing sweeps and the practice became wide-spread.[18] While most regional sweeps in the1840s had a first prize ranging from £50 to £300, by 1869 when a large-scale racing sweep known as the Deptford Spec was finally prosecuted (after operating for more than seven years) the police reported that prizes of almost £5,000 were commonplace.

Stories of good fortune achieved through a lucky win were such a feature of the life of the poor that social reformers and poor law guardians working to stamp out what they considered feckless behaviour had a high mountain to climb in debunking such myths. One hundred years after the worthies of Mary-le-Bone had tried to prosecute away the illicit gambling of the parish widows, Lady Florence Bell found gambling was common among workers in Middlesbrough. She commented that when one person had a good win it was widely reported in the community: "Such a stroke of luck happening to one house in the street is bound to be an encouragement to others" (Bell, 1907: pp. 257–258). The attraction of gambling was, she felt, understandable even if it should be deprecated, for:

> Every now and again a working man does win, and thereby acquires
> in one moment a lump sum of capital that would be accessible to
> him in absolutely no other way. (Bell, 1907: p. 260)

The music hall was "strongly rooted in the realities of working-class life" (Stedman-Jones, 1974: p. 491) and remained instrumental in the cultural transmission of the idea that luck was fundamental to escape from a life of drudgery. Stedman-Jones noted that popular songs in the halls mirrored the lives of the audience, "But the only real escape suggested in the songs is the surprise inheritance or the lucky windfall" (pp 492–493).

George Orwell was undoubtedly giving voice to the fundamental truth when he wrote in 1937:

> And above all there is gambling, the cheapest of all luxuries. Even
> people on the verge of starvation can buy a few days hope ('something
> to live for' as they call it) by having a penny on a sweepstake. (Orwell,
> 1937: p. 87)

The Quaker social investigator B.S. Rowntree had been a leading proponent
of the Street Betting Act (1906) and was dismayed to find that when he
conducted his second social survey of York in 1939 the legislation had been
unsuccessful at reducing gambling amongst the working classes. Indeed,
"a vast number of men and women indulge in this form of amusement"
(Rowntree, 1941: p. 400), and furthermore some people he questioned said
that they would "rather have six penn'orth of hope than six penn'orth of
electricity" (Rowntree, 1941: p. 403). The arrival of World War II did not
diminish the popularity of gambling. Indeed, when life is particularly risky
gambling may offer a chance to test luck, to control at least one aspect of
a life that is increasingly ordered by forces outside that which is normal.
Mass Observation reported on sport in wartime Britain and their observers
were surprised by the significance of sport-related gambling in the lives
of many of the people they interviewed:

> Then there are the incorrigible gamblers, the book-makers, 'George'
> of T. Webster fame, the vast organisations: Littlewoods, Vernons,
> etc ... This is the exploitation of partisanship, of the faith in a
> favourite, of the love of gambling and, last but not least, of the dazzling
> hope of colossal gain. Parasites, yes. But would organised sport
> be the same without them? (Mass Observation, 1939: p. 32)

The "hope of colossal gain" was not ignored by Mass Observation, who
reported on this aspect of working-class gambling in a number of studies.[19]
Gambling on horses could net a large prize if an outsider came in, and
large wins were well-reported. Foreign travel, albeit enforced, offered people
the chance to buy exotic lottery tickets and UK winners of large overseas
lottery prizes, and the Irish Hospitals Sweepstake, were well-documented
in the press.[20] Mass Observation found that people who filled in a pools
coupon were "predominantly thinking in terms of winning" although ideas
about winning the jackpot were mixed; many preferred the idea of one of
the consolation prizes (Mass Observation, 1947: p. 102). Nevertheless,
although most people lost their stake on the pools most weeks, the pleasure
of choosing the teams (which diaries collected by B.S. Rowntree show occupied
the entire Thursday evening in many families), either through intuition
or studying form, the anticipation of Saturday teatime and seeing if they
had won, the knowledge that people like them could win, all of this was a
tangible element of working-class culture (Rowntree, 1941: pp. 429–445).
    Press reports of a lucky win in the Irish Hospitals Sweep, newsreel
interviews with miners who had won the pools, music hall songs about

the impact of a big win on working-class lives, all add weight to the idea that knowledge of gambling as a route out of poverty was embedded in working-class popular culture. Pools wins generated huge publicity, *Picture Post* and the *Pathe Newsreel* ran regular features that detailed how big wins had changed lives, and in the 1937 to 1938 season there six dividends from Littlewoods (Clegg, 1993: p. 83).[21] Mass Observation found at least one large winner (of around £100) whose win could be substantiated among every group they interviewed, providing further evidence for a widespread knowledge-base of the role of gambling in providing significant cash-boosts to the average working-class bettor and therefore encouraging the belief that gambling was a justifiable endeavour through which life could be improved (Mass Observation, 1947: p. 50). Mass Observation established that stories of large gambling wins and good fortune (alongside wins and subsequent misfortunes) were common knowledge:

> Whatever social circles he moves in anyone … is likely to have met one or two one-time winners of substantial sums. (Mass Observation, 1947: p. 50)

The overwhelming impression of the role of gambling amongst the working classes in this period is that it offered the mass of the people a pleasurable leisure activity that had, as an added bonus, a sense of hope.

A bookie's wife told Mass Observation that betting was effectively a religion for most working-class bettors; after all, the working classes who gambled rarely took part in organised religion.

> What else have they got to look forward too? They would never hope to get out of their rut, only with a little bit of luck they hope to find in gambling. You'd be surprised if you knew how heavily and regularly the working man bets. It's his kind of religion — it brings him some hope. He's got no interest in religion, he knows it's only a money-making racket — the Parson's getting a good living out of it — same as my chap gets out of his. (Mass Observation, 1947: p. 59)

In a letter to his daughter Betty in 1944 John Moores, the man behind the Littlewoods pools empire, showed how well he realised the value of hope to the bulk of the people who participated in his football pools: "The poorest person in the country can be more joyously optimistic than the richest man in the world" (Clegg, 1993: p. 108). Similarly, when the Pilgrim Trust conducted a study among unemployed men in Liverpool in 1937 they found that the pools and betting on horses and dogs were extremely important in the lives of the men they were studying. Gambling gave the men "something to hope for" (Pilgrim Trust, 1938: p. 100); stories of winners and periodicals containing pools analysis or forecasting tools were the most thumbed parts of newspapers in the libraries and winners were people accorded status

---

— men and women whose opinions "on very different matters are heard with respect" (Pilgrim Trust, 1938: p. 99). Gambling mattered to the poor in a way that was barely understood by even the non-gambling working classes of the time, and was certainly outside the experience of the most of the rest of the population.

Mass Observation also found that luck featured prominently in discussions with gamblers about the way life treated them, gamblers held clear-cut beliefs that some people were generally luckier than others. While opposition to gambling was strongly associated with a rejection of ideas of luck, opposition to gambling was less strongly associated with religious practice (Mass Observation, 1947: p. 256). As a bingo player later described it:

> Well, put it this way. A lot of people don't believe that there's a God up there, but I do. If you're right good, you'll get luck put on to you. Do you know what I mean? If you do your work and don't do anything bad, the luck comes on. (Dixey with Talbot, 1982: p. 85)

This fits with the findings of Halliday and Fuller that most gamblers:

> ... share beliefs that there is an external being more powerful than themselves, whose favours can be sought, and who can be influenced by...physical and psychological activities here on earth. (Halliday and Fuller, 1974: p. 55)

As gambling is primarily a pursuit of the working classes, with the manual groups those most likely to have a flutter on the horses, a punt on the lottery or an evening at the dogs or bingo, then it is classes C2, D and E who are more likely to have a range of beliefs similar to those described by Halliday and Fuller and found running as a theme throughout the historical record on gambling; and the same groups are therefore more likely to transmit such beliefs down the generations.

Cultural transmission

Culture is not necessarily coherent or consistent. Cultural knowledge is often implicit — people often do not know why or how they believe something, they just do. However, there is not a vacuum. Knowledge impacts on actions and interactions, it is received and transmitted, as ideas are received and transmitted they develop and change, and a modified version may well gain currency albeit in the way that the game of 'Chinese whispers' works rather than in the way that evolution works; so cultural beliefs become part of the pattern and practice of everyday life and ideas that are culturally constructed have to be understood in their cultural context.

Cultural transmission, unlike evolution, is not based around survival of the fittest. Many of the ideas that are transmitted through generations deal with the elemental aspects of life and its processes. Rationality and science are useful where people live comfortable lives; they can be used to provide explanations when the unexplained or unexpected occurs. However, people who live life on the edge financially or socially often need comfort and may seek explanations and processes that more nearly fit with their experience of the unexpected; the uncontrollable events of life have greater impact the further down the social scale you are. Halbwachs (1992) pointed out that a whole range of beliefs and superstitions are invisible to the more cultivated circles of society. They assume that because they have rationalised such practices out of their lives, so too has the whole of society. However, he noted that a wide range of beliefs and superstitions have "a tenacious hold among the common people" (Halbwachs, 1992: p. 84). Life is complex and each individual has an intellectual life that contains elements of the irrational and the rational working alongside each other in varying proportions to provide clarification or solutions to the problems that occur in day-to-day life.

Halbwachs believed that ideas about good fortune were particularly prone to become part of the cultural fabric of lives, commenting that "those who possess it must appear to be favoured by destiny not for their wealth but because they were born under a favourable star" (Halbwachs, 1992: p. 147). Belief in luck is an idea, and all ideas are transmissible. "Customs and beliefs arise and are propagated that impose themselves on everybody, referencing nobody in particular" (Halbwachs, 1992: p. 184). The process of cultural transmission is difficult to document and the literature is not extensive, but nevertheless:

> The implications of focusing on the ability of humans to borrow
> information and then pass it on to another by non-genetic means
> is genuinely far-reaching. It is what makes culture possible. (Bloch,
> 2005: p. 7)

Cultural transmission of ideas and beliefs is an extremely important element of the glue that holds together social groups and the resultant behaviours can be viewed as constants in a social environment that is constantly changing. Constants in life enable people to cope with change. In fact, the continued existence of social practices amongst certain groups in society, even if ignored, or unacknowledged or unknown by the ruling classes, may help those groups both in coping with social change, but perhaps also provide a route of resistance to social change.

Knowledge is culturally constructed and has to be understood in its cultural context. It may not be irrational to believe that one has been born lucky or that there is a lucky seat at bingo in the context of personal knowledge. So when in 2002 the winner of £102,000 in a linked bingo game was insistent that he owed his success to a lucky charm he was not necessarily deluded, he may simply have been applying knowledge created from his belief in luck coupled with the fact that he had won:

> The sun was shining on this object and it gleamed like gold, I picked it up and saw it was a sort of bolt, though most unusual. I'm an engineer and normally recognise bolts, but this is one I have not seen before. I thought, is this an omen? A bolt from the blue? And I decided to take it with me to bingo. I also won another £30 house later that evening, and my wife borrowed it to take to bingo on Monday afternoon and won £10! I am going to take good care of that bolt. (*The Independent* 31st July 2002).

There is often a breach between cultural lifestyle desires and social reality. Where the size of the breach is so large that people cannot realistically hope to cross it then there is a need for assistance, and a cultural belief in luck coupled with gambling on the risky results of an event may provide either actual assistance in breaching the gulf (through a win) or at the very least the hope to keep people going in a society where they feel ever more left behind. Industrialisation, commercialisation and urbanisation have encouraged an increasing perception of paucity among the poor: "poverty becomes a greater problem the moment wealth is perceived as a definite possibility" (Eriksen, 2002: p. 251). The poor working classes may be relatively better off than their grandparents, but they see the products of consumerism around them and desire a share in this new society. As they cannot hope to earn through waged labour the means of full participation in a society of goods, they instead hope for a stroke of good fortune, a lucky lottery ticket, winning the draw for the Deptford Spec, for their number to come up on the link game at bingo or to have picked eight from ten matches correctly one weekend.

If gambling is seen as a bridge to lifestyle desires, and enough people make their way over and are reported as having made it, then this encourages hope to survive and even flourish in the lives of the working classes who gamble. The role of agents of change that are controlled by luck, fate and chance are set in narrative frames that are so well-understood that they do not need to be articulated. Arbitrary and random events are given status in the lives of the poor as they are seen as signs, signals of the direction life might take. Gaining control over chance, or at least taking a chance through a gamble or bet, is a way of increasing self-worth as well as potentially increasing actual worth. Gamblers fervently long for something outside their control (a win) and therefore they have hope, at least until the race is run or the game is over. They can then pursue that desire through placing another bet, trying again. Life does not offer many consecutive rays of hope. The power that determines what will happen with gambling is external to self;

the lottery ticket, betting slip or £1 coin in the slot represents power. So gambling becomes a way through which personal fate is questioned, over and over again, a way of testing a relationship with the gods. People recognise the stories of escape from poverty through a range of luck-based routes including gambling. These stories are usually told as an almost miraculous setting-apart through good fortune, and have become part of the cultural background of the gambling working classes, so that the child who says "When we win the lottery we will have a farm and a pony", and refuses to accept that this is such a remote possibility that it will not happen, is simply plugged in to their cultural background rather than being entirely irrational.[22] Everyone has heard of the mill girl who married well or won Miss England, the Gran whose bingo win hit the headlines or Jade Goody who made success out of failing to win a reality TV show. In part the development of literacy and printing which allowed the development of the popular press, printed ballads, sheet music and almanacs all aided the building of a mythology of hope. Stories of good fortune are popular, they help sales and once something has been published it is likely to also be spread and embellished by word-of-mouth. The urban myth is a product of urbanisation and is not a new creature. These stories show that there is hope; gambles do pay off; luck can fall on ordinary working-class people. All it takes is the courage to risk the shilling that was for the meter on a tip for the Oaks. Then, until the race is won, the lottery drawn, hope is alive in the heart, giving those whose lives are made drab by poverty a glimmer of joy. Such memories and understandings are often implicit but they exist and are important in understanding why some people continue to look for hope through routes that other groups in society consider irrational and irresponsible.

Potential responses to the Gambling Act (2005)

The Gambling Act (2005) states that all parties involved in gambling provision and regulation shall have a duty to prevent harm to children and vulnerable people but does not define what might constitute a vulnerable person. Where people view gambling as an investment in the future, and when money is short view wins as a valid way of attempting to meet a shortfall, they are likely to spend a regular weekly amount on gambling, budgeted-for like insurance. In such circumstances it is important that they are not tempted to risk more in order to pursue the increased prizes that appear to be suddenly more widely available. If a group in society are culturally inclined to view gambling as a form of insurance or investment in providing the hope of a better life for themselves and their family, then perhaps those responsible for framing regulations that allow the masses to pursue pleasures that can have consequences beyond the individual into the family and wider society need to take account of such cultural differences in the mechanisms designed to protect the vulnerable (Huggins, 1999: p. 92).

The increased availability of gambling opportunities in new settings moves gambling in Britain into untried and poorly understood areas. It is well-established that machine gambling, especially where there is a rapid rate of play, is significantly more addictive than many other types of gambling and that young working-class men are particularly vulnerable to becoming addicted to these machines.[23] The increased availability of high-stakes, high-jackpot fixed-odds-betting-terminals, which can now be found in every betting shop and a range of other venues, is illustrative of the potential problem. Betting shop workers have been facing increased levels of violence from mainly young male customers who have lost significant amounts of money playing these machines, but the machines are now providing up to 40% of the profits in many betting shops (*Observer*, 22nd July, 2007 and *Guardian* 13th August, 2007). The industry is not going to want to lose these machines but clearly the machines are encouraging growth of a problem that had previously only been documented in limited circumstances (Parke and Griffiths, 2005: pp. 255–272). These machines are not only located in betting shops, they are in a range of easily accessible venues and up to 150 may sited in each of the eight new large casinos that have been licensed. If poor people played the slots when the jackpot was limited to £25, "because, like, when you're skint you think, just put a pound in and get twenty quid", then the new machines with jackpots of up to £4,000 are infinitely more attractive (Casey, 2003: p. 251). Another factor that needs considering is that if poorer groups in society traditionally understand gambling as more investment than unrecoverable leisure spending, they may also be more likely to chase losses. This is well-nigh impossible with many of the more traditional gambling activities that the working classes participate in on a regular basis. The pools, lottery draws and bingo all tend to limit spending, while betting shops at least used to shut reasonably early. The impact on vulnerable adults of widespread availability of FOBTs is clearly an area where urgent action may be needed to prevent further harms developing.

There are similar problems emerging with remote gambling. Internet availability has spread through the social classes. Government schemes are increasing access to low-cost rebuilt computers for poorer families who may also subscribe to one of the cheap phone, satellite and Internet packages now available and making access to online gambling sites ever easier.[24] The type of games offered on the Internet gambling sites and via FOBTs are often those that are the most addictive. They adopt rapid rates of play, encourage regular gamblers with 'results boards' that show the punter to be an 'expert player', allow free plays and make regular use of the 'near win' that acts to draw in gamblers. If the vulnerable are to be protected from harm then where is the line drawn under vulnerability? Should a cultural tendency to view gambling as a reasonable strategy for income generation be a warning signal for intervention to prevent harm? If it may be the case that some sections of the working classes could be culturally vulnerable to gambling harm, should policies be modified?

Just as the working-class poor are the group most likely to develop gambling problems and are more likely to gamble than other social groups the working-class poor are also the group in society with the highest proportion of non-gamblers (Sproston, Erens and Orford, 2000: p. 24).[25] These dichotomies cause problems for policy makers; they prefer a simple picture to allow for ease of implementation. The tendency of policy makers to look for a simplistic analysis may explain why so many social policies are ineffective. In the case of gambling some governments appear to have legislative blinkers. They are able to accept that gambling is an activity that causes pleasure, offers an exciting leisure activity, allows people to expand an interest in a sport through following form and offers the hope of a win, but appear less concerned that at the same time it can lead to significant social problems, disproportionately harming some vulnerable groups in society. In the United Kingdom this blinkered view is illustrated by the decision to fund gambling research through a voluntary levy on the gambling industry. There are a range of potential solutions that could allow a liberalised and profitable gambling industry to provide pleasure for the many people who enjoy a regular flutter while providing a reasonable standard of protection to vulnerable groups, but in large part this depends on defining exactly which groups are vulnerable. Some new approaches are being tried in the fulcrum of societies where gambling was deregulated with too little thought about cultural vulnerabilities. This has led to a range of social problems amongst groups that research after the liberalisation of gambling has shown to be culturally vulnerable to gambling harms. So in New Zealand the indigenous Maori and South Pacific island population groups have been excessively harmed by access to increased gambling facilities.[26] A similar pattern has been observed in Australia, both among aboriginal groups but also among the poorer white groups in society. In the USA and Canada indigenous populations and poor black communities have suffered a higher rate of problems associated with gambling. The common features of worldwide experiences of cultural differences in dealing with liberalised gambling regimes are that investigation and action has been started well after the harms have begun to be apparent. It is always far more difficult to find an effective solution in such circumstances.

In the United Kingdom it seems likely that a public health approach will be developed in an attempt to minimise gambling harms across the board. Such an approach involves education about gambling and its dangers in schools to 'inoculate' young people against the vector (disease) of gambling; while there will be widely publicised treatment options available for those who despite education are harmed by gambling. The approach is similar to that used in alcohol, drugs and sex education programmes, although with varying degrees of success. However, in the case of gambling it may be that there needs to be an understanding of just who might be vulnerable before the vulnerable are harmed as a by-product of changes to established practices. If knowledge that some cultural groups are more likely to be harmed by gambling than others is applied to education, well-funded research, harm reduction and treatment packages, it might be possible that changes to gambling laws that make an activity that has always been the pleasure of the masses still freely available to the mass of the people while protecting all vulnerable groups.

Gambling is not a ritual of modernity, it is an ancient ritual that has evolved and re-evolved to fit the circumstances and groups who use it. To some groups it has become symbolic of irrationality, a pointless pursuit, a waste of time. To other groups in society gambling signifies a family ritual as lucky numbers are selected, and the lottery draw is watched on a Saturday evening; still other groups routinely request a scratchcard along with the morning paper or loaf of bread, lifting life out of the routine as they reveal the will of the gods and collect their prize. However, gambling also retains elements of risk, of playing with fire, and those who edge to close to the flames are consumed by a powerful magic that can lead them and their families into the depths of despair. The vulnerable must be identified before irreparable harm is done.

Notes

1   These findings may also have implications for other areas of risky behaviour including alcohol and substance misuse.

2   The term 'working class' is not generally applied to social groups by historians until the industrial revolution (the mid to late eighteenth century). In earlier periods the usual description might be the labouring classes, or the labouring poor. However to change terminology midway through an argument is confusing to readers not well-versed in historical terminology and so for ease of readership the term working class or classes will be used throughout.

3   See for example, M.W. Abbott, and Brian G. McKenna, 'Gambling and Problem Gambling among Recently Sentenced Male Prisoners in Four New Zealand Prisons', *Journal of Gambling Studies* Vol. 21, No. 4 Winter 2005; P.Adams Gambling Impact Assessment: For Auckland City Council, Manukau City Council, North Shore City Council, Waitakere City Council, Franklin District Council, Papakura District Council, and Rodney District Council Auckland City Council: Gambling Impact Assessment for the Seven Auckland Territorial Authorities — Part 1: January 2004; Tse Samson, Wong John & Kim Hyeeun 'A public health approach for Asian people with problem gambling in foreign

countries', *Journal Of Gambling Issues*: Issue 12, December 2004 and notes 12 and 23 for further sources.

4   The study is being conducted by Rebecca Cassidy, Anthropology Department, Goldsmiths College, University of London. See footnote 3 for further reading on overseas research.

5   Remote gambling includes Internet gabling, gambling via interactive television and gambling via the mobile phone network. Betting exchanges are a means by which punters can get together to bet with each other on the outcome of any event.

6   The legislation was fully implemented on 1st September 2007.

7   See for example David Dixon, From Prohibition to Regulation: book-making, anti-gambling and the law. Oxford, 1991 and David Miers, Regulating Commercial Gambling: past present and future, Oxford, 2004.

8   The difficulties that the magistracy continued to experience with enforcing the laws against betting and gaming were illustrated when several members of the bench at Smethwick in Staffordshire refused to try seven gaming cases because they had themselves placed bets. *The Times* 18 Nov 1949 6c.

9   The government introduced a Betting Duty between 1926 and 1929. It proved so difficult to collect that this attempt was abandoned. There was a Royal Commission on Lotteries and Betting in 1932 (Cmd. 4341), The Betting and Lotteries Act (1934) which regulated lotteries held in support of charities and authorised football pools was a result of the recommendations of this committee. Sir Alan Herbert brought forward a private members bill, the Betting Bill in 1939 but this was lost due to lack of parliamentary time.

10   The Churches Council on Gambling were active in providing the press with details of the danger of commercial gaming. By July 1961 an adjournment debate on the subject of commercial gaming in the House of Commons attracted more than seventy speakers despite taking place well after midnight. *The Times*, 20th July 1961 p. 9 column g.

11   The case for a regional casino will be reconsidered once the Gambling Prevalence Study and the Gambling Impacts Scoping Review are published in the autumn of 2007.

12   For cultural vulnerability see for example, J Rankine and D. Haigh, 'Social impacts of gambling in Manukau City: A report for Manukau City Council', New Zealand, 2003, Diane Tran Asian Gambling Family Losses: a study of gambling related violence in the Vietnamese community The Ignatius Centre for social policy and research Jesuit Social Services 1999 plus New Zealand social impacts studies cited in note 3.

13   See the extensive work by Mark Griffiths and also that of Richard
      Wood, Adrian Parke and Jonathon Parke into slot machines and young
      men.

14   The figure of 44% does not include lottery and bingo gambling. The
      market research company YouGov interviewed 2,015 GB adults (18+)
      between 23rd and 25th July 2007 for www.moneysupermarket.com
      and found that 44% of people surveyed who gambled had done so
      on the Internet and that of these 10% were using their credit cards
      to fund this activity. This figure for Internet gambling is considerably
      higher than that found in other surveys of gambling behaviour. It
      may be that only Internet users were interviewed and that this has
      had an impact on the results.

15   It is important to make clear that while poorer groups in society make
      up the largest proportion of gamblers on most types of gambling games
      (excluding casino gaming), poorer people are also the largest group
      of non-gamblers.

16   This song is one of several about gambling and luck written and
      performed by the music hall soliloquist and actor Jack Warner (Dixon
      of Dock Green). He was born to a poor family in the East End of London.
      He and his sisters (Elsie and Doris Waters) escaped through lucky
      breaks in the entertainment business, a recognised 'lucky break' for
      the working classes.

17   A prize of £1250 equates to about £74,000 today.

18   See Mike Huggins, *Flat racing and British Society 1790–1914: a social
      and economic history*, London, 1999 for a consideration of regional
      racing sweeps in the 1840s.

19   See for example the Penguin Factory study, files on Worktown, Sport
      in Wartime and Superstition all held in the Mass Observation Archive
      at Sussex University.

20   For a consideration of the impact of the Irish Hospitals Sweepstakes
      in Britain see Marie Coleman ' "A Terrible Danger to the Morals of
      the Country": the Irish hospitals' sweepstake in Great Britain, 1930–
      87', *Proceedings of the Royal Irish Academy,* Vol. 105C, No. 5, 197–
      220 (2005)

21   See for example *Picture Post* 13 December 1947.

22   A conversation on a school bus between two twelve-year old girls noted
      on the 18th May 2007.

23   See for example T. Yeoman, and. M.D. Griffiths,. 'Adolescent machine
      gambling and crime.' *Journal of Adolescence*, 19, 1996 183–188 Adrian
      Parke and Mark Griffiths, 'Aggressive behaviour in adult slot machine
      gamblers: an interpretative phenomenological analysis' *Journal of*

Community and Applied Social Psychology Vol. 14, No. 4, 2005 July-August, pp. 255–272.

24   In East Manchester 'Eastserve' offers broadband Internet with no phone-line required for £6 per month alongside recycled computers. The market research organisation YouGov interviewed 2,015 GB adults (18+) between 23rd and 25th July 2007 and found that 44% of gamblers were borrowing money to pay gambling debts and that credit cards were the most common source of funds. 'Gamblers are Dicing With Debt' www.moneyexpert.com accessed on 20 August 2007.

25   See also Creigh-Tyte and Lepper *Survey of Participation in, and Attitudes Towards, Gambling* 2004.

26   Articles that address such issues include, M. Abbott and B. McKenna (2005) 'Gambling and problem gambling among recently sentenced male prisoners in four New Zealand prisons', *Journal of Gambling Studies* Vol. 21, No. 4 (Winter); V. McGowan, L. Frank, G. Nixon, M. Grimshaw (2001) 'Sacred and secular play in gambling among Blackfoot peoples of Southwest Alberta' in A Blaszczynski, (ed) *Culture and the gambling phenomenon*, pp 241–255; I. Light (1977) 'Numbers gambling among Blacks: a financial institution', *American Sociological Review* Vol. 42, No.6: pp 892–904; T. Samson, Wong John & Kim Hyeeun (2004) 'A public health approach for Asian people with problem gambling in foreign countries', *Journal of Gambling Issues* No.12 (December); J Rankine and D. Haigh (2004)*Social impacts of gambling in Manukau City. A report for Manukau City Council*, New Zealand, http://www.manukau.govt.nz/documents/gambling.pdf; Steffensmeier, D. and Ulmer, J. T. (2006) 'Black and white control of numbers gambling: a cultural assets — social capital view'. *American Sociological Review Vol. 71, No. 1* (February): pp 123–156. http://www.ingentaconnect.com/content/asoca/asr/2006/00000071/00000001/art00006;jsessionid=1f921mj6amgp6.alice#avail

References

Bell, Lady Florence (1969) *At the works: A study of a manufacturing town (Middlesbrough)*. First published 1907, London, this edition New York: Augustus M Kelley.

Bloch, M. (2005) *Essays on cultural transmission*. LSE Monographs on Social Anthropology, Vol 75. London: Berg.

Boiwers, Si. (2007) 'Virtual racing claims 17% of betting on horses', *Guardian:* 13th August.

Creigh-Tyte, S. and Lepper J. (2004) *Survey of participation in, and attitudes toward gambling: Key findings from the 2004 NOP survey*. Technical Paper No 4 (April). London: HMSO.

Casey, E. (2003) 'Gambling and consumption: Working-class women and National Lottery play', *Journal of Consumer Cultur* No. 3: pp. 245–263.

Clegg, B. (1993) *The man who made Littlewoods: The story of John Moores*. London: Hodder and Stoughton.

Dawson E. (1961) *Mother made a book*. London: Geoffrey Bles.

Dixey R. with Talbot, M. (1982) *Women Leisure and Bingo*, Leeds: Trinity and All Saints College.

Dixon, D. (1991) *From prohibition to regulation: Bookmaking, anti-gambling and the law*. Oxford: Clarendon.

Erens, B., Orford, J. and Sproston, K. (2000) *Gambling behaviour in Britain: Results from the British Gambling Prevalence Survey*. London: Gamcare.

Eriksen, T. H. (2001) *Small places large issues: An introduction to social and cultural anthropology*, 2nd edition. London: Pluto Press.

Halbwachs, M. (edited and translated by L. A. Coser) *On collective memory*. Chicago, Chicago University Press.

Halliday, J., and Fuller, P. (1974) *The psychology of gambling*. London: Allen Lane.

Hansard (1809) P.P. 1808/9, Sessional Papers, Select Committee on Laws Relating to Lotteries, Second Report mf 9.11–12

Hobsbawn, E. (1992) 'Mass producing traditions: Europe 1870–1914', in E. Hobsbawm and T. Ranger (eds) *The invention of tradition*. Cambridge: Cambridge University Press, pp. 263–307.

Hobsbawm, E. and Ranger, T. (eds) (1992) *The invention of tradition*. Cambridge: Cambridge University Press.

Huggins, M. (1999) *Flat racing and British Society 1790–1914: a social and economic history*, London: Frank Cass.

Hutchins, A. (2002) 'Bingo: The brain game', *Independent* 31st July 2002 accessed online at *http://enjoyment.independent.co.uk/low_res/story.jsp?story=320169&host=5&dir=53*

Kempson, E. (1997) *Life on a low income*. York: Joseph Rowntree Foundation Social Policy Research.

Kemsley W.F.F. and Ginsberg, D (1951) *Betting in Britain*. London: Central Office of Information.

Mathiason, N. (2007) 'Bookmakers under fire over assaults', *Observer*: 22nd July.

Mass Observation (1939) 'Sport in Wartime' File Report 13 6, October.Mass Observation (1947) 'Mass gambling' File Report 2545c.

McKibbin, R. (1979) 'Working class gambling in Britain 1880–1939', *Past and Present* No. 82: pp. 147–78, 1979.

Miers, D. (2004) *Regulating commercial gambling: Past present and future*. Oxford: Oxford University Press.

Parke, A. and Griffiths, M. (2005) 'Aggressive behaviour in adult slot machine gamblers: An interpretative phenomenological analysis', *Journal of Community and Applied Social Psychology* Vol. 15, No. 4 (July-August): pp. 255–272.

Reith, G. (1999) *The age of chance: Gambling in western culture*. London: Routledge.

Rowntree, B. S. (1941) *Poverty and progress: A second social survey of York.* London: Longmans, Green and Co.

Skolnick, J. K.(1978) *House of cards: The legalisation and control of casino gambling.* Boston Mass.: Little Brown and Co.

Stedman-Jones, G. (1974) 'Working-class culture and working-class politics in London 1870–1900: Notes on the re-making of a working-class', *Journal of Social History*: pp. 460–508

Thomas, K. (1971) *Religion and the decline of magic.*London: Weidenfeld and Nicholson.

Yeoman, T. and. Griffiths, M.D. (1996) 'Adolescent machine gambling and crime', *Journal of Adolescence* No. 19: pp. 183–188.

YouGov (2007) *Gamblers are dicing with debt www.moneyexpert.com* accessed on 20 August 2007.

III

TOURIST SPACES:
TRADITIONAL AND EMERGING
VISITOR AND TRAVEL

FROM BOUTIQUE TO BOHO:
THE ART OF THE LUXURY HOTEL

Nicky Ryan

University of the Arts London, UK

Introduction

> A great hotel is not just a building, it is an individual with personality,
> spirit and authenticity. It's original, romantic, surprising, poetic
> and whimsical. It evokes an emotional response like a work of art.
> (Gramercy Park Hotel Website).

In 2006 hotelier Ian Schrager opened Gramercy Park Hotel in New York
designed by artist Julian Schnabel and featuring art by Andy Warhol, Cy
Twombly and Damien Hirst. The opening was covered by prestigious
magazines such as *Vogue*, *Time* and *Wallpaper*, international broadsheets
including *The International Herald Tribune* and *The Financial Times* and
numerous trade publications. Media interest in Gramercy Park was due
in part to the reputation of its owner, the historical associations of the hotel
and the anticipation that Schrager was moving hotel design in a new direction.
Schrager, in common with renowned property developers such as Steve
Wynn, had a reputation as an innovative entrepreneur and was considered
to be a formative influence on the development of the hotel business. *Vogue*
congratulated Schrager on "raising the bar" (McSweeney, 2006: p. 532)
while *Time* proclaimed the hotel to be "another lifestyle revolution" (Betts,
2006). With late business partner Steve Rubell, Ian Schrager has been credited
with pioneering the boutique hotel, marked by the opening of Morgans in
1984, which was designed by Andrée Putman. In 1988 Schrager hired Philipe
Starck to design the Paramount in New York and there followed a collaboration
which produced a succession of theatrical and elegant hotels that became
tourist destinations in their own right. As the trend for sleek minimalist
hotels gathered global momentum and boutique hotels proliferated at every
price level, Schrager launched a new type of luxury hotel, Gramercy Park,
in what he claimed to be in a dramatically different style.

This paper aims to explore the use of art in hotels as a key signifier of a new kind of luxury. The Gramercy Park Hotel is analysed from an art historical perspective, interpreting the hotel as emblematic of specific historical, social, political, and economic conditions. Preziosi (1993: p. 218) suggests that in this regard art history has been fundamentally semiological in nature from its beginnings: "By and large, disciplinary practice has construed artworks as intensely polysemous cultural artefacts, signalling many layers or dimensions of meaningful reference." The significatory properties of hotel design are explored and institutional rhetoric analysed in order to reveal "the social practices both in which that production is embedded and which it itself produces" (Rose, 2001: p. 142). A critical engagement with the dominant narratives of promotional literature such as the Gramercy Park Hotel Website provides an insight into the way that a company constructs and presents an image of itself to its various stakeholders. The paper is divided into three sections beginning with a brief historical overview of the development of modern hotel architecture. This is followed by a consideration of the boutique hotel phenomenon and the growing importance of the hotel lobby as site of spectacle and social ritual. The final section focuses on the 'artistic' narratives communicated by Gramercy Park and the significance of art and artists for hotels. The argument that art has been appropriated as a mark of distinction by hotels, as corporate identity is increasingly aligned with notions of 'artistic creativity', is contextualised within theoretical discourses surrounding the concept of luxury.

Re-imagining the luxury hotel

> Gramercy Park is the ultimate anti-brand. Luxury is not a price point or a logo on a handbag — it's an experience. (Schrager quoted by Gandee, 2006)

Luxury has been defined as an indulgence in, and enjoyment of, rich, comfortable and sumptuous living; an extravagance rather than a necessity; something pleasant and satisfying (Collins English Dictionary, 1994: p. 930). But luxury is a far more complex term than a dictionary definition would suggest and its meaning has shifted over time and in relation to different contexts. As French historian Fernand Braudel (1967: p. 122) argued, "superfluity and bare necessity" have always co-existed, but luxury itself "has many facets, according to the period, country or civilisation in question". Political historian Christopher Berry (1994: p. 242) maintained that "the persistence of the term 'luxury' indicates that even its contemporary usage is not merely casual or peripheral to the large questions of social and political theory, but rather, provides an illuminating insight into those questions". A consideration of the meaning and history of the concept of luxury is necessary to elucidate its re-interpretation and signification at Gramercy Park Hotel. Historically the idea of luxury was related to excess and moral corruption, but under Christianity, a distinction was drawn between 'luxus' meaning abundance and pleasure, and 'luxuria' meaning grossness. In the eighteenth century the politics of luxury changed as luxury began to lose its association with corruption and vice and "came to include production, trade and the civilising impact of superfluous commodities" (Berg and Eger, 2003: p. 7). A history of the idea of luxury from the classical period to the present day reveals how luxury has shifted from being a predominately negative term threatening social virtue, to a ploy supporting consumption (see Berry, 1994 and Twitchel, 2002).

The hotel has been a key signifier of luxury since the early nineteenth century and the rise of the mercantile bourgeoisie. Along with department stores, arcades and offices, the modern hotel was a new building type that responded to the changes wrought by capitalist industrialisation and its innovative modes of transportation and communication. The Tremont Hotel in Boston, for example, built in 1829, was a forerunner of the contemporary urban hotel in terms of size, service and style. Designed by professional architect Isaiah Rogers, it featured the latest in technology, and as Donald Albrecht (2002: p. 11) has argued "established the aristocratic palace as the model for hotel architecture". It was Thorstein Veblen, in his attack on the inequalities of the capitalist system in *The Theory of the Leisure Class* (1994 [1899]), who forged the association between luxury, class hierarchy and status. Veblen argued that "in order to gain and hold the esteem of men, it was not sufficient merely to possess wealth or power. The wealth or power must be put in evidence, for esteem is only awarded on evidence". Conspicuous consumption, conspicuous leisure and conspicuous waste were, according to Veblen, the markers of social positioning and hierarchical status. The aristocratic model of luxury established by grand hotels such as the Ritz in Paris, London's Savoy and the Waldorf-Astoria Hotel in New York provided a key site for the staging of conspicuous consumption and conspicuous leisure. Here the bourgeoisie enjoyed socialising and fine dining in opulent interiors that provided a glamorous environment in which to see and be seen.

By the 1950s the idea of what constituted luxury was rapidly changing as critics and designers rejected the pretensions of palatial décor in favour of the austerity of the International Style. Modernist architecture and Scandinavian furniture began to be promoted as the choice of preference for the discerning consumer. This can be demonstrated by the commercial success, but critical failure of the hotels at Miami Beach created by Morris Lapidus during this decade. The Fontainbleau (1954) and Eden Roc (1955) drew on the glamour and fantasy of Hollywood movies but were castigated by critics as "an architecture of excess" (Josephson, 1971: p. 109) and "stereo-

types of postwar American consumerism, of pretence, artifice, and vulgarity"
(Friedman, 2000). In the 1950s Robert Steiner and Joseph Weiss (1951:
p. 263) revised Veblen's theory of conspicuous consumption, arguing that
in a prosperous American society where an increasing number of people
could afford luxury goods, the old elite was forced to create new status
symbols so that they could maintain their position in society as tastemakers.
A "counter snobbery" came into play demonstrating a lack of interest in
money, dislike for flamboyant design, and an appreciation of simplicity.
This trend towards a pared down style of luxury, or "inconspicuous consumption" highlighted the importance of class distinctions and marked
out the clientele of Lapidus' ostentatious hotels as lacking the prerequisite
"cultural capital" (Bourdieu, 1984).

The period following World War II witnessed a growth in air travel and
mass mobility that created the ideal conditions for hoteliers to locate their
properties abroad as well to open additional sites in the domestic market.
Global chains were able to offer customers a consistent experience with
reliable service in a range of international locations. Standardisation and
uniformity was emphasised with profits maximised through economies of
scale. This was the birth of the 'box' hotel, or the "McDonaldisation" of the
hotel concept with its standardised operational procedures, strong branding
and architectural uniformity. "McDonaldisation", a term coined by sociologist
George Ritzer (1998: preface), was characterised by "efficiency, predictability,
calculability and control" but it was a process that could result in sameness
and cultural homogeneity. To avoid the latter condition, global chains such
as Hilton International designed their hotels to communicate a strong brand
identity inflected with local or regional characteristics. This guaranteed
guests a consistent level of service in a range of different architectural environments. In the 1980s the boutique, designer or lifestyle hotel emerged as
an antidote to the standardisation and anonymity of many corporate global
chains. Small-scale, usually fifty to one hundred rooms, non-chain operated
and individual in design, boutique hotels were at the cutting edge of fashion.
Attractions in their own right and flagships for the city, they became
destinations for both tourists and local residents. It was a hotel type that
reinvigorated the idea of the hotel as a design palace with the lobby providing
a key site of ritual display for the new cultural elite.

The Boutique Hotel

An entirely new genre of hotel — one that will change the game
again and raise the bar [...] As Morgans marked a paradigm shift
in hotels twenty years ago and created a new industry, so the new
Gramercy Park Hotel will accomplish the same impact today.
(Gramercy Park Hotel Website)

From its beginnings the public spaces of the hotel, and in particular the lobby, has provided a stage for the enactment of social relations and hierarchy. The lobby is a semi-private, semi-public place which marks the border between the public realm of the street and the private realm of the hotel bedroom. It is a threshold, a liminal space between inside and outside where people meet, wait and observe others. A space of possibility and indeter-minacy, the lobby has provided rich subject matter for artists, novelists and cultural commentators. The lobby was a new form of space that emerged from the nineteenth century revolution in travel and transportation which had transformed the modern city. For Siegfried Kracauer (1995), a cultural theorist writing in Weimar Germany, the lobby was an emblematic space of modernity, "a space of unrelatedness", of boredom, alienation and displacement where individuals sat isolated in silence, reading to avoid eye contact. The theme of disconnection is further elaborated by Fredric Jameson (1991) in his analysis of John Portman's Bonaventure Hotel in Los Angeles. The hotel is used to illustrate the changes in aesthetic production that Jameson claimed were characteristic of postmodernism. The Bon-aventure aspired to be "a total space, a complete world, a kind of miniature city" that eschewed the utopian language of modernism and drew on the vernacular of the American city. For Jameson the hotel lobby immersed guests in its vast "milling confusion", it was a "postmodern hyperspace" which transcended the "capacities of the individual human body to locate itself [...] to map its position in a mappable external world".

Adorned with chandeliers, rich draperies and monumental staircases or formed of multi-storey atria surrounded by restaurants and shops, the hotel lobby operated as a key signifier in the communication of an aestheti-cised corporate identity through design. In the boutique hotels of Ian Schrager which opened throughout the 1980s and 1990s, the stylish but small bed-rooms, encouraged guests to spend more time in the lounges, bars and lobbies. Schrager coined the phrase "lobby living" to promote his development of the hotel lobby as a fashionable site of entertainment and spectacle. With his background in nightclubs such as Studio 54 in the 1970s, Schrager declared his intention to make hotels the nightclubs of the 1990s (Ryder, 2002). He transformed the hotel lobby into the location for exclusive social gatherings framed against a backdrop of spectacular lighting and theatrical visual effects. On special occasions the lobby was roped off and surrounded by a crowd of spectators watching celebrities arrive and hoping to gain access to the spectacle within. In *The Society of the Spectacle* written in 1967, Guy Debord argued that society had become a spectacle over which individuals have no control. The spectacle was "capital become an image", a site of illusion and ideology that constituted a form of domination. The reinvention of the lobby as a new kind of gathering place embodied in the concept of "lobby socialising" was part of a strategy to compete with other leisure destinations. In *The Experience Economy*, business strategists Joseph

Pine and James Gilmore claimed that experiences represented the foundation for future economic growth. They argued that experiences were central to "a new, emerging economy" (1999: p. 11) and represented "an existing but previously unarticulated genre of economic output" (p. ix). In order to be distinctive, Pine and Gilmore advocated that hotels should provide more than good service and an attractive environment but should also create memorable experiences.

The concept for the first boutique hotel, Morgans in New York, was influenced by the private gentleman's club and featured leather chairs, panelled walls and chequered marble flooring. However it was Schrager's collaboration with Philippe Starck, which produced the boutique's signature style, the hotel as theatre with over-scaled baroque furniture and fluid draperies juxtaposed against a minimalist backdrop. Minimalist interiors have been referred to as "interchangeable and typologically neutral" (Zabalbeascoa and Rodriguez Marcos, 2000: p. 110) but as Brian O'Doherty (1999: p. 79) has argued in *The White Cube*, white is not neutral but has an authority that can transform ordinary objects into something distinctive. From the 1980s onwards the extreme reductionism of "the white cube", a style which dominated museum, gallery and exhibition spaces, became popular in commercial buildings. By appropriating the form of the art gallery, stores and hotels invested their properties with the values associated with this elite environment. By the 1990s minimalism provided the major design statement at the luxury end of both retail and hotel developments. The slick and stylised aesthetic favoured by Schrager was rapidly emulated throughout the hotel industry and numerous boutique hotels emerged targeting a wide range of customers. Traditional box companies such as Starwood Hotels & Resorts, the largest hotel company in the United States moved into the lifestyle sector with its W hotels, promoting the business hotel as boutique.

The democratisation of luxury is "the single most important marketing phenomenon in modern times" and occurred as a direct result of the market economy and democratic political system (Twitchell, 2002: p. 29). Since the 1970s luxury has been defined downward into ordinary goods and services, "even as we have increased our ability to consume objects and sensations hitherto beyond our reach". Instead of luxury products and services being the preserve of the wealthy and upper classes, what Twitchell refers to as the "old luxe", the new consumers of luxury have a sense of entitlement that is unrelated to class. "Commodified mini-milieus" have developed with their own luxury markers and shared stylistic tastes based on "status goods, and the drive for self-expression though consumption" (Gottdeiner, 2000: p. 17). Increasingly a mix of 'high' and 'low' goods and services were being consumed as people combined luxury with value products to satisfy their individual requirements. If luxury was no longer something that was desired by many but consumed by few, nevertheless the need to retain an aura of exclusivity remained important to 'premium' brands. Schrager claimed that the minimalist boutique concept had been "co-opted by the mainstream" (quoted by Betts, 2006) and sought to redefine luxury in his new venture, the Gramercy Park Hotel.

In 2005 Schrager sold the Morgans Hotel Group and developed the Ian Schrager Company which owns, develops, manages and brands hotels, residential and mixed-used projects. Announcing that the boutique hotel was dead, Schrager declared that Gramercy Park Hotel heralded the invention of a new genre (Gramercy Park Hotel Website). Luxury is a social construct subject to continual reinvention and the idea of luxury embedded in Schrager's new enterprise lay in its uniqueness and individuality delivered through what was claimed to be an "eccentric" and "unorthodox" style aesthetic (Gramercy Park Hotel Website). Against the backdrop of ubiquitous minimalism and affordable luxury, Schrager turned to art as a marker of distinction. His strategy was similar to that of luxury fashion brands in the retail sector such as Prada, Comme des Garçons and Louis Vuitton where the work of cutting-edge artists and architects was incorporated into flagship stores in order to appeal to a niche consumer culture that prized 'artistic' sensibility. As Bourdieu argued in *The Field of Cultural Production* (1993), the prestige of the 'avant-garde' producer can only be sustained through a symbolic opposition to the mainstream. Working with neo-expressionist artist, sculptor and film director Julian Schnabel, the hotelier created an eclectic and idiosyncratic space where the overarching concept that endowed the project with cutting-edge status was contemporary art.

The Bohemian Hotel

> A unique atmosphere imbued with the same spontaneous, haute bohemian, eclectic, eccentric and edgy sophistication one would find in an artist's studio or home. (Gramercy Park Hotel Website)

The design for Gramercy Park Hotel was conceived by Schnabel, edited by Schrager and realised by in-house architect Anda Andrei and business partner Michael Overington. The original hotel, an eighteen-storey Renaissance Revival building (1925–30), was located in an L shape overlooking the only remaining private park in New York. With former famous guests including artists, filmmakers, fashion editors, architects and actors such as Humphrey Bogart, the hotel had a bohemian heritage which Schrager's refurbishment renewed and accentuated. Modelled on Schnabel's own home, the design concept made public the private and personal preferences of the artist in terms of interior layout and décor. With its rich renaissance colours, sensuous textures, voluptuous forms and huge canvasses of museum-quality contemporary art, Gramercy Park appeared to represent a dramatic departure from the Spartan and glossy boutique hotels that had preceded it.

The lobby was the prime site for the communication of corporate identity as it had been in the boutique hotels. Twenty feet high and decorated with furniture and fittings collected in flea markets, made to order by craftsmen or designed by Schnabel, the lobby was intended to create a bohemian atmosphere and resemble an artist's studio or home. The look was not based on a poverty stricken artist's garret but drew inspiration from the residence of a "bohemian with money" (Schrager quoted by Blum, 2006). Schnabel designed the bronze tables, lanterns, rug, door handles, curtain rods and finials, and the huge ten-foot hand-carved fireplaces. Nothing in the hotel was mass-produced or generic but was either custom-made like the Venetian chandelier and Aubusson rug, or a renovated found piece. Each guest room was different and designed to reference the past but "not to be The Four Seasons, not to be imitative of the old, not to be Disney" (Andrei quoted by Nobel, 2006). In the Rose and Jade bars, handmade tiles, reclaimed wood, hand tufted rugs and extravagant draperies combined to create an aesthetic described by Schrager as "rock'n'roll baroque" (Nobel, 2006). Throughout the public spaces of the hotel, paintings worth millions of dollars, by Schnabel, Jean-Michel Basquiat, Cy Twombly and Andy Warhol adorned the walls. The art which had been loaned was due to change periodically as different guest curators were invited to curate collections. Even the guest rooms were hung with contemporary and vintage photographic images to reinforce the centrality of art to the new hotel concept.

Displaying art in hotels is not a new idea but the reputation of hotel art had significantly declined with the rise of the chains and the proliferation of low quality prints as a form of inexpensive wall decoration. However in the 1980s and 90s an interest in displaying authentic works of art grew as demonstrated by Schrager's use of artists such as Robert Mapplethorpe to produce art for Morgans' guest rooms. A trend towards the incorporation of art into the interior design of the hotel can also be witnessed in the recent proliferation of 'art hotels'. At the Hotel Max in Seattle, Hotel Fox in Copenhagen and the Hotel des Arts, San Francisco, art was painted directly on the walls by local artists or loaned for free in return for publicity. The benefit for the hotel was that art created a point of difference from competitors; it provided interest for guests and could attract attention from the media. Visitors were offered an alternative venue to the museum in which to enjoy an immersive art experience while the artist was liberated from the conventions of the gallery system. The rise of the 'art hotel' is one manifestation of a growth in cultural tourism that has occurred since the 1980s and is evidence of the increasing fashionability of art as "a metropolitan mass pursuit" (Wilson, 1999). The utility of art for the hotel industry also underlined the importance of 'creativity' to economic life and the central role that culture played in the knowledge economy and in the construction of global corporate identity.

Schrager vigorously refuted the categorisation of Gramercy Park as an 'art hotel' and the significance of his project resided in the way in which an 'artistic' lifestyle was invoked through the creation of a space that resembled an artist's studio. Historically viewed as the centre of the artistic universe and imagination, the studio was the context for the creation of 'masterpieces' and "the unique place of art's production" (Buren, 1979). In his essay *The Function of the Studio*, conceptual artist Daniel Buren announced the demise of the studio arguing that art produced in this context failed to engage with the site where it was eventually to be shown. The studio has nevertheless continued to be the location where many artists produce their work and remains an emblematic site of 'creativity'. At Gramercy Park the colour scheme of the lobby with its deep red and ochre palette, the richness of the soft furnishings, the central chandelier, wooden ceiling and black and white floor tiles bore a striking resemblance to the interior featured in Johannes Vermeer's *The Art of Painting* (1666). This work depicts an artist in his studio sitting in front of an easel observing an elaborately dressed female model. From the seventeenth century onwards the studio became a familiar subject through which artists could explore ideas about art and the nature of their vocation. Vermeer's painting which appears to portray an everyday scene is in fact an allegory about art and inspiration. The model is dressed as Clio, the muse of history wearing a crown of laurel that signifies glory. In one hand she holds a trumpet representing fame and in the other a book symbolising history. The artist is dressed in fine clothing to indicate his status and provides the conduit through which the muse finds expression (see Wheelock, 1995). Although this specific work of art is not alluded to by Schrager in interviews about the hotel, the hotelier confirmed that the rooms were designed to evoke paintings. If the boutique hotel had appropriated the cultural authority of the museum and commercial gallery, Gramercy Park by contrast was associated with the symbolic values of the studio, the prime locus of artistic individuality and creativity.

Institutional rhetoric played a key role in the communication of narratives that emphasised the hotel's 'artistic' theme. The Gramercy Park Hotel website referenced art historical discourses surrounding Romanticism and the bohemian highlighting notions of individuality, uniqueness, authenticity and creativity. The hotel was described as "the new high Bohemia" and "Bohemia re-invented for the 21st century" and Gramercy Park's 'authentic' bohemian credentials were set against the falseness and commercialisation of mass culture exemplified by "copycat" boutique hotels. The idea of the bohemian and the construction of a bohemian identity originally arose out of the transformation of cultural production and consumption in the nineteenth century when market relations replaced traditional forms of patronage (Rykwert, 1997). The Romantic movement elevated the artist to the status of creative genius and established him as a heroic rebel rejecting bourgeois convention through the creation of radical experimental art.

Gramercy Park tapped into what Griselda Pollock (1996) has referred to as bourgeois concepts of art that celebrate individualism by means of the idea of the artist "as the feeling being whose works express both a personal sensibility and a universal condition". Wilson (1999) however has demonstrated that as the bohemians continually pushed the boundaries of bourgeois taste, so consumer culture rapidly absorbed their stylistic innovations. Gramercy Park appeared to represent a further stage in the commodification of artistic lifestyles already evident in the gentrification of many urban districts such as Soho New York, formerly occupied by artists (Zukin, 1982).

Conclusion

> In today's world, luxury is increasingly defined as an expression of individuality, through the unique and highly personal experience that luxuries help provide. (Graham and Matthews, 2004)

Reports from market researchers and brand consultants on the current state of the luxury sector emphasise that luxury is more than a product or service but is about providing "authentic", "unique, memorable experiences that are differentiated" (Coupe, 2007). At Gramercy Park Hotel customers were promised an "idiosyncratic, eclectic vision that offers a perfect modern alternative to the institutional approach one now finds in even the most high-end boutique design hotels" (Gramercy Park Hotel Website). The grand urban hotel had been refashioned in the guise of the artist's studio. The bohemian lifestyle it evoked was emblematic of a new kind of idiosyncratic and individualistic luxury aimed at a footloose, affluent and increasingly art-savvy leisure class. The myth of the artist as an eccentric and bohemian figure was used as a metaphor for creativity and high culture, thereby associating the narratives of imagination, passion and vision with the image of Gramercy Park Hotel and by extrapolation the Schrager brand. The cultural capital of contemporary artist Julian Schnabel was appropriated to produce symbolic capital for the Ian Schrager Company. Bourdieu (1984: p. 2) has argued that "a work of art has meaning and interest only for someone who possesses the cultural competence, that is, the code into which it is encoded". Gramercy Park was designed to appeal to an audience who possessed the requisite knowledge or 'cultural capital' to 'read' its multiple and complex cultural coding. Here the 'artistic' theme served to communicate a superior aesthetic 'taste' as art fulfilled the key role of marking out and maintaining brand distinction.

References

Albrecht, D. (2002) *New hotels for global nomads*. London: Merrell.
Arnold, A. (2000) 'Luxury and restraint: Minimalism in 1990s clothing', in N. White and I. Griffiths (eds) *The fashion business*. Oxford: Berg, pp. 167–181.
Berg, M. and Eger, E. (2003) *Luxury in the eighteenth-century: Debates, desires and delectable goods*. Basingstoke: Palgrave Macmillan.
Berry, C. (1994) *The idea of luxury: A conceptual and historical investigation*. Cambridge: Cambridge University Press.
Betts, K. (2006) 'A hotel guru changes rooms', *Time* Vol. 168, No. 7.
Blum, A. (2006) 'Welcome to the art hotel', *Business Week* 25 May.
Bourdieu, P. (1984) *Distinction: A social critique of the judgement of taste*. London: Routledge.
——— (1993) *The field of cultural production*. Cambridge: Polity Press.
Bourdieu, P. & Delsaut, Y. (1975) 'Le couturier et sa griffe: contribution à une théorie de la magie', *Actes de la recherche en sciences sociales* No. 1.
Braudel, F. (1967) *Capitalism and material life, 1400–1800*. New York: Harper Torchbooks.
Buren, D. (1979) 'The function of the studio', *October* Vol. 10: pp. 51–58.
Collins English Dictionary (1994) London: Harper Collins.
Coupe, S. (2007) 'The changing face of luxury travel', *Locum Destination Review* 19. Online. Available HTTP: http://www.locum-destination.com/pdf/LDR19TheChangingFaceOfLuxury.pdf (accessed 2 September 2007).
Debord, G. (1994 [1967]) *The society of the spectacle*. New York: Zone Books.
Friedman, A. (2000) 'The luxury of Lapidus: Glamour, class, and architecture in Miami Beach', *Harvard Design Magazine* Summer, No. 11.
Gandee, C. (2006) 'Staying power', *Sunday Times Style* 10 September.
Gottdeiner, M. (2000) *New forms of consumption: Consumers, culture, and commodification*. Langham, Maryland: Rowman & Littlefield Publishers.
Graham, P and Matthews, M. (2004) 'The changing face of luxury', *Knowledge Networks*. Online. Available at HTTP: http://www.knowledgenetworks.com/know/2004/spring/1-1_graham.html (accessed 25 May 2007).
Gramercy Park Hotel Website. Online. Available at HTTP: http://www.gramercyparkhotel.com/index.html (accessed 10 May 2007).
Jameson, F. (1991) *Postmodernism, or the cultural logic of late capitalism*. London: Verso.
Josephson, M. (1971) 'Lapidus' pornography of comfort', *Art in America,* March.
Kracauer, S. (1995) *The mass ornament: Weimar essays*. Cambridge: Harvard University Press.
McSweeney, E. (2006) 'Up at the old hotel', *Vogue* September, pp. 532–533.
Nobel, P. (2006) 'Julian Schnabel, reluctant decorator', *The New York Times*, 3 August.
O'Doherty, B. (1999 [1976]) *Inside the white cube*. Los Angeles: University of California Press
Pine, J. and Gilmore, J. (1999) *The experience economy: Work is theatre and every business a stage*. Boston: Harvard Business School Press.

Pollock, G. (1996) 'Art, art school, culture', in J. Bird, *et al.* (eds) *The Block reader in visual culture*. London: Routledge, pp. 50–67.

Preziosi, D. (1993) 'Seeing through art history', in E. Messer-Davidow, D. Shumway and D. Sylvan (eds) *Knowledges: Historical and critical studies in disciplinarity*. Charlottsville, Virginia: University Press of Virginia, pp. 215–231.

Ritzer, G. (1998) *The McDonaldisation thesis: Explorations and extensions*. London: Sage.

Rose, G. (2001) *Visual methodologies: An introduction to the interpretation of visual materials*. London: Sage.

Ryder, B. (2002) *Bar and club design*. New York: Abbeville Press.

Rykwert, J. (1997) 'The constitution of bohemia', *Res* No. 31: pp. 109–127.

Steiner, R. and Weiss, J. (1951) 'Veblen revised in the light of counter-snobbery', *Journal of Aesthetics and Art Criticism* Vol. 9, No. 3: pp. 263–268.

Twitchell, J. (2002) *Living it up: Our love affair with luxury*. New York: Columbia University Press.

Veblen, T. (1994 [1899]) *The theory of the leisure class*. New York: Dover Publications.

Wheelock, A. (1995) *Vermeer and the art of painting*. New Haven: Yale University Press.

Wilson, E. (1999) 'The bohemianisation of mass culture', *International Journal of Cultural Studies* Vol. 2, No. 1: pp. 11–32

Zabalbeascoa, A. and Rodriguez Marcos, J. (2000) *Minimalisms*. Barcelona: Gustavo Gili.

Zukin, S. (1982) *Loft living: Culture and capital in urban change*. Baltimore: John Hopkins Press.

LIVE ENTERTAINMENT AT THE SEASIDE — HOW FAR A PART OF THE CULTURAL OFFER?

Steve Hayler

Canterbury Christ Church University, UK

Introduction

The British seaside resort was created ostensibly for leisure; it is a unique environment that exhibits many key features arising from a particular set of circumstances. In part this reflects its physical geography and marginal location (Ryan, 1997; Shields, 1991; Walton, 2000) but resorts are dynamic places and their environments are the product of change, displaying a range of both modern and relic features.

In analyses of these changing landscapes, most attention has focused on the attractions of the sea, beach, promenade and various forms of accommodation (Cooper, 1997; Demetriadi, 1997; Shaw and Williams, 1997; Pearce, 1995) and how these and visitors' interests in them have changed over time (Agarwal, 1994; Butler, 1980; Cooper, 1990). However, one particular element that has clearly been part of this physical and cultural environment but which has received scant attention is that of live entertainment. Yet live entertainment has been part of the physical fabric and social construction of resorts from the outset. From the mid nineteenth century to the 1960s there is no doubt that live entertainment was an important part of what visitors expected to see and it is generally assumed that it provided an important motive for visiting; if not the prime motive at least an important secondary one, with Blackpool, for example, boasting as many as fourteen live shows in the 1950s (Parry, 1983, quoted in Urry 2002). However, while live entertainment may have been important in the past, how far is this still the case and, more precisely, what part does it continue to play in the tourism product, particularly the broader cultural offer provided by seaside resorts at the beginning of the 21st century? This paper seeks to provide a basic framework to explore this question and briefly discusses preliminary research in this field.

Cultural tourism and the cultural offer at the seaside

Cultural tourism is credited as being one of the largest growing segments of global tourism (WTO, 2004) and is increasingly being utilised as a means of social and economic regeneration. Culture has become a basic resource from which the themes and narratives essential to 'place-making' can be derived (Gottdiener, 1997). This, according to Richards and Wilson (2006), often involves tying the physical assets and living culture together. Although there has been substantial research of the use of culture and heritage in tourism, few studies attempt to differentiate culture in the context of tourism and focus on its constituent parts (Hughes, 2000). Thus, much discussion has focused on heritage centres, art galleries, castles, historic houses, festivals, events, indigenous culture and, on film and literary-induced tourism and there has been less consideration of the performing arts and entertainment (Hughes, 2000). This is surprising — particularly for English seaside resorts, given that they have been traditionally associated with the pleasure-periphery. Such pleasures have always featured live entertainment, primarily focused around the (popular culture) summer variety show (Hayler, 1999) — which had continued to be a central aspect of the seaside cultural offer during the late 19th and 20th century. It may no longer be such a prominent aspect of cultural activities at the seaside in the 21st century (particularly in relation to variety shows) but live entertainment in various forms is still an important part of the seaside cultural offer which includes such diverse attractions as amusement arcades, roller-coaster rides, up-market fish restaurants and increasingly, cultural and arts centres, and festivals of various descriptions.

There will also be a place for live entertainment in the 'cultural capital' at seaside resorts — an amorphous concept in its broadest sense that has a range of definitions which refer either to an individual (person-based) or to a destination (destination-based). Historically, interpretations of cultural capital have been person-based as it is usually understood to encompass the collection of non-economic forces such as family background, social class, varying investments in, and commitment to, education and to different resources which influence academic success (Hayes and MacLeod, 2006; Savage *et al.*, 2005). But cultural capital need not relate solely to the possession of, say, graduate qualifications: it can be accumulated over time through talent, skills, training and exposure to cultural activity (Bordieu, 1984), such as provided at English seaside resorts since their inception. However, at the English seaside there has been a paucity of research of the utilisation of culture within the cultural capital framework, which may perhaps be explained by the fact that studies of cultural capital traditionally focus on individual or personal capital at the expense of broader consideration of destination-based cultural capital such as live entertainment, and the built infrastructure (the theatres, Pier Pavilions and Winter Gardens) that are themselves reflections of the cultural experience of a visit to the seaside. Additionally, Amin and Thrift (2002) and Pine and Gilmore (1999) state that increasing competition in the market means that goods and services are no longer enough by themselves, and that producers must differentiate their products by transforming them into 'experiences' which engage the consumer (Richards and Wilson, 2007). This symbolism might usefully be extended to English seaside resorts as they attempt to adapt to changing consumption patterns and changing cultural tastes and attitudes during the early years of the current century. In this context this paper is concerned with a preliminary discussion of the role of live entertainment within the (popular) cultural capital offer at seaside resorts, including the symbolism of live entertainment as a reflection of the acquisition of cultural capital.

Live entertainment at the English seaside, with a comment on the role of local authorities

Certainly up to the 1950s seaside live entertainment had established itself as the popular culture of the day, particularly when the 'season' shifted to the seaside. At the beginning of the 21st century live entertainment continues to be a given in the mosaic of the cultural offer at the seaside but has become less focused on 'traditional' seaside entertainment and is now an eclectic mix of some 'high' (ballet, opera, classical music etc.) but mostly 'low' arts (performing arts and live entertainment such as comedy, rock and pop, tribute bands, children's theatre etc.), that cater for residents, people within a 45-minute drive-time, and tourists — including long-stay, short-stay, and day-trippers (Hayler, 2004). In relation to the ownership and management of the seaside venues, and therefore with some influence on the programming for live entertainment, there remains a strong local authority presence and none of the local authorities in a recent study see a future without live entertainment or without council involvement of some sort (Hayler, 2004). Currently, there is a trend towards involving the private sector in running seaside theatres so there may be less direct council involvement; but whether such political 'fashions' fade or fail, the local authorities will be there to 'pick up the pieces'. This is because live entertainment is seen as an essential part of the cultural offer, part of the image of the resort location — even if it has always proven difficult to quantify, or justify in terms of how far it persuades particularly tourists to visit a certain location and how far it contributes to the acquisition of cultural capital.

Issues of the image of seaside resorts are also, significantly, a general reflection of prevailing cultural attitudes, relating to the perceived importance of cultural factors in the total seaside destination experience. This relates to how far seaside tourism is itself a reflection of 'cultural capital' as a part of cultural tourism, and then, in turn, to attitudes towards providing particular cultural activities, including live entertainment, and any particular expectations of live performance that might influence (seaside) tourist/resident decision-making in relation to cultural symbolism and, potentially, destination imagery. This informs the debate about the importance of cultural motives in the decision to visit a destination, and reinforces the need to understand the role of the traditional activity of seaside entertainment as a particular attribute of the location, but with strong links to cultural perceptions — past, present and future, personal and universal.

Notwithstanding the lack of hard evidence, live entertainment, as suggested, continues to be part of the cultural offer, whether it is provided by the public authorities, the private sector, or sometimes by the two working in partnership. Historically, live entertainment has been a 'given', so there has been no real necessity, until recently, to assess it as part of the cultural capital at seaside resorts. Additionally, there has been little interest in its place in seaside cultural capital. There have been no systematic attempts to quantify the effect of live entertainment and how changes in its provision (including the amount and types of live entertainment provided) might affect the image, the cultural capital of a resort location (also, in relation to personal cultural capital acquisition) and, in turn, what potential consequences this may have for the economic, social and cultural well-being of English seaside resorts. This comment refers to all the various markets that the live enter-tainment is aimed at — not just short or long-stay tourists, but also day visitors (deliberately attending shows, or not), and increasingly the residents and people within a 45 minute drive time. It also refers to the consequent move at the seaside towards 52-week programming — the result of changing audiences and tastes (Hayler, 2004). At the seaside this is well illustrated by the popularity of 'quality' touring musicals of the West End variety, such as 'Joseph', 'Phantom' and 'Cats', that now regularly visit provincial theatres, including those in seaside resorts. There is certainly a 'blurring' between the live entertainment offer at many seaside resorts and the theatre programmes at non-West End provincial locations, as well as 'scaled down' versions of West-End productions.

Public policy and live entertainment at the seaside

The changing economic fortunes and cultural aspects of seaside resorts are, as indicated, linked with the other key influence concerning the future role of live entertainment at the seaside — the role of the local authority. Local government, within parameters set by central government, fundamentally has co-ordinated and sometimes directly controlled the economic and cultural activities of the location and its role in managing live entertainment over the last hundred years or more, as has already been noted. Despite a general image that projects much of the seaside experience as 'tired', tourism remains the economic base for most seaside resorts. Economic restructuring is the key to economic survival and there may be a role in such restructuring for particular cultural activities, e.g. festivals that include live entertainment.

There is no legal obligation for local authorities to provide live entertainment, but they have a long history of going beyond their statutory duties in the funding of the performing arts, and cross-party political consensus has allowed them to provide a wide range of leisure facilities and cultural locations and activities, including live entertainment. More recently, however, a slightly different attitude to that of its predecessors would appear to have emerged with New Labour involving a more directional, if not direct, role for central government, making local authorities articulate clear cultural strategies 'directly' to the Department for Culture, Media and Sport (DCMS, 2000).

The impact at the seaside promises to be significant and could have an important influence on live entertainment provision. Furthermore, the promotion of clear cultural strategies with defined cultural activities is reinforced by the requirement of the Department for the Environment, Transport and the Regions for local authorities (since the late 1990s) to provide Best Value (DETR, 1999), a key element of which is that local government should be more responsive to customer needs that 'put people first'. This places greater pressure on local authorities to broaden their cultural offer which in the past may have been too narrowly focused on 'the arts'. Thus, local authorities at seaside locations may well see live entertainment as a useful contribution to a local cultural strategy that can link to acquiring a broad range of 'cultural capital'.

At seaside locations this practical approach requires the gathering of statistics measuring and comparing the live entertainment at seaside theatres, and so the author is working with the British Resorts Association (now the British Resorts and Destinations Association) via the Centre for Resort Theatre (CRT), run by the author, since 2000. Agreed Performance Indicators (benchmarking criteria) gathered for this exercise include:

- number of performances;
- number of performance days;
- average ticket price;
- percentage of seats sold;
- net income;
- contribution (net, actual contribution, and by criteria, i.e. type of performance, such as comedy, variety, 'musical theatre' etc.).

CRT has now been in operation for eight years and detailed analysis of trends emerging from the database suggests that aspects of live entertainment have been changing, thus affecting the acquisition of cultural capital (Hayler, 2004). Variety shows have declined considerably at the beginning of the

21st century. Musical theatre (increasingly in the form of travelling West End productions), along with pantomime, are the two highest percentage categories of live performance (around 14%), followed by a broad spread of categories such as comedy, children's/family, drama — all at about 6% of all performance categories, and tribute bands at about 8%. All 'high' arts combined constitute only a small percentage of performances, approximately 5.5%. The rise of tribute bands is a phenomenon of the last 15 years: there are, for example, 8 ABBA tribute bands, but only some of these sell a good proportion of available seats. The preceding comments are well documented and further explained in Hayler (2004). The CRT database provides facts, but not reasons why people attend particular performances. Further research to establish motivation, cultural perceptions, changing cultural attitudes, and the location of patrons, for example, needs to be combined with the data before the (cultural) role for live entertainment at seaside resorts can be adequately understood in relation to the cultural capital of the seaside.

Conclusion

At the beginning of the 21st century, in any future vision for seaside resorts, it would appear that there is a role for live entertainment in relation to the perceived image, status and character and cultural perception of the location. At every resort in the CRT database (17 locations at its peak), there is continued support for the provision of a varied live entertainment programme. This does not mean that there is any particular consistency, even across similar-size resorts, regarding the understanding and role of live entertainment in the economic and cultural life of the resort, but that there is a universal, tacit understanding that it should continue. Particular live entertainment provision is resort-specific and the importance of the local context needs to be investigated further, along with consumers' and potential consumers' cultural perceptions. However, in general terms, it is interesting to note that live entertainment at the seaside is gradually moving away from traditional seasonal entertainment towards a year-round mix of mostly 'low' but with a small amount of 'high' (performing) arts provision. In this respect, as noted, seaside theatres, despite their often distinctive appearance, are becoming increasingly similar to provincial, non-seaside, theatres. Given such a development, a new morphology is emerging as seaside live entertainment changes to sit somewhere between the exclusive entertainments provided at the early spa resorts and the traditional live entertainments provided during the period of mass tourism. Furthermore, it may also be part of a broader shift which is seeing seaside resorts being transformed into 'towns by the sea'. These shifts can accommodate an emerging description of aspects of the cultural capital (yet to be agreed) that might be acquired by visiting live entertainment performances at seaside resorts. This paper has suggested that 'hard' data from the CRT database can be utilised via an emerging research agenda in attempting to evaluate the relative effect of live entertainment when acquiring cultural capital at the seaside.

References

Amin, A. and Thrift, N. (2002) *Reflections on current developments in contemporary urban geography*. Cambridge: Cambridge University Press.

Agarwal, S. (1994) 'The resort cycle revisited — implications for resorts', *Progress in Tourism, Recreation and Hospitality Management* 5: pp. 194–207.

Butler, R.W. (1980) 'The concept of a tourist area cycle of evolution: Implications for management of resources', *Canadian Geographer* 24: pp. 5–12.

Bourdieu, P. (1984) *The life distinction: A social critique of the judgement of taste*. London: Routledge.

Cooper, C. P. (1990) 'Resorts in decline: The management response', *Tourism Management* Vol. 11, No. 1: pp. 63–67.

Cooper, C. (1997) 'Parameters and indicators of the decline of the British seaside resort', in Shaw G. & Williams A.M. (eds) (1997) *The rise and fall of British coastal resorts*. London: Pinter.

Demetriadi, J. (1997) 'The golden years: English seaside resorts 1950–1974', in Shaw G. & Williams A.M. (eds) (1997) *The rise and fall of British coastal resorts*. London: Pinter.

DCMS (2000) *Creating opportunities: Guidance for local authorities in England on Local Cultural Strategies*. London: HMSO.

DETR (1999) *Modernising local government, in touch with local people* (CM 4014). London: HMSO.

Gottdeiner, M. (1997) *The theming of America*. Boulder: West View Press.

Halsey, A.H., Kelly, C. and Levin, H. (1997) *Education: Culture, economy and society*. Oxford, OUP.

Hayes, D. and MacLeod, N. (2006) 'Packaging places: Designing heritage trails using an experience economy perspective to maximise visitor engagement', *Journal of Vacation Marketing* Vol. 13, No. 1: pp. 45–58.

Hayler, S. M. (1999) 'Live entertainment at the seaside', *Cultural Trends* No. 34: pp. 63–98.

———— (2004) 'Live entertainment at the seaside: A benchmarking exercise for Local Authority theatres', *Cultural Trends* No. 51: pp. 41–75.

Hughes, H. (2000) *Arts, entertainment and tourism*. Oxford: Butterworth-Heinemann.

Parry, K. (1983) *Resorts of the Lancashire coast*. Newton Abbot: David & Charles, quoted in Urry (2002).

Pearce, D. (1995) *Tourism today: A geographical analysis*. Harlow: Longman.

Pine, B. H. and Gilmore, J. H. (1999) *The experience economy: Work is theatre and every business a stage*. Harvard: Harvard Business Schools Press.

Richards, G. and Wilson, J. (2007) 'Developing creativity in tourist experiences: a solution to the serial reproduction of culture?', *Tourism Management*, Vol. 27, No 6: pp. 1209–1223.

Ryan, C. (1997) *The tourist experience: A new introduction*. London: Cassell.

Savage, M., Gayo-Cal, M., Warde, A. and Tampubolon, G. (2005) *Cultural capital in the UK: A preliminary report using correspondence analysis*. CRESC Working paper No. 4. Manchester: Centre for Research on Socio-Cultural Change, University of Manchester.

Shaw, G. and Williams, A. (1997) 'The private sector: Tourism entrepreneurship — a constraint or resource', in Shaw G. and Williams A.M. (eds) (1997) *The rise and fall of British coastal resorts*. London: Pinter.

Shields, R. (1991) *Places on the margin: Alternative geographies of modernity*. London: Routledge.

Urry, J. (2002) *The tourist gaze (Theory, Cultural and Society* Series). London: Sage Publications.

Walton, J. K. (2000) *The British seaside: Holiday and resorts in the twentieth century*. Manchester: Manchester University Press.

WTO (2004) *World Tourism Organisation: The Asia-Pacific perspective*. WTO Seminar Proceedings, Cambodia, 8 June 2004.

HOMELAND SECURITY IMPACT ON THE ROOSEVELT CAMPOBELLO INTERNATIONAL PARK [1]

Glyn Bissix, Nick Baker, and Liesel Carlsson

School of Recreation Management and Kinesiology, Acadia University, Nova Scotia, Canada

As recently as June 2007, implementation of the more stringent regulations for tourists traveling across the USA-Canada border was postponed because of passport application backlogs. While welcome news in the short term for both the Canadian tourism industry and tourism operators in northern USA, this temporary policy reversal has added to the confusion surrounding tourism destination planning along the Canada-USA border. The Roosevelt Campobello International Park (RCIP), situated on Campobello Island in southern New Brunswick, Canada, is only a few minutes drive across an international bridge from Lubec, Maine in the USA. The park relies heavily on American tourists to fill its visitor ranks and future visitation levels might be expected to be adversely impacted by more stringent border crossing regulations unless creative ways of sustaining American visitations can be found. The park's proximity to the international border suggests that it can serve as a bellwether for examining the evolving challenges for cross-border tourism.

The security intensification precipitated by the 9/11 attack on the USA has complicated travel between the USA and Canada. This, in turn, has put pressure on the tourism industry on both sides of the border to revise marketing and management strategies. To put post 9/11 impacts in perspective, however, it is important to note that the RCIP has experienced gradual reductions in visitations over two decades (see **Figure 1**). This trend is largely attributed to a dwindling population with a direct connection to the presidential era of Franklin D. Roosevelt and the special place it had in mid-twentieth century American life. Despite this ongoing drift, reductions have been clearly exacerbated by the consequences of 9/11, thus raising concerns about sustaining park visitations once cross-border regulations are further tightened.

As a result of the prevailing uncertainty, this study was initiated to gain a better understanding of the factors influencing park visitor preferences,

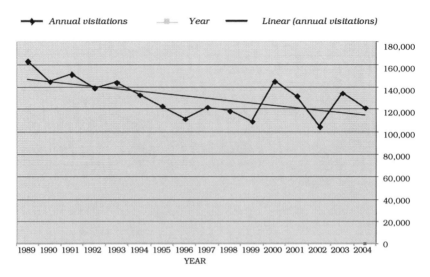

Figure 1: RCIP Annual Visitations 1989–2004

experiences and behaviours and how these have changed in response to increased border crossing regulations, as well as to determine the potential implications of a further intensifying of cross-border regulatory requirements. Reference to Manning's 1989 study enabled comparison of visitor behaviour separated by approximately twenty years, allowing specific insight into the effects and implications of evolving cross-border regulations. Based on this comparison and a more detailed analysis of the most recent visitor survey, this chapter examines the lessons learned, and suggests possible strategies to mitigate the most adverse effects of regulatory intensification.

The Roosevelt Campobello International Park

Franklin D. Roosevelt, the 32nd President of the United States, led America from the Great Depression through the Second World War and is the only American president to have been elected four successive times. Despite a polio infirmity that restricted him to a wheelchair, Roosevelt was, by and large, a respected international statesman. The gift of his family retreat to the people of Canada and the USA has, for many years, proved a magnet for those wishing to understand more about the life of a president who had such a considerable impact on ordinary Americans and Canadians. The park assets include the Roosevelts' country home, several 'cottages' acquired by the Park Commission from the Roosevelts' neighbours, and the country estate which is made up of natural coastlands, woodlands and pathways. RCIP is situated on Campobello Island, an island whose economy is dominated by summer tourism and a year round commercial fishery.

The park is administered by a commission established under a treaty signed in 1964. It has six members, three from each country, and is equally funded by Canada and the USA. The RCIP is seen as an important symbol of international friendship and cooperation; it is the only park in the world jointly owned by two countries and administered by an international joint commission. As implied above, cross-border travel between Campobello Island and Lubec, Maine was relatively simple prior to 9/11; park visitors, staff, and islanders generally traveled freely and with little delay across the border. Travelers experienced only occasional requests to show a driver's license, and were rarely interviewed at length or had their vehicles inspected. Nowadays, there are increasing cross-border formalities with the prospect that, in the very near future, all travelers will be required to show a valid passport or high-tech identity card.

The mail-in survey of park visitors conducted on behalf of the RCIP Commission in 1989 (Manning, 1990) indicated a very high level of satisfaction with the RCIP experience. Since that survey, the Park Commission has worked diligently to maintain and improve the park experience, including increased management and marketing of the park's natural areas. Beyond the difficulties presented by increasing cross-border regulation, the Park Commission has identified the changing demographic as a particular challenge to maintaining visitor levels. Those Americans and Canadians with a personal and emotional connection to Roosevelt's presidency are aging and decreasing in numbers, a fast disappearing clientele, who are less able or willing to travel. The need to understand the modern traveler and park visitor is therefore of particular importance in guiding park management planning and marketing. The surveys conducted in the summer of 2006 (Baker & Bissix, 2006; 2007) focused on visit satisfaction, cross-border experiences, barriers or impediments to visit, and pre- and post-visit experiences that might have affected their overall experience. It is expected that this study will be repeated within the next few years to monitor the ongoing impacts of cross-border regulations on park visitors and consequent changes to RCIP management and marketing strategies.

A review of the literature

This study is structured around three distinct literatures, two contextual and one methodological. The first section examines park visitor behaviour, the second explores the emerging literature on post 9/11 tourism, while the third section considers the efficacy of on-line surveys compared to other approaches such as traditional mail-in surveys. The literature on visitor studies is broad-ranging and includes, for example, a detailed study of visitor behaviour within park settings under various management arrangements.

It also includes changing visitor tastes and adaptations in marketing, the impacts of crowding and conflicting uses; and the barriers and constraints experienced in visiting or attempting to visit a park setting. This study is particularly concerned with three fundamental visitor study themes that consequently frame this literature review. The first concerns the quality and relevance of the park experience on visitation levels; the second concerns the commitment of visitors toward a particular park setting; and the third concerns the barriers and constraints, real or perceived, that park visitors experience. The first theme in particular relates to the enduring challenge of maintaining product quality while ensuring that the product or service remains attractive and relevant to a viable market.

Standards of quality

In calling for a more systematic process to assess the quality of tourism facilities in New Brunswick that might lead to infrastructure improvement, Eiselt and Eiselt (1998) emphasized the tourism industry's sensitivity to economic swings and evolving customer tastes: "Clearly, being a nonessential product, it is among the first activities to be affected by an economic downturn and the changing interests of tourists" (np). Two important questions to ask then are, to what extent does enduring product quality cushion economic downturns, and what else is involved? One consideration for mitigating any barriers to accessibility is understanding when a commitment to visit is made and how promotional efforts affect that decision. According to O'Neill (2000), tourism promotion has predominantly focused on the pre-visit decision with insufficient attention given to confirming the perceptions formed during previous visits, perceptions which may lead to repeat visits or translate to positive word-of-mouth marketing (WOMM).

Citing O'Neill (2000), Palmer and O'Neil (2003) pose three important marketing questions: "What do [park visitors] consider the important features of services to be? What level of those features do they expect? [and] How do [park visitors] perceive service delivery?" The first question challenges park managers to more fully assess visitors' needs and hone pre-visit marketing accordingly. Park quality can then be further supplemented with on-site customer services and the tailoring of the park experience to better meet visitor needs. In a practical sense the question concerning "service quality can be conceptualized as the difference between what a customer expects and [his/her] perceptions of actual delivery (O'Neill, 2000: p. 47)". In this context Eiselt and Eiselt (1998) suggest that it is actually possible to lower visitor expectations to more realistic levels but this is generally considered counter-productive as it reduces commitment to visit, return, or recommend the site to others. They additionally argue that "today's travelers demand higher standards for accommodation, parks, and tourist sites in general (np)," signifying that quality enhancement must endure, especially as client tastes evolve.

The last of O'Neill's marketing questions, how visitors perceive quality, should be a primary concern for park managers. Perceived quality is a key to influencing future visitation decisions and word-of-mouth marketing (Hogan, Lemon & Libai, 2004). Interestingly park visitors and managers can have very different perceptions of quality. In backcountry campsites, for example, Stankey and Lucas (1984) found that some park users consider certain park conditions as assets while managers view them as environmental deficits. For instance, trampled vegetation around campsites was tolerable for users while managers considered such conditions unacceptable. It is therefore important to note that objective reality and managerial perceptions of quality are not necessarily as important for marketing a venue as the valuations of the visiting public. It should be noted however, that evidence from marketing museums suggests that an agency's core values should never be compromised. Friedman (2007) for example, chronicles several examples where museums sacrificed historical authenticity for short-term visitor gains but to the detriment of long-term goals.

The changing marketplace and 9/11

In broadly considering the barriers and constraints facing American visitors to Canada, it is sobering to realize that numerous countries impose constraints on international visitors including Americans and Canadians with little negative impact. For example, Antigua and Barbuda require of visitors a minimum passport validity of six months and proof of sufficient funds (Levack, 2006). Australia similarly requires a ten-year passport valid for at least six months and an electronically sourced visa which can be conveniently processed by home-country travel agents (Australia, 2007). Such constraints provide little solace for tourism operators along the USA/ Canada border whose client base traditionally enjoyed largely unfettered cross-border access. As always, vigilant Canadian tourism operators have kept a close eye on USA travel behaviour to stay on top of trends. To this end the magazine *Tourism* tracks the American visitation patterns and monitors destination awareness as well as perceived travel barriers (Jan/ Feb 2006). Such publications allow tourism managers to keep abreast of constraints and proactively adjust marketing effort.

Be that as it may, it is clear from the popular media that the impact of 9/11 on travel patterns was swift and intense. Once the US government realized the gravity of the attacks on 9/11, it immediately declared the whole of the continental USA a no-fly zone (Smith & Carmichael, 2005). Hundreds of transatlantic and transborder flights heading to the USA were diverted to Canadian airports or back to Europe and Africa. Halifax International Airport, for example, received forty unscheduled passenger planes requiring emergency immigration processing and accommodation for 8,400 passengers until new flights to the USA could be sanctioned. Regional hotels quickly filled to capacity necessitating a governmental call for local billeting. The response was overwhelmingly positive; Nova Scotians welcomed thousands of strangers into their homes and cared for them for days until flights resumed (*Chronicle Herald*, 2001).

The first academic and tourism industry literature concerning 9/11 initially focused on crisis management (Evans & Elphick, 2005; Fall, 2004; Fall & Massey, 2005) but evolved to a more reflective review on tourism impact. Eisinger (2004) for instance, found an early shock response to tourism in American cities with substantial visitor reductions. He also noted a fast rebound to, or near to, pre 9/11 levels. Similar conclusions were drawn by Enz and Canina (2002) who examined the immediate impact of 9/11 on American hotels, and by Greenbaum and Hultquist (2006) who looked at hotel accommodation levels in Italy. While the immediate visitor impact is largely understood and reported in the popular press, there is, to date, little academic literature on its longer-term impact on park visitation patterns. Daerr (2002) reported a 6% overall reduction in national park visitations in 2001 (although some of this decline was due to security induced park closures), while noting that places like Washington DC and New York City experienced the biggest decline (over 19%). The North East, the area in the USA adjacent to RCIP, experienced a relatively large decline with a 10.2% decrease compared to the year before, while the Midwest and Southeast had modest increases. Of particular note, was that the Grand Canyon National Park had a large drop in attendance, attributed mostly to its international popularity.

While it will become obvious when viewing this study's results that the number of people making a spontaneous decision to visit RCIP is relatively small, it is also clear that this visitor segment will be profoundly affected by new controls, in fact largely lost from the RCIP visitor profile. The liter-ature notes that visitors to a tourism destination traditionally "have varying motives, interests, and means in selecting specific venues for overnight accommodations and dining experiences as well as recreational and entertainment experiences" (Rompf, DiPietro,& Ricci, 2005: p.11). As Rompf *et al.* (2005) point out, critical decisions about selecting services and attractions "can [normally] be made at any or all journey points" (2005: p. 11) whether that is before the trip begins, while in transit, or at (or near) the intended destination. In the case of the RCIP in the future, whether travelers are adventuresome, risk-averse, inexperienced, or disinclined decision-makers will matter little, as all will be denied access to the RCIP from the USA unless they present the appropriate travel documents. The impact of lost visitors to the RCIP will therefore be felt beyond the park itself, to the surrounding communities on both sides of the border. While it is beyond the scope of this report to examine in detail the lost economic surplus to border communities, this study provides some initial insights.

One factor in the general control of park managers is managing the quality of the park experience. To buffer against the expected impact from increased regulations, it is therefore important to assess whether the quality of the RCIP experience has decreased sufficiently to explain the perpetual decline in visitor levels over the last twenty years and more recently since 9/11. It is also important to assess whether visitor tastes have changed sufficiently to further contribute to the observed decline. In assessing the particular impact of 9/11 and the extent to which changing border regulations contribute to changes in visitor levels, this study considers the perceived barriers to visiting RCIP and the changes since 9/11. In this context it is important to examine whether these real or perceived barriers pose an enduring threat to park visitation and whether adjustments in management and marketing can compensate for expected changes. To address these concerns, this study was designed to generate baseline data so that future visitor studies might better distinguish between ongoing trends in RCIP visitors' motivations and the impact of barriers inflicted by more stringent international border crossing regulations.

On-line surveys

Since the proposed changes in cross-border regulations would be enacted swiftly, it was necessary to devise a research process for accessing impacts quickly. It was recognized that the traditional mail-in survey would be costly, time-consuming and would not meet the immediate needs of park managers. For that reason, an on-line visitor survey was considered in the spring of 2006. The literature on web-based surveys, while limited, is nevertheless quite optimistic about their potential value. Young and Ross, for example, pointed toward their promise in 2000, suggesting an impressive potential for web-based surveys in the recreation management field; Kiernan *et al.* (2005) argued five years later that greater use should be made of them. The latter research team found no evaluative bias in a web and paper administered experiment while McMullin, Hocket and McClafferty (2006) found no appreciable differences in reliability or validity between on-line and mail-in surveys in a national USA survey. In a reliability comparison with older rural women, average 58 years, using both pencil and paper and on-line versions of a standard dietary questionnaire, Boeckner *et al.* (2002) found minimal appreciable differences in ease of completion or comprehension levels. The latter study's conclusions were important to this study, as the vast majority of visitors to RCIP were elderly and, it was surmised, might have difficulty responding to an on-line survey. Boeckner *et al.* (2002) recommended that greater use could be made of on-line questionnaires without fear of selection (age) bias.

Most recently in the journal *Visitor Studies*, Parsons (2007: pp. 24–5) made a comprehensive review of web-based surveys and provided a useful list of advantages and disadvantages as well as tips based on best practices.

He based this list on the available literature and his own consultative experience. His list of advantages and disadvantages of using Web-based surveys are shown in **Table 1** and **Table 2** below.

Table 1   Advantages of Web-Based Surveys

- Convenience
- Quick and timely dissemination
- Quick response/replies
- Customizable with filter questions and skip patterns
- Flexible format
- Ability to randomize response choices, even questions
- Ability to provide pop-up boxes with more information/explanation/directions
- Ease of adding 'bells and whistles' multimedia (video, audio, photos)
- Automated data entry with fewer data errors
- Quicker data processing and reporting (and in some cases real-time results)
- Cheaper than paper (no paper, postage, mailing or data entry: cheaper reminders)
- Reduced (almost negligible) costs for additional respondents
- Ability to export data into data analysis software
- Ability to track respondents' answering behaviours
- No paper waste
- Wider distribution, even to international audiences (overcomes international boundaries)
- Larger sample sizes, maybe even ability to survey entire populations eliminating need for sampling
- Respondents can take [survey] at their own pace
- Data collection available to everyone/anyone.

Table 2   Disadvantages of Web-Based Surveys

- Coverage (not everyone has Internet access)
- Challenge with probability sampling
- Computer literacy/technology skills needed
- Unfamiliar format
- Technology glitches can create problems
- Different browsers or different monitors may show different surveys
- Lower response rate
- Difficulty getting random sample and so possibility of sampling bias
- Verification of responses (who is responding: is one person responding many times)
- Abandonment
- Potential culture and language issues
- New method with little research
- Data security and privacy concerns
- Survey fatigue (as with telemarketing).
- Difficulty getting random sample and so possibility of sampling bias
- Verification of responses (who is responding: is one person responding many times)

Given this limited but generally positive literature, there appears to be no substantive methodological grounds for dismissing on-line surveys as a legitimate approach to social science research; they, in fact appear particularly useful for a study of this kind.

Methodology

Due to the confidence of the literature, the cost savings in questionnaire distribution and retrieval, as well as the substantial advantages in data processing costs and time, it was decided that this study would use an on-line survey approach. We used a short, one page on-site survey of park visitors to obtain basic visitor information, combined with a more extensive on-line follow-up questionnaire. As already indicated, there was some initial hesitation over using an on-line survey, due to the older-than-average age of the typical RCIP visitor (compared to most park visitor populations) and the assumption that they would not be comfortable using the Internet. While our study did not have the benefit of Parson's attribute list (see Tables 1 & 2) at its commencement, we had recognized many of the same benefits prior to the study and inadvertently profited from others. Most notably, one of the greatest advantages to an Internet study based in Canada and conducted by a Canadian university lay in the assumption, eventually proven correct, that a substantial majority of respondents were from the USA. Initially we had envisioned a mail-in survey, and in anticipation of the difficulty and added costs of return mail across an international border, we had provisionally arranged cooperation with an American university to reduce mail and data processing costs, although due to time constraints this strategy was abandoned.

We experienced a substantially lower response rate than Manning did in his 1989 survey: nonetheless we argue that our sample is as representative as Manning's was. However, we have no way of knowing whether conducting the study through a USA-based university would have elicited a greater response rate. Also, although by using an in-house, university based, on-line survey system we were able to assure our research ethics board (REB) and the RCIP of respondents' anonymity, this did not necessarily reassure potential respondents: they had to take our word that anonymity would be protected. To avoid an individual being counted more than once, we made visual inspections of the database to determine whether obvious duplications existed. We were able to identify a few such cases and eliminated these from the dataset. Software is available to deal with this issue but was not used in our study because of budget and time limitations. As we deliberately avoided entering the respondents' e-mail address in the data record to ensure anonymity, we had less control over deliberate double entry. We did, however, make a visual comparison of comments, home state/ province location etc. and noted no obvious "stacking" of the dataset. We did receive one dubious on-site response from a certain "Tony Blair" from the United Kingdom, and upon checking the authenticity of the e-mail address we eliminated this response.

As noted in the list of disadvantages (see Table 2), we identified a problem in properly displaying the survey on-screen with some computer monitors. We therefore coded the display to be easily read by the smallest and oldest laptop computer screen in our research laboratory. We also noted that a few respondents had clearly and consistently reversed their answers to certain multiple part questions. In the process of inspecting respondents' on-line answers and matching these to their written comments, we identified six with a clear and unequivocal disparity in their assessment of park facilities and services. In these cases we concluded that there had been obvious and consistent respondent coding error, and so confidently reversed the responses to these questions in the offending surveys. There were a few other surveys where we suspected response errors but their submitted comments (or lack thereof) were not sufficiently persuasive for us to make adjustments. By not adjusting the responses to these surveys the overall quality ratings of some park features and services may be lower than they might otherwise have been. While we recognize that this type of respondent error is also possible in a paper survey, we nevertheless hope to minimize this error in the future by incorporating more user-friendly on-screen formatting.

Before publishing on-line, we tested the survey with several different types of Internet browsers and found it worked satisfactorily with each. However, one additional adjustment was made while transferring the database from our web-based survey system to a Microsoft Excel© database. We found that we could not use the Microsoft Internet Explorer browser to transfer data to Excel, so we tried Mozilla Firefox instead, which worked successfully. We suspect the problem lies in an overzealous firewall embedded in the Microsoft Browser which cannot easily be corrected because of its hidden and proprietary coding. Once the dataset was transferred to Excel using Mozilla Firefox, we experienced no further difficulties in the transference of the data to SPSS version 14 for Windows (2007) for subsequent data analysis.

Prior to formally publishing the survey on-line, several trial iterations were developed in consultation with RCIP park management. Once a first draft of the complete survey was agreed upon, the questionnaire was compiled using Microsoft Publisher and uploaded for testing on Acadia University's on-line survey system. Using a restricted access URL, a small group of students, staff and community members (6) were invited, in series, to complete the survey. They were asked to note the time for completion, and any difficulties in comprehension or in the performance of the on-line survey. Minor adjustments were made after each tester completed the survey. When a consistently satisfactory performance was attained, with no reported difficulties, park staff was then invited to test the on-line version, report any deficiencies, and make further suggestions for refinement; this testing phase also led to a few minor changes.

Simultaneous with this testing process, a protocol for soliciting potential respondents was developed with senior park staff. Three strategies were adopted. The first was to approach park visitors as they walked from the RCIP Visitor Centre to the main attraction of the park, the Roosevelt Cottage; the second involved setting up a table between the parking lot and the Visitor Centre, a route through which almost all visitors are funneled; and the third approach used park interpretive staff at the completion of the Roosevelt Cottage tour, which was the most popular park attraction. All three strategies involved approaching park visitors opportunistically who appeared to be 19 years or older. Each of the first two strategies utilized one of three trained senior undergraduate students from Acadia University, who were also employed to conduct a biodiversity study. The third strategy used park interpretive staff after the Acadia students returned to campus in mid-August. In all three situations, visitors were asked to answer a few short questions and then invited to participate in the on-line survey, and if the response was affirmative they were asked to provide an e-mail address for future contact. Of the 607 who completed the initial one page survey, 505 supplied a usable e-mail address and 143 subsequently submitted usable on-line surveys from this sample frame. This translates into a 28.3% sample response rate.

In his 1989 study, Manning attempted a random survey by selecting a sample-frame of ten survey days from July 25 to September 23 including weekdays and weekends with an hourly sampling schedule. As explained earlier, the 2006 survey involved using personnel with other responsibilities, such as interpretation or field research, to solicit survey participants. Using a similar response solicitation strategy to that utilized by Manning, the 2006 canvassing team operated over 47 days beginning August 22 and ending October 19, with weekends and weekdays proportionally represented. While the size of the samples is quite different in the three surveys, the basic respondent characteristics are similar. For example, in Manning's study, of the 890 respondents 115 (13%) were Canadian and 775 (71.1%) American; and of the 607 respondents in the on-site survey in 2006, 59 (9.7%) were from Canada and 538 (88.6%) from the USA. There were an additional 10 (1.6%) respondents from Europe. When considering only Canadian and American respondents, this translated to 9.9% Canadians and 90.1% Americans (N=597). Of the 116 on-line respondents 8 (7%) were from Canada and 108 (93%) from America. Interestingly, despite increased cross-border regulations, there was a greater proportion of Americans responding in the 2006 surveys compared to the 1989 survey (see **Table 3**).

**Table 3   Proportion of Canadian and American Respondents
(1989, 2006(1) and 2006(2))**

Survey	Americans	Canadians
Manning 1989 Mail-in	(775) 87.1%	(115) 13.0%
Baker & Bissix 2006 On-site	(538) 90.1%	(59) 9.9%
Baker & Bissix 2006 On-line	(108) 93.0%	(8) 7.0%

While the results section that follows compares the respondents of the various surveys in some depth, an interesting preview is that in Manning's study, 43.3% of respondents visited RCIP in pairs, a percentage that climbed to 54.4% in 2006. Also experiencing an increase in 2006 were the respondents who visited the park alone.

Results

The results of the surveys are presented using descriptive rather than inferential statistics. Neuman (2000) describes descriptive statistics as: "a general type of simple statistics used by researchers to describe basic patterns in the data" (p. 508). This approach was endorsed in the literature by Mitra and Lankford (1999) and by Veal (1997) to reveal the overall sample's responses which can be used to support management decision-making.

Most parks and recreation facilities depend heavily on repeat visits to swell their attendance figures but, for many, a visit to the RCIP is a once-in-a-lifetime experience (see **Table 4**).

Table 4   Expectations to Revisit RCIP

Do you expect to visit the Park again in the next few years?		
	2006	1989
Yes	54%	59%
No	46%	41%

The overall rate of repeat visitors is remarkably similar when comparing the 1989 and 2006 surveys, 24% and 26% respectively. Also similar are the numbers of those who intend a repeat visit to the RCIP, 59% in 1989 and 54% in 2006. While we have no way of accurately monitoring how many respondents follow through on their intent to return, a drop-off between intention and actual practice is hardly surprising when taking into account the many intervening factors which complicate people's lives. To get insights on why visitors do not return it is useful to look at the comments of those who have no intention of returning. As with Manning's study, when asked to elaborate on why they would not be returning, respondents indicated that it was too far to travel, they would not be returning to the area, and there were many other interesting places to visit. Given the location of RCIP and its main focus on history, these reasons seem perfectly logical and provide important clues as to where and how to focus marketing resources in the future.

There are relatively few heavy users (6 or more visits) of the RCIP (see **Table 5**); and while there appears to be a modest increase in 2006 compared to 1989 (6% and 3.6% respectively), this segment does not appear to be large enough to concern the RCIP's marketing attention. However, having a roughly one in four chance of attracting a visitor back to RCIP makes this focus on marketing very appealing, especially when one compares the effort necessary to commit new visitors from the American and Canadian populations-at-large. Even more critical to the marketing effort, given the constant need of park managers to attract approximately 75% of visitations from brand new clients, is the importance of word-of-mouth marketing (WOMM). Manning found in 1989 that 99% of park visitors that year were willing to recommend a visit to RCIP to others; a rate which remained constant in 2006 (see **Table 6**). Given the acknowledged importance of WOMM in the literature, the high approval ratings of RCIP visitors, and the likely impact of cross-border regulations on translating initial intentions to visit into actual visitations, more attention needs to be given to how effectively WOMM translates into actual commitment to visit the RCIP.

Table 5   Frequency and Intensity of Park Visitations

Have you visited the Park previously?			*How many times?*		
	2006	*1989*		*2006*	*1989*
Yes	26%	24%	1	13%	10.8%
No	76%	76%	2	1%	5.3%
			3	4%	2.2%
			4	1%	1.4%
			5	1%	0.9%
			6–10	6%	1.7%
			> 10	0%	1.9%

Table 6   Willingness to Recommend RCIP to Others

As a result of your border experience, would you recommend others visit?

	2006	1989
Yes	99%	99%
No	1%	2%

Figure 2 compares the household income of survey respondents in 1989 and 2006; however, before any meaningful comparison could be made of income ranges, 1989 dollars had to be adjusted to 2006 values. In addition, with the vast majority of respondents coming from the USA, all household incomes were treated as if they were based on American dollars. The average monthly US Consumer Price Index (CPI) was calculated for the years 2006 and 1989 using 1982–4 as base years; a quotient of 1.63 was used to adjust 1989 household incomes to 2006 dollars. Unlike Manning in 1989, in 2006 we offered respondents the option to not disclose household income; we considered this an added assurance of anonymity and 12% of respondents took advantage of this option.

When comparisons were made no substantial differences in household income were noted; there were however, some small differences. A shift was seen in fewer visitors in the $20,000–$50,000 income bracket in 2006 compared to 1989 and a correspondingly larger representation in the over $100,000 household income bracket was noted for 2006. This upward shift in household income reflects the increase in educational attainment and greater representation of mid-life visitors. More visitors to the RCIP in 2006 had graduate, undergraduate and college degrees, and a larger proportion of visitors in 2006 came from the 50–60 age range which tend to be years of strong income potential. Furthermore there were fewer visitors in retirement, when income potential tends to decrease, in 2006 compared to 1989.

While the household income of visitors showed some variation, the motivation for travel was remarkably similar. The RCIP remains a major reason for travel to the region. In 2006, 50% indicated that RCIP was the

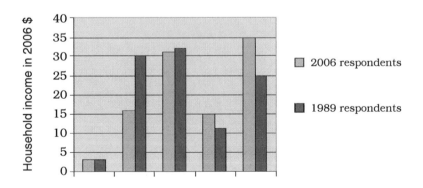

Figure 2   Total annual household income for 2006 and 1989 (Adjusted to 2006 Dollars)

primary purpose of their trip; in 1989 it was 51%. Travel by recreational vehicle (RV) had reduced from 10% in 1989 to 5% in 2006; bus travel dropped from 5% in 1989 to 1% in 2006; however, travel by car, truck, SUV or minivan increased slightly from 83% in 1989 to 89% in 2006. Interestingly, 10% of our 2006 sample traveled alone to the RCIP while only 1% did so in 1989. In a corresponding drop, only 59% traveled as a family compared to 66% in 1989.

In 2006, 88% of respondents toured the historic cottages (down from 94% in 1989), 54% engaged in photography in 2006 (up from 45% in 1989), there was an increase in beachcombing (34% up from 29%) and nature study increased from 9% to 12%. Other park activities remained surprisingly similar including visiting the flower gardens (42% in 2006 compared to 43% in 1989) and driving the scenic roads (49% in 2006 compared to 50% in 1989). Additionally visitors in 2006 took in the Eagle Hill Bog and the Seaside Interpretive tours (9% and 5% respectively), that did not exist before 1989. When asked simply "What areas did you visit?" it became clear that the natural areas were more popular in 2006 compared to 1989 and, while fewer visited the interpretation center, the use of park interpretation services within the centre saw a substantial increase. Eighty-five percent viewed the park's interpretive film in 2006 compared to 72% in 1989 and 76% visited the Visual Aids Room in 2006 which was up from 46% in 1989. The rise in popularity of the backcountry reflects the efforts of park managers to promote the natural sites and introduce visitors to the special places that the Roosevelts came to the Island to enjoy.

In general the quality of the experience for park visitors has not declined appreciably in the intervening survey years, nor surprisingly has it increased despite the continuing efforts of park managers to maintain and improve the park experience. These results were presented in a detailed report to the RCIP (Baker and Bissix, 2007). By and large the satisfaction ratings for the park's attractions are down five to fifteen points from extremely high levels in 1989. In part, this may be attributable to: reverse coding errors in completing the on-line survey, a more discerning clientele in the year 2006; and, more worryingly, to higher dissatisfaction. Possible sources of dissatisfaction may be parking lot repairs during the summer of 2006 and the closure of some cottages for special events; the latter was a repeated feature of written comments among several survey participants. While the ratings on park quality remains very high, its comparatively lower assessment in 2006 compared to 1989 is cause to make further assessments of quality over the next few years.

Cross-border issues

Of particular relevance to this study are the issues concerning cross-border travel regulations. It was already noted that a larger proportion of survey respondents in 2006 was from the USA compared to the 1989 survey.

This possibly suggests that American visitors are presently coping well with the additional cross-border formalities; it could also mean that marketing the park in Canada has become less effective compared to that in the USA. Of the 83% of respondents who approached the park from the Maine side of the border: none had no delay, 99% experienced a short delay, 0% had a substantial delay and 1% indicated an unreasonably long delay entering Canada. Traveling in the opposite direction to the United States, 58% had no delay, 29% a short delay, 5% indicated a substantial delay while 1% had an unreasonably long delay. Eight percent did not return immediately across the border at Lubec. It is clear that the pattern of delay at the two border crossings is different; more are experiencing some level of delay coming into Canada than going out. It is unclear, however, what might be done about this except provide more information in the park's website to prepare potential visitors for what they might expect. Such warnings may nevertheless detract some potential visitors from making a commitment to travel. It is important to note that no one denied access to Canada from the United States would show up in this survey, and conceivably these travelers would also be missing in any future RCIP visitor survey.

Compared to 1989, more visitors in 2006 realized that they would have to cross the international border to visit Campobello (89% in 2006 compared to 77% in 1989), suggesting greater awareness of the cross-border formality. Only one respondent indicated that this would have been a deterrent to travel if known in advance; this compares to 3% in 1989 (interestingly, the person indicating a reluctance to travel also stated a willingness to visit again). In general, when respondents were asked whether they would recommend a visit to the RCIP as a result of cross-border travel formalities only 1% said no. This was even more positive than 1989 when less stringent requirements were in force, and then 2% indicated reluctance. Of particular significance to future RCIP marketing is the level of awareness in 2006 regarding the need for photo identification; 9% said they were unaware of this requirement. Despite this, their completion of the survey indicated that they had the necessary documents.

When asked whether the requirement for passports in the future would deter a return visit, 8% said it would. Clearly a potential 8% drop in US visitors resulting from passport requirements would have serious consequences for the RCIP and its surrounding communities; however, responses concerning visitor reaction to present cross-border formalities are encouraging. None of the visitors who experienced a delay at the border indicated a reluctance to re-visit RCIP as a result of future passport requirements. Indeed, there was only a 5% drop from 1989 levels in expressed intent to return (54% compared to 59%) when asked immediately after the passport requirement question whether they were likely to return to the RCIP.

Discussion

The RCIP has experienced a gradual decline in visitations over the past two decades that can best be explained by an American and Canadian populace becoming less personally attached to the F. D. Roosevelt presidency. A notable exception to this decline was a rise in visitors during the 2000 season. It is interesting to speculate on whether this reversal might have continued in subsequent years had it not been for the immediate impact of 9/11. Importantly, for many aspects of North American life, the aftermath effects of 9/11 were short-lived. A notable example was in the travel industry where hundreds of passenger airliners were temporarily mothballed throughout the world; however, a rebounding economy soon led to new industry highs. The impact of 9/11 lingers, however, and this is a key concern for the RCIP and other cross-border tourism attractions as homeland security continues to ratchet-up travel regulations rather than relax them. For the RCIP, the spectre of potential American visitors being stopped at the international border in 2008 because they lack appropriate travel documents is increasingly possible.

Spontaneous visitors, those who decide to visit the park while in the general vicinity, are at present an important visitor segment for the RCIP and its surrounding communities on both sides of the border. Thirty-three percent of RCIP visitors in 2006 indicated that the park had little to no influence in drawing them to the immediate vicinity of North-east Maine or South-east New Brunswick. It is this travel segment, those visiting the RCIP largely on impulse, that are most likely to be lost to the RCIP in future unless some acceptable solution for cross-border travel becomes broadly available. While tourists often adjust their itinerary while on route, travel to the RCIP from northern Maine will be impossible if they are not carrying acceptable travel documents. If, in future, all drivers' licenses issued in North America meet the required border-crossing standard, and children can be provided acceptable documentation, then much of this problem will disappear over time. However, as it is unlikely that such documentation will be available by the summer of 2008, a drop in visitors to RCIP can be anticipated.

Is it possible that enhanced word-of-mouth marketing (WOMM) can soften the adverse impact? As the literature suggests, WOMM is particularly useful for those tourism products with a reputation for high quality. There is little doubt that the RCIP enjoys such a reputation, so the question remains whether the RCIP's full potential for WOMM can be exploited, and its core of annual visitors mobilized as promotional agents of the park to compensate for the projected drop in casual cross-border visitations. Unfortunately, the specific mechanisms of WOMM, in the influencing of purchasing decisions, are among the least understood of all promotional strategies: thus the most effective prescription for action is by no means clear. One possible strategy is to distribute complimentary postcards to visitors and invite them to mail the cards to friends, co-workers and relations; an incentive program might also be devised at reasonable cost, to encourage visitors to participate in word-of-mouth marketing. Another possible strategy is the use of Internet mailing, where RCIP visitors are encouraged to send greetings from the RCIP by e-mail to friends, co-workers and relations. However, given the proliferation of SPAM, this option needs careful evaluation. As inferred by Hogan, Lemon and Libai (2004), a significant challenge is dovetailing the timing of visitor WOMM efforts with the optimal time to influence travel commitment.

Regardless of timing, a key factor in the RCIP's favour is its consistent product quality. Over the past decade or so the RCIP has attempted to maintain and raise its product quality within its core business of interpreting the life and times of F. D. Roosevelt. It has also broadened its product mix to give greater emphasis to presenting the natural features of the park to visitors, and connecting these to life on Campobello Island for the Roosevelts. As the literature examined earlier suggests, there is no guarantee that the efforts of park managers to improve certain park features will be fully appreciated by park visitors. It behooves park managers therefore, to better understand the perceptions of park visitors and determine the extent to which they can, without compromising core park values, accommodate the needs and desires of its clientele. The evidence of the 2006 on-line survey points to visitors that generally appreciate these efforts, although the closing of certain cottages for conferences that restrict visitor access have in some cases diminished the visitors' experience. As potential visitors' tastes and demands evolve, it will be increasingly important to assess their perceptions of the RCIP, to determine how park managers might respond.

In this time of evolving perceptions and tastes it is important to recognize that the continuance of the downward trend experienced over the last two decades is not necessarily inevitable. It is, for example, likely that the historic value of the RCIP will increase in the years to come as its antiquity grows. Unfortunately, the relative isolation of Campobello Island from major population centres is likely to become a more pressing problem for RCIP managers as the impacts of the "end of oil" (Roberts, 2004; Silverthorn & Greene, 2004), and the societal changes induced by climate change, affect regional, national and international travel patterns. The discussion of such profound drivers of recreation travel is however beyond the scope of this paper and must necessarily be left for another chapter to be written on the life of the RCIP and Campobello Island.

Acknowledgements

1   This research was aided and funded by the Office of the Vice-president Academic, the Harriet Irving Botanical Gardens, the Acadia Institute for Teaching and Technology, and the Office of the Dean of Professional Studies Faculty Research Support Fund, Acadia University; the Social Sciences Humanities Research Council Institutional Grant; and the Roosevelt Campobello International Park.

We wish to acknowledge the support of Mr. Peter Romkey, Director of the Harriet Irving Botanical Gardens, Mr. Terry Aulenbach, BCS. Institute for Teaching and Technology and Dr. Brian Vanblarcom, Department of Economics, Acadia University; Mr Harold Bailey, Roosevelt Campobello International Park and Ms. Samantha Bissix, BA, for their technical assistance during this study.

References

Australia (2007) Australia Travel Information: Visa — Traveling to Australia from the Americas. http://www.australia.com/ (Accessed: November 10).

Baker, N. and G. Bissix. (2006) *Analysis of an on-site survey of Roosevelt Campobello International Park Visitors— Summer 2006*. Wolfville, NS: School of Recreation Management and Kinesiology, Acadia University.

Baker, N. and G. Bissix. (2007) *Analysis of an on-site survey of Roosevelt Campobello International Park Visitors — Summer 2007*. Wolfville, NS: School of Recreation Management and Kinesiology, Acadia University.

Boeckner, L.S., C.H. Pullen, S.N. Walker, G.W. Abbott, and T. Bloc (2002) 'Use and reliability of the world wide web version of the block health habits and history questionnaire with older rural women', *Journal of Nutrition Education* 34, Suppl 1, pp. S20–S24.

Chronicle Herald (2001) 'Terror aftermath: Hamm says thanks for helping out', Nova Scotia, Wednesday, September 19: p. A11.

Daerr, E.G. (2002) 'Americans seek solace in parks after September 11', *National Parks* Vol. 76, No. 1/2: pp. 26–27.

Eiselt, H.A. & M. Eiselt. (1998) 'Grading procedures in the tourism industry: The case of New Brunswick', *Revue Canadienne des Sciences de l'Administration* Vol. 15, No. 1: pp. 65–75.

Eisinger, P. (2004) 'The American city in the age of terror', *Urban Affairs Review* Vol. 40, No. 1: 115–30.

Enz C. and L. Canina, 2002. 'The best of times, the worst of times: Differences in hotel performance following 9/11', *Cornell Hotel and Restaurant Administration Quarterly* (October): pp. 41–52.

Evans, N. and S. Elphick. (2005) 'Models of crisis management: An evaluation of their value for strategic planning in the international travel industry', *International Journal of Tourism* No. 7: pp. 135–150.

Fall, L.T. (2004) 'The tourism industry's reaction in action: Re-strategizing promotional campaigns in the wake of 9/11', in R. Denton (ed) *Language, symbols, and the media: Communication in the aftermath of the World Trade Center attack*. New Brunswick, NJ: Transaction Publishers.

Fall, L.T. and J.E. Massey. (2006) 'The significance of crisis communication in the aftermath of 9/11: A national investigation of how tourism managers have re-tooled their promotional campaigns', *Journal of Travel & Tourism Marketing* Vol. 19, No. 2/3: pp. 77–90.

Friedman, A. J. (2007) 'The great sustainability challenge: How visitor studies can save cultural institutions in the 21st century', *Visitor Studies* Vol. 10, No. 1: pp. 3–12.

Greenbaum, R. and A. Hultquist. (2006) 'The economic impact of terrorist incidents on the Italian hospitality industry', *Urban Affairs Review* No. 42: pp. 113–130.

Hogan, J.E.; K.N. Lemon and B. Libai. (2004) 'Quantifying the ripple: Word-of-mouth and advertising effectiveness', *Journal of Advertising Research* Vol. 44, No. 3 (September): pp. 271–280.

Kiernan, N.E., M. Kiernan, M.A. Oyler and C. Gilies. (2005) 'Is a web survey as effective as a mail survey? A field experiment among computer users', *American Journal of Evaluation* Vol. 26, No. 2 (June): pp. 245–252.

Levack, K. (2006) 'Passport requirements', *Successful Meetings* Vol. 55, No.12 (November): p. 54.

McMullin, S.L., K. Hockett and J. McClafferty. (2006) 'Validity and reliability of an internet-based survey conducted simultaneously with a mail survey', Abstract Database: ISSRM 2006 — 12th International Symposium on Society and Resource Management. Vancouver, BC, Canada. June.

Manning, R.E. (1990) *Roosevelt Campobello International Park: Visitor use report, June 1990*. School of Natural Resources, University of Vermont.

Mitra, A. and S. Lankford (1990) *Research methods in parks, recreation and leisure services*. Champaign, IL: Sagmore Publishing.

Neuman, W. L. (2000) *Social research methods: Qualitative and quantitative approaches* (4th Ed). Toronto: Allyn and Bacon.

O'Neil, M. (2000) 'The role of perception in disconfirmation of service quality', *Quality Focus: Second Quarter* 4, No. 2: ABI/INFORM Global pp. 46–59.

Palmer, A. and M. O'Neill (2003) 'The effects of perceptual processes on the measurement of service quality', *The Journal of Services Marketing* Vol. 17, No. 2/3: ABI/INFORM Global: p. 254.

Parsons, C. (2007) 'Web-based surveys: Best practices based on the research literature', *Visitor Studies* Vol. 10, No.1: pp. 13–33.

Roberts, P. (2004) *The end of oil: On the edge of a perilous new world*. Boston: Houghton Mifflin.

Rompf,P.; R.B. DiPietroand P. Ricci(2005) 'Locals' involvement in travelers' informational search and venue decision strategies while at destination', *Journal of Travel & Tourism Marketing* Vol. 18, No 3: pp. 11–22.

Smith, W. W. and B. A. Carmichael. (2005) 'Canadian seasonality and domestic travel patterns: Regularities and dislocations as a result of the events of 9/11', *Journal of Travel & Tourism Marketing* Vol. 19, No. 2/3: pp. 61–76.

Silverthorn, G. and G. Greene, eds. (2004) *The end of suburbia: Oil depletion and the collapse of the American Dream* [video recording]. Toronto: The Electric Wallpaper Co.

Stankey, G.H. and R.C. Lucas (1984) *The role of environmental perception in wilderness management.* Wilderness Management Research Unit, USDA Forest Service, Missoula, Montana. Available at: http://leopold.wilderness. net/pubs/157.pdf (accessed April 5, 2008).

Tourism on-line (October 2007) http://www.corporate.canada.travel/corp/media/ app/en/ca/magazine/showSubmitArticle.do (accessed October 12, 2007).

Veal, A. (1997) *Research methods for leisure and tourism: A practical guide* (2nd Edn.) London: Pitman Publishing, 1997.

The Importance of Developing Networks in the Leisure Industry: Attitudes to Competition along Australia's Murray River

Clare Lade

School of Sport, Tourism and Hospitality Management,
La Trobe University, Australia

Introduction

This research examines the importance and the opportunity for network development within the leisure industry of four regional centres located along Australia's Murray River. Cluster theory serves as the broad theoretical orientation, with the attitudes towards competitive behaviour and the receptiveness to network development examined. While cluster theory has primarily been applied in the manufacturing industry in the past, its use in the leisure industry is relatively new. Great opportunity exists for co–operation and networking relationships to be developed in the leisure industry due to its heterogeneous nature. The results of this research may be used to facilitate future initiatives to promote development within leisure and tourism related industries.

Background to the research: Competitive business theory

Role of competitive advantage in achieving industry success

As a progression from the theory of comparative advantage, researchers have turned to alternate approaches to achieving industry success through competitive advantage. While comparative advantage relates to resources available to a region, competitive advantages concern the ability for a region to effectively manage and use these resources more over the long term (Ritchie and Crouch, 2003).

A region's competitive advantage is determined by its skills and resources, use of technology, branding and strategic management. How well a region copes with its competitors in order to reduce costs and increase differentiation will determine how effective is the utilisation of these skills

(Porter, 1990). Achieving a competitive advantage involves creating and maintaining a favourable position of competitiveness relative to those of existing and potential competitors and may be considered an absolute concept, regarded as looking within an industry (Poon, 1993; Porter, 1985, 1990; Rosentraub and Przybylski, 1996).

Porter's theory of competitive advantage

Porter (1990) further developed the theory of competitive advantage with his 'diamond' model. Porter (1990) believes each industry differs substantially and, consequently, so too will the nature of competition and sources of advantage. In a regional context, firms within a region must recognise their capabilities and select accordingly the most appropriate industries to compete in, bearing in mind that different industries require differing sources of advantage and a single industry should not be solely relied upon.

Competition is vital to the success or failure of a region, with Porter (1990) devising four broad determinants of competitive advantage — factor conditions; demand conditions; related and supporting industries; and firm strategy, structure and domestic rivalry — influencing the external environment to which a region will or will not benefit. These determinants may be regarded as the forces that provide a region with motivation, capabilities and pressures that encourage innovation and creative initiatives (Crocombe *et al.*, 1991). In addition, two variables of government and chance may also influence the development of competitive advantage.

Competitiveness at a regional and destination level

Porter (1990) discusses competitive advantage at a firm level relating to the manufacturing industry however, much confusion still exists "as to what the concept (of competitiveness at a regional or destination level) actually means and how it can be effectively operationalised..." (Bristow, 2005: p. 286).

A number of difficulties arise in discussion of regional and destination competitiveness. Firstly, problems exist with transferring a concept traditionally used to describe firm performance to a regional or destination scale. Firm competitiveness relates to two principle sources; economics and business community. In economic terms, the market is the ultimate decider of appropriate behaviour in the economy and "competitiveness simply describes the result of responding correctly to market signals" (Schoenberger, 1998: p. 3). In other words, competitiveness may be considered as survival of the fittest, driven by profit maximisation. Business community represents 'external validation of a firm's ability to survive, compete and grow in markets subject to international competition' (Bristow, 2005: p. 287) and so therefore used to explain firm behaviour. Ultimately a firm must perform in a certain manner in order to be competitive (Schoenberger, 1998) and as a result, there is a clear meaning of competitiveness at firm level, relating to the ability 'to compete, grow and be profitable in the marketplace' (Bristow, 2005: p. 287).

Porter (1985; 1990) believes firm competitiveness is a proxy for productivity with competitiveness and productivity described as equivalent terms — competitiveness is productivity. Porter (1985; 1998) has extended his theory of firm competitiveness to regions, nations and locations in general, relating to the level of productivity with which human capital and natural resources are used. It is Porter's (1985; 1998) belief that places are equivalent to corporations, competing for market share in a competitive global economy and acknowledges a clear connection exists between productivity and regional living standards, with productivity having a major influence on the cost of living, cost of doing business and the level of wages in the region. Porter does however fall short of asserting that regional competitiveness and regional prosperity are equivalent notions.

Storper (1997: p. 264) defines regional competitiveness as "the capability of a region to attract and keep firms with stable or increasing market share in an activity, while maintaining stable of increasing standards of living for those who participate in it". Although this definition is related to the global competitiveness perspective, emphasis is placed on that it asserts that regional competitiveness and regional prosperity are interdependent upon one another if not directly equivalent notions, which Porter (1985; 1990) falls short of suggesting. This definition deliberately avoids equating regional competitiveness with productivity and has gained widespread acceptance and use amongst new regionalists (Huggins, 2003; Malecki, 2002; Maskell and Malmberg, 1999). Porter's (1990) general determinants applied to firm competitiveness are suggested as a 'one size fits all' approach without adequate empirical research to substantiate it (Deas and Giordano, 2001). As Reinert (1995) outlines, microeconomic productivity is considered necessary but not sufficient on its own for financial returns, increased market share or overall improved macroeconomic performance. Regional competitiveness involves possessing the conditions to enable the region to sustain winning outcomes. These conditions include a combination of the degree of human capital employed, along with the Porterian theory of competitive advantage for firms and attractiveness of the regional business environment. Ritchie and Crouch (2003) within their model consider the need for resources to be effectively deployed in order for a destination to successfully remain competitive and sustainable.

Role of co–operation

There has been debate around the comparative value of both co–operative and competitive behaviour in contributing to successful regional cluster development as a competitive strategy (Enright, 1996). Much attention (Enright, 1990; Scott, 1992;) in relation to the importance of co–operation, appears to be placed upon the consequences resulting from unco–ordinated behaviour of decentralised competitors. Conversely, Porter (1990) places greater weight on the need for competitiveness in order to stimulate innovation and production within the international markets. His viewpoint, along with that of Lazonick (1993), acknowledges the role of co–operation, however emphasises the role of strong rivalry within the formation of business cluster networks.

Although as noted by Scherer (1991) and also demonstrated by the textile-apparel production channel in both the US and Great Britain, competition by itself is no assurance of successful performance. Processes in the US case were delayed as part result of competitive rivalries among firms in the channel, while in Great Britain inconsistent formation of high performance collaborations within the production channel caused similar outcomes (Doeringer and Terkla, 1996).

Opportunity exists in the tourism and leisure industries for firms of different sectors to work in co–operation with one another. The opportunity exists due to the heterogeneous nature of the industry consisting of many related and supporting sectors such as accommodation, food and beverage, attractions and transport. If these various sectors participated in co–operative behaviour, the delivery of the leisure product to the consumer may be achieved more efficiently. Co–operation between firms within the same sector of the leisure industry may be facilitated through product differentiation.

Enright (1996) believes the question is not whether firms should co–operate or compete with one another, but rather on what dimensions they should co–operate and what dimensions they should compete on. The optimal mix of the two varies greatly, depending upon the industry and region therefore, "we need to develop an understanding of what types of competitive or co–operative behaviour are feasible and desirable under differing circum-stances" (Enright, 1996: p. 200).

Attitudes to competition

Competitiveness may be considered to encompass a combination of both competitive and co–operative elements and requires careful judgement of the dimensions to which regions should co–operate or compete on (Enright, 1996). In order to gain a competitive advantage more emphasis needs to be placed on innovation, differentiation and specialisation, rather than prior concentration on imitation and cost cutting measures (Jacobs and de Man, 1996).

A region that displays a shared understanding of competitive behaviour is one that is more likely to increase its competitive advantage in the long term (Porter, 1990). Indicators of a shared understanding of competitive behaviour by local businesses may include: incorporating measures to improve productivity; innovative product development; building relationships with local suppliers; participating in local tourism organisations involved in selling the destination; clearly differentiating products from other similar products; and working co–operatively with other similar businesses in the region. Measures such as reducing prices, imitating other successful businesses, increasing advertising expenditure and receiving government subsidies may be regarded as only a short term approach to raising overall competitiveness.

Business clusters

Increasing competitiveness through business clusters

For the purpose of the research, clusters are defined as "geographic concentrations of interconnected companies, specialised suppliers, service providers, firms in related industries, and associated institutions in particular fields that compete, but also co–operate" (Porter, 1998, pp. 197–198). Business clusters may be considered in conjunction with Porter's theory of competitive advantage and, by operating efficiently, will stimulate new business formation, increase productivity and allow room for innovation (Doeringer and Terkla, 1996). As Bordas (1994: p. 4) notes, the success of a cluster nowadays is less dependent "on its comparative advantages and more on its competitive ones".

Limited research has been published on clustering in Australia (Enright and Roberts, 2001), however knowledge about cluster theory has advanced on the world scale, particularly with publication of Porter's (1990) *The Competitive Advantage of Nations*, generating numerous cluster formation initiatives. Recent attempts to foster industry cluster growth in Australia has been regionally motivated with one belief that cluster development processes can assist in achieving positive economic outcomes and develop new industries for regions (Enright and Roberts, 2001). Business clustering may be regarded as a means of stimulating local businesses to contribute substantially to their own development, without reliance on government support (Jackson, 2006).

Both Porter (1990) and Waits (2000) maintain regional clusters of related industries, particularly within the advanced economies of today, contribute greatly to growth of employment opportunities, export and income. More emphasis, according to Jacobs and de Man (1996), is placed on innovation, differentiation and specialisation within cluster development, rather than previous concentration on imitation and cost cutting in order to gain a competitive advantage. In addition, researchers Doeringer and Terkla (1996) and Gordan and McCann (2000) believe co–operation between industry players is a vital factor influencing effective cluster performance.

Applications of cluster development in the tourism and leisure industry

Although as acknowledged previously limited research into the role of clustering and network development within the leisure industry exits, Hall *et al.* (1997) refer to network development more specifically within the wine industry. Although many regional wineries do not recognise themselves as operating completely in a tourism or leisure sense, their activities do appear to have some tourism and leisure focus. Hall and Macionis (1998) observed within their research, that many smaller winemakers often perceive tourism related leisure activities as undesirable, due to the visitor's tendency to taste the wines and engage in winery tours without any interest in purchasing the wine product. However evidence of wine and tourism related leisure activities network-like characteristics exist in regional South Australia, with the Barossa Valley having developed 'proactive wine tourism initiatives by regional wine industry associations, such as the Barossa Wine and Tourism Association' (Hall *et al.*, 1997: p. 15). Co–operation is required between local business operators, wineries, and tourism and accommodation oper-ators. Each of the case regions demonstrates to some extent the presence of a local wine region. The Rutherglen and Mildura wine regions may be considered more distinct than those in the Echuca and Swan Hill regions, with gourmet food and produce accompanying the wine product.

Hall (2004) further considers the link of clusters and network develop-ment within the rural wine and food sectors in New Zealand. Inter-sectoral linkages and network development must be encouraged to promote new product and service innovations that may assist in regional competitive advantage and resilience. Hall (2004) emphasises the importance for effective communicative relationships between these industries and the need for a champion and institutions to be recognised. Long term commitment to cluster and network development by these champions may assist in delivering mutual benefits to both industries concerned.

Jackson and Murphy (2002) discuss how Porter's (1998) cluster concept may build on the antecedent industrial district model to produce a paradigm in which tourist destinations may be studied further. Dimensions taken from Porter's cluster research have been applied to tourism destinations in both Australia and Canada within their research. Victoria, Canada demonstrated up until 1985 "tourism development along traditional industrial lines" (p. 50), however after the creation of Tourism Victoria (in Canada) a more management and co–operative development and marketing approach was adopted. Research was also undertaken in Albury Wodonga, Australia and the results indicated that this region may be regarded as a promising cluster. Certain dimensions that already exist within this region, however require further development in order to be fully activated.

Konsolas (2002) explores the degree to which Porter's elements of competitive advantage are present in relation to the Greek tourism industry. Although Greece is fortunate to possess a number of advantageous conditions, it has experienced very slow tourism growth in the past. Evidence suggests that the tourism industry has incorporated to an extent, facets of its other major industries however potential to develop other industries, particularly those offering services, does still exist. Cluster development incorporating related services and industries may be a means of raising its competitive advantage and thus, contributing to substantial growth of the industry.

Michael (2002) explores the role of clustering retailing activities, including antiques, memorabilia and collectables, in generating regional economic development. His research suggests that the antique trade exhibits characteristics that may be described in similar terms to tourism activity. The antique trade has the ability to attract visitation or add further value to existing destinations and generate economic benefits in the same way that tourism does. Often these antiquing related activities are located in similar areas and examples are given of where 'clusters' of antique and oldwares traders exist in regional areas, such as Chiltern and Malden in Victoria, Australia. Clusters of these activities and other niche markets may be considered a trip generator in which demand for a number of other visitor related services will be created, including travel, accommodation and the food and beverage sectors.

Further research by Michael (2003; 2006) explores the principles of micro–market clustering based on tourism, concentrating not only on the economic but social benefits associated with the clustering concept. Michael (2003) reiterates that clustering does not necessary offer an automatic solution for regional development, in terms of increasing competitive advantage, but instead may deliver considerable benefits and create opportunity for local growth "where particular market conditions favour cluster formation" (p. 134). Clusters may be considered a more effective influence on growth in regional areas through increasing the demand for travel and capitalising on this demand for further growth of complementary industries. Michael (2003) identifies three distinct forms of cluster formation including horizontal, vertical and diagonal clustering. Although each form separately is expected to improve market benefits to those participating, as a form of economic co–location, greater emphasis is placed on the overall structure of the cluster. Greater synthesis between organisations is likely to "enhance production synergies and increase the collective market size" (p. 138). This form of co–operative behaviour provides destinations with new opportunities to expand, while reducing costs and enabling regional clusters to compete more efficiently with other tourism destinations (Michael, 2006).

Business cluster characteristics

Key factors characteristic of a 'successful' cluster may be recognised in accordance with the following characteristics identified by Porter (1998): 1) interdependence of firms; 2) flexible firm boundaries; 3) co–operative competition; 4) trust in sustained collaboration; 5) community culture and supportive public policies; 6) shared understanding of competitive business ethic; 7) private sector leadership; 8) wide involvement of cluster participants; 9) appropriate cluster boundaries; 10) institutionalisation of relationships;

11) social structure and attention to personal relationships; and 12) life cycles (Jackson and Murphy, 2006: p. 38). The degree to which the four regional centres of Mildura, Swan Hill, Echuca and Albury Wodonga, all located on the Murray River, demonstrate these characteristics will be determined and regarded as one with highly significant clustering and networking potential. Absence of particular characteristics may be considered barriers to successful cluster and co–operative development.

The four cases

Albury Wodonga

The regional centre of Albury Wodonga is surrounded by a diversity of landscape, attractions, activities and heritage townships. The Murray River, mountains, Lake Hume, wineries and historical towns provide the region with a wide range of activities to satisfy both its visitors and local community. Lake Hume attracts various water sports and fishing enthusiasts, while the nearby mountains provide skiing in the winter and bushwalking and hiking activities in the warmer months of the year.

With a surrounding population of just over 100,000 people, Albury Wodonga experiences a climate marked by hot dry summers, mild autumns and springs and cool, wet winters. Major industry sectors of the regional centre include food processing, broad acre agriculture, specialist horticulture, engineering, textile, manufacturing, computer technology, education and tourism (Albury Wodonga Strategic Plan, 2004). Emerging industries of the regional centre thought to possess high potential include aquaculture and forestry.

Located on the Hume Highway, 300km north-east of Melbourne, 563 km south-west of Sydney and 360km south of Canberra along the main transport and communication corridor, Albury Wodonga is easily accessible by car, rail, coach and air services. Infrastructure within the region includes sporting facilities, garden and parkland and a variety of accommodation and conference facilities. Opportunity exists for this regional centre to further develop linkages and inter-firm relationships as well as strong and focussed leadership and river based industry co–operation in order to increase the value of its natural advantages.

Echuca

Echuca is located approximately 206 kilometres north west of Melbourne and with nearby Moama, is located on the border between Victoria and New South Wales. The regional centre has a population of approximately 12,000. Once home to the largest port in Australia, Echuca is now home to the largest collection of paddlesteamers. Completely restored paddle-steamers provide tourists with daily river cruises highlighting the history of the Murray River and the region. The local indigenous culture is considered a valuable natural advantage, with the Yorta Yorta people still today exhibiting their culture within the surrounding region.

A warm climate, similar to that of Southern Europe, is characteristic of Echuca with major industries of the regional centre including fine wine and food produce, dairying, tourism, forestry, beef, wool, grain, fruit, vegetables, horticulture and agriculture. A wide range of eating establishments, line the port of Echuca, ranging from restaurants to less formal cafes. Educational institutes in the regional centre consist of two secondary and primary schools, a catholic secondary and primary school, an Aboriginal learning centre and an adult education centre.

Echuca as a riverside regional centre experiences a variety of natural advantages in association with its location and by further exploring river-based initiatives and strategies these factor endowments may be further enhanced in the future.

Swan Hill

Swan Hill is located in Victoria's northwest 217km from Mildura and 340km from Melbourne. Swan Hill has a warm climate similar to that of the Mediterranean and has currently a population of 9,357 people, also servicing a further 40,000 people within the surrounding region. Swan Hill combines its own history with a range of modern facilities, while the River services irrigation districts extending into the Mallee region. Agriculture is the major supporting industry of the region with horticulture in recent years rapidly growing in popularity.

Swan Hill is regarded as a major market centre of New South Wales Riverina district however, production in both wine grapes/cultured table grapes, wheat, wool, dairy products, maize, fodder crops, fat stock, market store fruit, nuts and vegetables is apparent as a result of irrigation. The focus of local manufacturing is primarily on farm machinery. Major attractions of the region include the Burke and Wills tree, the Giant Murray Cod, Murray Downs, Hilltop Resort Fauna Park, Tyntynder Homestead, the Pheasant Farm and Lake Boga.Lake Boga, located south of Swan Hill, offers a range of water sports, including fishing, boating, swimming, sailing and water skiing, while the city itself offers a range of sporting and recreation venues.

Mildura

The regional centre of Mildura is located in the north west of Victoria and adjoining the far south west of New South Wales, making it accessible to major capital cities of Adelaide, Melbourne, Canberra and Sydney. The Mildura City Council encompasses an area of 22,330 square kilometres with a population of approximately 45,000 people (Sunraysia Area Consultative Committee, 2001). Mildura and region experiences a reasonably warm climate.

Grapes, wine, vegetables, citrus, food processing, wheat, sheep, beef production, tourism, education, health and welfare services are the region's current major industries. Technology and mineral sands mining are amongst new and emerging industries of the region.

Regional infrastructure includes the Murray and Darling Rivers, Northern Mallee Pipeline, natural gas, the interstate road linkages and rail links to major ports, all of which add value to the Sunraysia region. The Murray River is highly significant to the development of Mildura, particularly as a source of irrigation. 12.1% of the population are of indigenous background and a variety of programs are underway in association with the indigenous community, both promoting the culture and developing employment opportunities (Sunraysia Area Consultative Committee, 2001).

The education system employs a large proportion of the Sunraysia region's population with a variety of positions in the local university, TAFE institute and primary and secondary schools. Numerous opportunities also exist to further enhance the skills of the regional centre's workforce with a diversity of options available including flexible apprenticeship schemes, on the job training programs and distance education (Sunraysia Area Consultative Committee, 2001).

Although Mildura possesses a number of natural advantages, opportunities still exist to further exploit these natural advantages in order to attract tourism, increase general employment opportunities and gain additional economic benefits.

Methodology

The four regions were selected and used as the basis for investigation into the attitudes towards competition and the receptiveness to cluster development in order to increase competitive advantage along Australia's Murray River. These cases were expected to represent contrasting results with respect to the degree of industry success and competitiveness. For the purposes of this research a case study method was adopted and within this framework questionnaire surveys were distributed to between 85 and 100 tourism related businesses of each case region and in-depth interviews were also conducted with principal representatives of the relevant tourism and development organisations.

Quantitative data from the questionnaire surveys was subjected to non-parametric analysis procedures to test for differences between the multiple groups. Non-parametric tests make no assumptions about the parameters (such as the mean and variance) of a distribution, nor do they assume that any particular distribution is being used. Interview protocols were based on preliminary analysis of the questionnaire survey responses, along with cluster success factors identified in the literature and attributes of the competitive advantage concept as it applies to the development of regional locations.

Results

For the purpose of the research the level of competitiveness of each regional centre may be determined through consideration of both tourism expenditure and overnight visitation along with the presence of Porter's (1990) broad determinants of competitive advantage.

Tourism contribution to regional economic development along the Murray River

Tourist overnight visitation varied between each of the case regions between the years 2000 and 2005. In 2005 the total overnight visitation to the Murray East region (encompassing Albury Wodonga) was 9,984, the Central Murray region (encompassing Echuca) 13,251 and Murray West region (encompassing Swan Hill and Mildura) was 22,224 (Tourism Research Australia, 2005).

In 2003 the total overnight visitor expenditure in each of the four case regions varied with the Murray East region (encompassing Albury Wodonga) being $115 million. The Central Murray region (encompassing Echuca) $200 million and Murray West region (encompassing Swan Hill and Mildura) was $218 million (Bailey *et al.*, 2004). Using estimated expenditure by over-night visitors per capita of local population as a basic indicator of performance, the result for Echuca was $16,000, for Albury Wodonga $1,182 and combined Swan Hill and Mildura $3,872. The Echuca region attracts far greater total visitor expenditure per capita then the other three river towns. As a result, Echuca may be considered to be relatively more successful, in terms of tourist expenditure and visitation, than Swan Hill, Mildura and the Albury Wodonga region.

Competitive advantage in the four regions

In summary of the case region's competitive advantages, Echuca demon-strates a strong presence of each of Porter's (1990) determinants, with a tendency to display more man-made factor conditions than natural advan-tages. It is difficult to separately establish the degree of competitive advantage of both the Mildura and Swan Hill regions, due to being unable to disaggregate their tourism expenditure and tourist overnight visitation from the data provided for the Murray West region, which incorporates both of these regions.

However, Mildura demonstrates a high presence of man-made advan-tages, demand conditions, related and supporting industries and has a high regard for incorporating natural advantages into regional strategies. Considerable government support is received by the Mildura region, however the opportunity exists to increase support from the New South Wales state.

Swan Hill also demonstrates considerable government support for its development, however in comparison to the Mildura region has a lower presence of man-made advantages, demand conditions and related and supporting industries.

Overall in comparison to the other three regional centres, the Albury Wodonga region has a lower presence of Porter's (1990) determinants except in relation to factor conditions, where the region is inclined to display a greater range of man-made advantages.

Attitude to competition

Having a shared appropriate understanding of competitive behaviour displayed by the local business community may assist overall regional competitive development. Porter (1990) considers that business practices concentrating on product (or service) differentiation and innovation rather than cost cutting and imitation, will assist in increasing the overall competitive advantage of the region. Furthermore, increasing co-operation and improving relationships between local industries is inclined to increase competitive advantage.

Overall, the majority of respondents from each of the case regions indicated that they were prepared to work in co-operation with other businesses of the industry and recognise the importance of using innovation in order to differentiate their products or services, rather than relying on price based competition and imitation as strategies to improve their competitive position.

A comparison of the Albury Wodonga region with the other three case regions was performed, due to the substantial difference in Albury Wodonga's earnings from tourism. Interestingly enough, the results indicated that the Albury Wodonga region have a stronger regard for the use of product/service innovation, differentiation strategies and reduction of taxes and regulations and less consideration for imitation of successful businesses for increasing competitive advantage. According to these results, the Albury Wodonga region satisfies Porter's (1990) competitive behaviour in relation to competitive attitudes, which suggests that other underlying factors may have an influence on the successful development of this region in relation to tourism.

Characteristics used as a measure of the attitudes towards competition by those respondents from each case region are displayed in **Table 1**. The Albury Wodonga region demonstrates the most appropriate attitudes towards competition, followed by Echuca, with Swan Hill and Mildura considered to display less appropriate attitudes towards competition in comparison.

Table 1   Comparison of Attitudes to Competition Between the Regional Centres [Mean, Standard Deviation]

ATTITUDE TO COMPETITION	Mildura	Swan Hill	Echuca	Albury Wodonga	TOTAL
Improving productivity (more efficient use of resources)	3.8 (1.9)	4.8 (1.9)	4.5 (2.2)	4.8 (2.3)	**4.46 (2.1)**
Reducing prices	2.7 (1.8)	2.5 (1.8)	2.3 (1.4)	2.3 (1.7)	**2.45 (1.7)**
Imitating other successful businesses	3.3 (1.6)	3.6 (1.9)	3.0 (1.5)	2.7 (1.9)	**3.14 (1.7)**
Reducing production costs such as wages	3.9 (1.9)	4.0 (2.3)	3.6 (2.0)	4.4 (2.3)	**3.96 (2.1)**
Reduced taxes	4.5 (1.6)	4.9 (2.5)	5.2 (2.0)	5.7 (2.0)	**5.05 (2.0)**
Innovations in my product	5.0 (1.9)	5.0 (2.1)	5.4 (1.4)	6.3 (1.1)	**5.44 (1.7)**
Receiving government subsidies	3.5 (2.1)	3.7 (2.2)	4.1 (1.9)	4.0 (2.8)	**3.83 (2.3)**
Participating in local tourism organisations involved in selling the destination	5.5 (1.4)	4.8 (1.7)	5.6 (1.7)	5.4 (2.2)	**5.33 (1.8)**
Building relationships with local suppliers	5.0 (1.7)	4.7 (1.7)	5.2 (1.5)	5.4 (2.0)	**5.06 (1.7)**
Clearly differentiating my product from other similar products	5.5 (1.6)	5.6 (1.6)	5.4 (1.9)	6.1 (1.4)	**5.65 (1.6)**
Reduced government regulation in relation to taxes	4.3 (1.8)	3.9 (2.8)	4.8 (2.4)	5.5 (1.9)	**4.65 (2.3)**
Increasing my advertising expenditure	3.7 (1.5)	4.1 (1.8)	4.3 (1.9)	4.1 (2.1)	**4.03 (1.8)**
Working cooperatively with other similar businesses	4.9 (1.6)	4.7 (1.1)	5.1 (1.6)	5.2 (2.1)	**4.99 (1.7)**
Working cooperatively with other local businesses in the tourism industry	5.3 (1.3)	5.1 (1.8)	6.0 (1.2)	5.6 (1.8)	**5.5 (1.5)**

Presence of co-operation

The interdependence of firms, co-operative competition, trust in sustained collaboration, wide involvement of cluster participants, institutionalisation of relationships and social structure and attention to personal relationships have all been outlined by Porter (1998) as key characteristics of successful cluster development. These were all considered in association with the presence of co-operation in each of the case regions.

Various viewpoints regarding the role of co-operation in the development of regional competitive advantage exist. Some researchers (Enright, 1990; Scott, 1992) have placed greater emphasis upon the consequences resulting from unco-ordinated behaviour of decentralised competitors, while others (Lazonick, 1993; Porter, 1990) place greater importance on the need for competitiveness in order to stimulate innovation and production within the international markets. Enright (1996) suggests rather than considering both competition and co-operation as mutually exclusive factors in competitive development, consideration should be given to the dimensions on which a region should co-operate.

Results suggest a high level of co-operation exists within the Echuca region. The strong presence of related and supporting industries in the region, along with the ability for these to work together in order to assist in raising the competitive advantage of the entire region is evident. The strong leadership existing within the region may assist in the efficient co-ordination of related activities and communication of the benefits associated with working co-operatively, leading to an overall increase in co-operation between related industries of the region and their competitiveness.

There are fewer tendencies for related and supporting industries in the Albury Wodonga region to work co-operatively together. The lack of a cohesive tourism structure, teamed with an absence of strong local leadership has resulted in a lack of co-ordination of activities and subsequently less co-operation among related industry players to this point in time.

This evidence suggests that strong leadership is required in order to organise and provide co-ordination of activities to those related and supporting industries present within the region in order to encourage co-operation. Although some industries may work together naturally, it appears sound leadership increases the likelihood of co-operation occurring between related and supporting industries within the region.

Characteristics considered to be associated with the presence of co-operation within each of the regional centres are displayed in **Table 2**. The degree of presence has been ranked in accordance with the respondents' mean responses from the questionnaire survey. The Echuca region demonstrates the highest degree of presence overall, followed by the Mildura, Swan Hill and Albury Wodonga displaying the lowest presence of co-operation in comparison.

Table 2   **comparison of co-operation characteristics between the regional centres [mean, standard deviation]**

CO-OPERATION CHARACTERISTICS	Mildura	Swan Hill	Echuca	Albury Wodonga
Related/supporting industries are present within the region	3	4	1	2
Local tourism related industries often work together to raise competitive advantage of the region	2	3	1	4
Common technologies are often shared by industries of the region	1	3	2	4
Local industries of the region where possible share common resources and distribution channels	3	4	1	2
Supporting industries supply complementary products to assist production and distribution	1	4	2	3
Where possible I take the opportunity to work co-op with other local tourism related businesses to sell the destination first	2	3	1	4
I think that there is potential to increase linkages with other tourism related businesses in this region	1	4	2	3
The local industry needs help to develop and maintain linkages with other related tourism businesses	1	3	4	2
TOTAL RANKING	**2**	**3**	**1**	**4**

Presence of cluster characteristics

Each of the four case regions may be identified in accordance with the presence of those pre-conditions associated with cluster development. **Table 3** displays the degree to which each region conforms to the outlined cluster characteristics and hence, the potential for co–operative cluster development.

Echuca

Key factors characteristic of a 'successful' cluster may be recognised in accordance with the characteristics identified by Porter (1998). Currently there is a tourism related cluster operating within the Echuca regional centre, incorporating the port precinct and other attractions, the accommodation

Table 3   Presence of Successful Cluster Characteristics

+ indicates presence of characteristic
− indicates requires further development of characteristic

CLUSTER CHARACTERISTICS	Mildura	Swan Hill	Echuca	Albury Wodonga
Interdependence of firms	+	+	+	+
Flexible firm boundaries	+	+	+	+
Co-operative competition	+	+	+	+
Trust in sustained collaboration	+	+	+	+
Community culture and supportive public policies	+	+	+	+
Shared understanding of competitive business ethic	+	+	+	−
Private sector leadership	+	+	+	+
Wide involvement of cluster participants	+	+	+	+
Appropriate cluster boundaries	+	+	+	−
Institutionalisation of relationships	+	+	+	−
Social structure and attention to personal relationships	+	−	+	−
Life cycles	−	−	−	−

sector and food and wine related industries. Echuca Moama tourism is largely responsible for co–ordinating the cluster and organising these and other industry groups, particularly in relation to promotional initiatives and bulk marketing. The primary aim of Echuca Moama Tourism in relation to this co–ordinated approach to development is to place an emphasis on selling Echuca as a destination experience and using this co–operation between relevant sectors in order to deliver a quality visitor experience. The success of the region in relation to tourism expenditure and overnight visitation indicates that the presence of this tourism cluster, emphasising local co–operation between related industries in order to sell the destination as one, does contribute to successful tourism and related leisure development and in turn to raising the overall competitive advantage of the region.

Mildura

Within the Mildura region a greater emphasis was placed on the less formal establishment of tourism related clusters. Evidence suggests that the clustering concept is likely to be happening naturally within the region without any formal structural developments. These naturally occurring clusters are thought to be operating within the wine industry, accommodation and attractions sectors. The main benefits with working in co–operation with other similar businesses, in relation to information sourcing and reducing costs, are that similar benefits associated with formal cluster development may be achieved. The problem often associated with informal clusters is that they usually depend upon one or two energetic people or leaders and once those people leave, the cluster is likely to disintegrate as a result. Therefore, the role for formally supporting cluster development including funding, researching and educating is necessary.

It appears that cluster development is occurring more formally within the horticulture and agricultural industries. However with evidence of naturally occurring cluster development within a range of sectors constituting the tourism industry, huge potential exists for formal cluster development to occur within this area which draws together the various sectors of the tourism industry. Similar characteristics are associated with naturally occurring clusters as with formally developed clusters including co–operation and local leadership and therefore these may just require a formal structure and leadership to be developed in order to provide more substantial benefits to the region.

Swan Hill

While levels of co–operation exist separately between accommodation, cultural activities, attractions, a tourism and hospitality group, Murray River Golf cluster and the viticulture sectors in Swan Hill, further assistance is required in order to formally develop these individual tourism related sectors into the one tourism cluster. By combining these individual smaller 'clusters' and developing one large formal tourism cluster of the region, the potential benefits associated with the clustering concept may be fully achieved.

Albury Wodonga

Naturally occurring clusters appear to exist within the Albury Wodonga region however the development of more formal clusters is considered to be still within the early development phase. Co–operation exists in the accommodation sector with a Moteliers Associated formed, however potential exists to further develop this as part of a formal tourism cluster of the region incorporating the transport, attractions and food and wine sectors. In order for this to be achieved, though, willingness from all sectors needs to be established and a correct structure with appropriate leadership provided to co–ordinate the various activities. Difficulties have existed in the past in relation to structure and leadership and are areas that must be addressed if the region is to develop to its full tourism potential.

Presence of tourism clusters and economic benefits relationship

The results imply that those regions which have fully adopted the clustering concept are inclined to be more successful in terms of tourism expenditure and overnight tourist visitation.

Echuca is the only region that demonstrates a formal tourism cluster functioning as such, and, in terms of visitor expenditure and overnight visitation, the region may be regarded a success. While the other three river-based centres demonstrate some degree of cluster development in tourism related sectors, a more formal structure needs to be developed to incorporate these individual sectors. Realisation of this need, along with correct guidance and support, may result in the other three regional centres receiving the economic benefits that the Echuca region has come to achieve in the leisure industry.

Barriers to co–operative cluster development

The major barriers or obstacles preventing the potential development of successful clusters within the four case regions were identified within each of the case regions. The diagram below outlines the identified barriers in association with those characteristics of successful cluster development in **Table 4**.

Table 4   Barriers to Successful Cluster Development

CLUSTER CHARACTERISTICS	BARRIERS TO CLUSTER DEVELOPMENT
Interdependence of firms	
Flexible firm boundaries	
Co-operative competition	Reluctance to share knowledge and information
Trust in sustained collaboration	Greed and self interest
Community culture and supportive public policies	Lack of trust and co-operation between local businesses
Shared understanding of competitive business ethic	Backward and close-minded thinking
Private sector leadership	Lack of organisation and leadership
Wide involvement of cluster participants	Lack of time, interest and expertise
Appropriate cluster boundaries	Border anomolies
Institutionalisation of relationships	Business diversity
Social structure and attention to personal relationships	
Life cycles	

Similar responses arose between the four regions, and these are outlined and summarised further below.

Reluctance to share knowledge and information   —

A reluctance to share delicate information and knowledge amongst similar businesses of the region was recognised as a prime obstacle to effective cluster development. The competitive elements such as fear of local business competition, business protection and intense personal competition all may contribute to this lack of information sharing and thus prevent any form of co–operation between regional businesses and industries from occurring. This greedy type of behaviour — too many people regarded as wanting 'all of the cake' rather than just one piece — suggests a lack of trust in sustained collaboration and possibly co–operative competition, two characteristics identified in association with successful cluster development.

Greed and self interest   —

A major identified obstacle to cluster development was that of greed and selfishness of local businesses within the region. Self interest and egotism were recognised as primary impediments, along with the perception of the threat of competition. Some businesses were identified as being inclined to work independently and for themselves only and not think of the region as a whole. The presence of greed, self interest and egotism may be considered in relation to a lack of trust in sustained collaboration or relationship which was outlined as a pre-condition for successful cluster development.

Lack of trust and co–operation between local businesses —

Identified by all case regions was a lack of trust and co–operation between similar businesses that have the potential to form industry clusters as a major barrier. Co–operation may be considered a vital factor in successful cluster development and without it such development is very unlikely to occur. Businesses need to recognise the benefits associated with working together and put a certain degree of trust in those relationships formed. This lack of trust also may be considered in relation to a lack of presence of one of the key pre-conditions set for successful cluster development.

Backward and close-minded thinking —

Small business myopia was considered a major barrier with the competitive attitudes of some groups also having a negative influence on cluster development. Lack of forward vision, teamed with past bad habits and ignorance of new business arrivals all prevent the benefits associated with successful cluster development from being achieved. Porter (1998) outlined having a shared understanding of competitive business ethic as a requirement for successful cluster development, this backward and close minded thinking demonstrates there is a lack of this characteristic within the regions.

Lack of organisation and leadership —

Businesses within the case regions acknowledged their interest in being a part of an operating cluster, however believe their region lacks the organisation and leadership required to make a success of it. Lack of support from the local government and council was identified as a main hurdle by respondents in regards to providing the necessary organisation and leadership. Outlined as one of the pre-conditions for successful cluster development, was private sector leadership. A lack of organisation and leadership suggests an absence of this requirement.

Lack of time, interest and expertise —

A lack of time was acknowledged as a major constraint to successful cluster development, along with also genuine interest and the expertise to co–ordinate cluster development. Without initial interest and correct guidance and expertise, many businesses lose sight of the potential value clustering may bring to their own business as well as the entire region. Many businesses identified that they were 'flat out' with operating their own business, leaving little or no time to participate in additional business related activities. Regions demonstrating these characteristics may be considered as lacking wide involvement of cluster participants, one of the necessary characteristics associated with successful cluster development.

Border anomalies —

Results indicate that border anomalies contribute to a fragmented tourism industry structure and subsequently, a lack of strong industry leadership. Differing government authorities may impede effective cluster development and contribute to the region exhibiting an overall lower competitive advantage. Appropriate cluster boundaries are characteristic of a successfully operating business cluster and its absence (poorly defined cluster boundaries) therefore may restrict successful development.

Business diversity —

The variations existing between the local businesses of the regions were deemed a barrier due to differing management goals and diverse business needs. Major difficulties were considered to arise particularly in the subjects of joint goal setting and conflicting business needs. Team-working skills also were regarded as lacking as a result of diverse business activities. Institutionalisation of relationships may encourage parallel goal setting by businesses with the welfare of the destination as a focus within the regions and reduce the diversity which appears to currently exist.

Established conservative business clusters —

Previous formation of conservative business clusters was also regarded as an impediment to potential successful cluster development within the case regions. Well established clusters incorporating small town favourites may exclude new business arrivals from joining and therefore limiting the effectiveness of the business cluster. Wide involvement of cluster participants is necessary for a cluster to develop successfully and thrive and without it, the cluster is likely to disintegrate. Barriers to entry are also considered characteristic of anti-competitive behaviour, thereby contributing to a breakdown of the shared understanding of competitive behaviour characteristic associated with successful cluster development.

The cluster development barriers perceived by respondents represent an absence of the pre-conditions outlined by Porter (1998), therefore providing support for Porter's (1998) theory of cluster development.

Conclusion

Through analysis of the local business community's attitudes towards competition along with their receptiveness to cluster development in the four case regions located on the Murray River, insight may be provided into how a region's competitive advantage may be increased.

Although it is important for local businesses to gain an understanding of the elements underlying competitive behaviour and have an appropriate attitude towards competition, the research indicated that additional factors are necessary in order to operationalise these attitudes. A presence of strong local leadership and the ability for related and supporting industries in the region to work together were deemed vital to contributing to competitive advantage. Strong leadership may assist in efficient co–ordination of related activities and communication of the benefits associated with working co–operatively, leading to an overall increase in co–operation between related industries of the region and their competitiveness.

With respect to the pre-conditions for business cluster development as a competitive strategy, there was some variation between the regions. Specifically the Albury Wodonga region lacks strong the local leadership, co–operation, defined tourism industry structure and well defined boundaries required for successful cluster and co–operative development. The region however held high regard for innovation within development and expressed appropriate attitudes to competition. Both the Echuca and Mildura regions demonstrate high levels of strong local leadership, well defined boundaries and industry structure and regard for innovation within development. Swan Hill also has a strong regard for innovation within development and co–operation. The regard for high innovation within development was recognised by all of the four regions which may suggest this factor needs also to be teamed with other characteristics in order for successful clustering behaviour to occur.

Clusters may be considered to affect competition by increasing produc-tivity of the region, increasing the capacity for innovation and stimulating formation of new businesses that supports innovation and expands the cluster (Porter, 1998). The results imply that those regions which have fully adopted the clustering concept are inclined to be more successful also in terms of tourism expenditure and overnight tourist visitation.

In addition to the characteristics considered to play a key role in successful cluster development, those considered to impede cluster development were also recognised. Business clustering may be considered a valuable tool to assist in raising the competitive advantage of a region and therefore contribute to overall regional economic development, providing the correct local leadership and co–operation between sectors constituting the industry exists.

References

Albury Wodonga Area Consultative Committee (2004) *The Strategic Regional Plan 2004–2007.*

Bordas, E. (1994) 'Competitiveness of tourist destinations in long distance markets', *The Tourist Review* Vol. 3: pp. 22–34.

Brent Ritchie, J.R., and Crouch, G. I. (2003) *The Competitive destination: A sustainable tourism perspective.* CABI Publishing, Wallingford.

Bristow, G. (2005) 'Everyone's a 'winner': Problematising the discourse of regional competitiveness', *Journal of Economic Geography*, No. 5. pp. 285–304.

Crocombe, G.T., Enright, M.J. and Porter, M.E. (1991) *Upgrading New Zealand's competitive advantage — The Porter Project on New Zealand.* Auckland, New Zealand: Oxford University Press.

Deas, I. and Giordano, B. (2001) 'Conceptualising and measuring urban competitiveness in major English cities: An exploratory approach', *Environment and Planning* No. 33: pp. 1411–1429.

Doeringer, B.and Terkla, D.G. (1996, 'Business strategy and cross industry clusters', *Economic Development Quarterly* Vol. 9, No. 3: pp. 225–237.

Enright, M. (1990) in Porter, M.E. (2000) 'Location, competition, and economic development: Local clusters in a global economy', *Economic Development Quarterly* Vol. 14, no. 1: pp. 15–34.

———— (1996) 'Regional clusters and economic development: A research agenda' in U. Staber, N. Schaefer and B. Sharma, de Gruyter *(eds) Business networks: Prospects for regional development.* Berlin, New York, pp. 190–213.

Enright, M. J. and Roberts, B. H. (2001) 'Regional clustering in Australia', *Australian Journal of Management* Vol. 26: pp. 66–85.

Gordon, I. and McCann, P. (2000) 'Industrial clusters: Complexes, agglomeration and/or social networks', *Urban Studies* Vol. 37: pp. 513–532.

Hall, CM. (2004) 'Rural wine and food tourism cluster and network development', in D. Hall, I. Kirpatrick and M. Mitchell (eds) *Rural tourism and sustainable business.* UK: Channel View Publications.

Hall, C.M., Cambourne, B., Macionis, N. and Johnson, G. (1997) 'Wine tourism and network development in Australia and New Zealand: Review, establishment and prospects', *International Journal of Wine Marketing* Vol. 9, No. 2/3: pp. 5–31.

Hall, C.M., and Macionis, N. (1998) 'Wine tourism in Australia and New Zealand', in R.W. Butler, C.M. Hall, and J. Jenkins (eds), *Tourism and recreation in rural areas*. Sydney: John Wiley and Sons, pp.197–224.

Huggins, R. (2003) 'Creating a UK competitiveness index: Regional and local benchmarking', Regional Studies No. 37: pp. 89–96.

Jackson, J. A. (2006) 'Developing regional tourism in China: The potential for activating business clusters in a socialist market economy', *Tourism Management* Vol. 27, No. 4: pp. 695–706.

Jackson, J. A., and Murphy, P.E. (2002) 'Tourism destinations as clusters: Analytical experiences from the New World', *Tourism and Hospitality Research Vol. 4*, No. 1: pp. 36–52.

—— (2006) 'Clusters in regional tourism development: An Australian case', *Annals of Tourism Research* Vol. 33, No. 4: pp. 1018–1035.

Jacobs, D. and de Man, A.P. (1996) 'Clusters, industrial policy and firm strategy: A menu approach', *Technology Analysis and Strategic Management* Vol. 8, No. 4: pp. 425–437.

Konosolas, I. (2002) *The competitive advantage of Greece: An application of Porter's diamond*. USA: Ashgate Publishing Company.

Lazonick, W. (1993) 'Industry clusters vs global webs: Organizational capabilities in the American economy', *Industrial and Corporate Change* Vol. 2: pp. 1–24.

Malecki, E. (2002) 'Hard and soft networks for urban competitiveness', *Urban Studies* No. 39: pp. 929–945.

Maskell, P. and Malmberg, A. (1999) 'Localised learning and industrial competitiveness', *Cambridge Journal of Economics* No. 23: pp. 167–185.

Michael, E.J. (2002) 'Antiques and tourism in Australia', *Tourism Management* Vol. 23, No. 2: pp. 117–125.

—— (2003) 'Tourism micro–clusters', *Tourism Economics* Vol. 9, No. 2: pp. 133–146.

—— (2006) *Public policy: The competitive rramework*. South Melbourne: Oxford University Press.

Poon, A. (1993) *Tourism, technology and competitive strategies*. Wallingford, UK: CAB International.

Porter, M.E. (1985) *Competitive advantage — creating and sustaining superior performance*. New York: The Free Press.

—— (1990) *The competitive advantage of nations*. London: The Macmillan Press Ltd.

—— (1998) *On competition*. Boston: Harvard Business Review Press,.

Reinert, E.S. (1995) 'Competitiveness and its predecessors — A 500 year cross national perspective', *Structural change and economic dynamics*, No. 6: pp. 23–42.

Rosentraub, M.S. and Przybylski, M. (1996) 'Competitive advantage, economic development, and the effective use of local public dollars', *Economic Development Quarterly* Vol. 10, No. 4: pp. 315–330.

Scherer, F.M. (1991) 'Research, development, and technological innovation,' in I. Yamazawa and A. Hirata (eds) *Industrial adjustment in developed countries and its implications for developing countries*. Tokyo: Institute of Developing Economics.

Schoenberger, E. (1998) 'Discourse and practice in human geography', *Progress in Human Geography* No. 22: pp. 1–14.

Scott, A.J. (1992) 'The Roepke lecture in economic geography. The collective order of flexible production agglomerations: Lessons for local economic development policy and strategic choice', *Economic Geography* Vol. 68, No. 3: pp. 219–233.

Storper, M. (1997) *The regional worl.* New York: Guilford Press.

Sunraysian Area Consultative Committee. (2001) *Strategic Regional Plan 2001–2004*, available http://www.sunraysiaacc.com.au/strategic_regional_plan.htm, [accessed September 9, 2002].

Tourism Research Australia (2005) October 2005 Forecasts, Tourism Forecasting Committee.

Waits, M.J. (2000) 'The added value of the industry cluster approach to economic analysis strategy development and service delivery', *Economic Development Quarterly* Vol. 14, No. 1: pp. 35–50.

Leisure Studies Association

LSA Publications

LSA

An extensive list of publications on a wide range of leisure studies topics, produced by the Leisure Studies Association since the late 1970s, is available from LSA Publications.

Some recently published volumes are detailed on the following pages, and full information may be obtained on newer and forthcoming LSA volumes from:

LSA Publications, c/o M. McFee
email: mcfee@solutions-inc.co.uk
The Chelsea School, University of Brighton
Eastbourne BN20 7SP (UK)

Among other benefits, members of the Leisure Studies Association may purchase LSA Publications at preferential rates. Please contact LSA at the above address for information regarding membership of the Association, LSA Conferences, and LSA Newsletters.

ONLINE

Complete information about LSA Publications:

www.leisure-studies-association.info/LSAWEB/Publications.html

WHATEVER HAPPENED TO THE LEISURE SOCIETY? THEORY, DEBATE AND POLICY

**LSA Publication No. 102.   ISBN 978 1 905369 13 3   [2008]
eds. Paul Gilchrist and Belinda Wheaton**

Contents

SPORT, LEISURE, CULTURE AND SOCIAL CAPITAL: DISCOURSE AND PRACTICE

LSA Publication No. 100.   ISBN 978 1 905369 11 9   [2007]
eds. Mike Collins, Kirsten Holmes, Alix Slater

Contents

MAKING SPACE: MANAGING RESOURCES FOR LEISURE AND TOURISM

LSA Publication No. 99.   ISBN 978 1 905369 10 2   [2007]
eds. Tim Gale, Jenny Hill and Nigel Curry

Contents

SOCIAL AND CULTURAL CHANGE: MAKING SPACE(S) FOR LEISURE AND TOURISM

**LSA Publication No. 98.   ISBN 978 1 905369 09 6   [2007]
eds. Maria Casado-Diaz, Sally Everett and Julie Wilson**

Contents

URBAN TRANSFORMATIONS: REGENERATION AND RENEWAL IN LEISURE AND TOURISM

LSA Publication No. 97.   ISBN 978 1 905369 00   [2007]
eds. Cara Aitchison, Greg Richards and Andrew Tallon

Contents

URBAN TRANSFORMATIONS: REGENERATION AND RENEWAL IN LEISURE AND TOURISM

**LSA Publication No. 96.   ISBN 978 1 905369 00   [2007]
eds. Cara Aitchison, Greg Richards and Andrew Tallon**

Contents

SERIOUS LEISURE: EXTENSIONS AND APPLICATIONS

LSA Publication No. 95.   ISBN 978 1 905369 006 5   [2006]
eds. Sam Elkington, Ian Jones and Lesley Lawrence

Contents

FESTIVALS AND EVENTS: CULTURE AND IDENTITY IN LEISURE, SPORT AND TOURISM

LSA Publication No. 94.   ISBN 978 1 905369 05 8 [2007]
eds. Cara Aitchison and Annette Pritchard

Contents

EVENTS AND FESTIVALS: EDUCATION, IMPACTS AND EXPERIENCES

LSA Publication No. 93. ISBN 978 1 905369 04 1 [2006] eds. Scott Fleming and Fiona Jordan

Contents

CASE STUDIES IN EVENT MARKETING AND CULTURAL TOURISM

LSA Publication No. 92. ISBN: 978 1 905369 03 4 [2006]
eds. Jane Ali-Knight and Donna Chambers

Contents

SPORTING EVENTS AND EVENT TOURISM: IMPACTS, PLANS AND OPPORTUNITIES

LSA Publication No. 91. ISBN 978 1 905369 02 7 [2006]
ed. Martin Robertson

Contents

ETHICAL ISSUES IN LEISURE RESEARCH

LSA Publication No. 90. ISBN 978 1 905369 01 0 [2006]
eds. Scott Fleming and Fiona Jordan

Contents

DEFINING THE FIELD: 30 YEARS OF THE LEISURE STUDIES ASSOCIATION

LSA Publication No. 89. ISBN 978 1 905369 00 3
eds. Eileen Kennedy and Helen Pussard

Contents

EVALUATING SPORT AND ACTIVE LEISURE FOR YOUNG PEOPLE

LSA Publication No. 88.   ISBN: 0 906337 99 2 [2005] pp. 236+xviii
eds. Kevyn Hylton, Anne Flintoff and Jonathan Long

Contents

YOUTH SPORT AND ACTIVE LEISURE: THEORY, POLICY AND PARTICIPATION

**LSA Publication No. 87. ISBN: 0 906337 98 4 [2005] pp. 185 + xii
eds. Anne Flintoff, Jonathan Long and Kevyn Hylton**

Contents

SPORT AND ACTIVE LEISURE YOUTH CULTURES

**LSA PUBLICATIONS NO. 86. ISBN: 0 906337 97 6 [2005] pp. 238 + xxii
eds. Jayne Caudwell and Peter Bramham**

Contents

LEISURE, SPACE AND VISUAL CULTURE: PRACTICES AND MEANINGS

LSA Publication No. 84. ISBN: 0 906337 95 X [2004] pp. 292+xxii
eds. Cara Aitchison and Helen Pussard

Contents

LEISURE, MEDIA AND VISUAL CULTURE: REPRESENTATIONS AND CONTESTATIONS

LSA Publication No. 83. ISBN: 0 906337 94 1 [2004] pp. 282
eds. Cara Aitchison and Helen Pussard

Contents

SPORT, LEISURE AND SOCIAL INCLUSION

**LSA Publication No. 82. ISBN: 0 906337 933 [2003] pp. 296
ed. Adrian Ibbetseon, Beccy Watson and Maggie Ferguson**

Contents

ACCESS AND INCLUSION IN LEISURE AND TOURISM

LSA Publication No. 81. ISBN: 0 906337 92 5 [2003] pp. 288
eds. Bob Snape, Edwin Thwaites, Christine Williams

Contents

VOLUNTEERS IN SPORT

**LSA Publication No. 80. ISBN: 0 906337 91 7 [2003] pp. 107
ed. Geoff Nichols**

Contents

LEISURE CULTURES: INVESTIGATIONS IN SPORT, MEDIA AND TECHNOLOGY

**LSA Publication No. 79. ISBN: 0 906337 90 9 [2003] pp. 221 + xii
eds. Scott Fleming and Ian Jones**

Contents

PARTNERSHIPS IN LEISURE: SPORT, TOURISM AND MANAGEMENT

**LSA Publication No. 78. ISBN: 0 906337 89 5 [2002] pp. 245 + iv
eds. Graham Berridge and Graham McFee**

Contents

LEISURE STUDIES:
TRENDS IN THEORY AND RESEARCH

**LSA Publication No. 77. ISBN: 0 906337 88 7 [2001] pp. 198 + iv
eds. Stan Parker and Lesley Lawrence**

Contents

SPORT TOURISM: PRINCIPLES AND PRACTICE

LSA Publication No. 76. ISBN: 0 906337 87 9 [2001] pp. 174 + xii
eds. Sean Gammin and Joseph Kurtzman

Contents

VOLUNTEERING IN LEISURE: MARGINAL OR INCLUSIVE?

LSA Publication No. 75. ISBN: 0 906337 86 0 [2001] pp. 158+xi eds. Margaret Graham and Malcolm Foley

Contents

LEISURE CULTURES, CONSUMPTION AND COMMODIFICATION

LSA Publication No. 74. ISBN: 0 906337 85 2 [2001] pp. 158+xi
ed. John Horne

Contents

LEISURE AND SOCIAL INCLUSION: NEW CHALLENGES FOR POLICY AND PROVISION

**LSA Publication No. 73. ISBN: 0 906337 84 4 [2001] pp. 204
eds. Gayle McPherson and Malcolm Reid**

Contents

JUST LEISURE:
EQUITY, SOCIAL EXCLUSION AND IDENTITY

LSA Publication No 72. ISBN: 0 906337 83 6 [2000] pp. 195+xiv
Edited by Celia Brackenridge, David Howe and Fiona Jordan

Contents

JUST LEISURE:
POLICY, ETHICS & PROFESSIONALISM

LSA Publication No 71. ISBN: 0 906337 81 X [2000] pp. 257+xiv
Edited by Celia Brackenridge, David Howe and Fiona Jordan

Contents

WOMEN'S LEISURE EXPERIENCES: AGES, STAGES AND ROLES

LSA Publication No. 70. ISBN 0 906337 80 1 [2001]
Edited by Sharon Clough and Judy White

Contents

MASCULINITIES: LEISURE CULTURES, IDENTITIES AND CONSUMPTION

LSA Publication No. 69. ISBN: 0 906337 77 1 [2000] pp. 163

Edited by John Horne and Scott Fleming

Contents

GENDER ISSUES IN WORK AND LEISURE

LSA Publication No. 68.ISBN 0 906337 78 X
Edited by Jenny Anderson and Lesley Lawrence [pp. 173]

Contents

SPORT, LEISURE IDENTITIES
AND GENDERED SPACES

LSA Publication No. 67. ISBN: 0 906337 79 8 [1999] pp. 196
Edited by Sheila Scraton and Becky Watson

Contents

HER OUTDOORS: RISK, CHALLENGE AND ADVENTURE IN GENDERED OPEN SPACES

LSA Publication No. 66 [1999] ISBN: 0 906337 76 3; pp. 131
Edited by Barbara Humberstone

Contents

POLICY AND PUBLICS

LSA Publication No. 65. ISBN: 0 906337 75 5 [1999] pp. 167
Edited by Peter Bramham and Wilf Murphy

Contents

CONSUMPTION AND PARTICIPATION: LEISURE, CULTURE AND COMMERCE

LSA Publication No. 64. ISBN: 0 906337 74 7 [2000]
Edited by Garry Whannel

Contents

GENDER, SPACE AND IDENTITY: LEISURE, CULTURE AND COMMERCE

LSA Publication No. 63. ISBN: 0 906337 73 9 [1998] pp. 191
Edited by Cara Aitchison and Fiona Jordan

Contents

THE PRODUCTION AND CONSUMPTION OF SPORT CULTURES: LEISURE, CULTURE AND COMMERCE

LSA Publication No. 62. ISBN: 0 906337 72 0 [1998] pp. 178
Edited by Udo Merkel, Gill Lines, Ian McDonald

Contents

TOURISM AND VISITOR ATTRACTIONS: LEISURE, CULTURE AND COMMERCE

LSA Publication No 61. ISBN: 0 906337 71 2 [1998] pp. 211
Edited by Neil Ravenscroft, Deborah Philips and Marion Bennett

Contents

LEISURE PLANNING IN TRANSITORY SOCIETIES

LSA Publication No. 58. ISBN: 0 906337 70 4
Edited by Mike Collins; pp 218

Contents

LEISURE, TIME AND SPACE: MEANINGS AND VALUES IN PEOPLE'S LIVES

LSA Publication No. 57. ISBN: 0 906337 68 2 [1998] pp. 198 + IV
Edited by Sheila Scraton

Contents

LEISURE, TOURISM AND ENVIRONMENT (I)
SUSTAINABILITY AND ENVIRONMENTAL POLICIES

LSA Publication No. 50 Part I; ISBN 0 906337 64 X
Edited by Malcolm Foley, David McGillivray and Gayle McPherson
(1999);

Contents

LEISURE, TOURISM AND ENVIRONMENT (II) PARTICIPATION, PERCEPTIONS AND PREFERENCES

LSA Publication No. 50 (Part II) ISBN: 0 906337 69 0; pp. 177+xii
Edited by Malcolm Foley, Matt Frew and Gayle McPherson

Contents

LEISURE: MODERNITY, POSTMODERNITY AND LIFESTYLES

LSA Publications No. 48 (LEISURE IN DIFFERENT WORLDS Volume I)
Edited by Ian Henry (1994); ISBN: 0 906337   52 6, pp. 375+

Contents